FOR ALL THOSE WHO LOVE MAGIC, MYSTERY, AND MIRACLES ...

"Every page invites you to a more perfect connection to your soul. Beautifully done."
—Wayne Dyer, author of *Manifest Your Destiny*

"Good stories remind us that there is a collective, mutual power that connects us all. This book is a sharing of the insights and triumphs of people like us. It reminds us of something we often forget: we are not in it alone."
—Larry Dossey, M. D., author of *Prayer Is Good Medicine*

ARIELLE FORD is the president of her own highly successful public relations firm, The Ford Group. Her clients have included Deepak Chopra, Wayne Dyer, Marianne Williamson, Louise Hay, Jack Canfield, Mark Victor Hansen, Joan Borysenko, and Neale Donald Walsch. She lives in La Jolla, California, with her two feline furry angels, J.B. and Montana.

HOT CHOCOLATE
FOR THE
MYSTICAL SOUL

101 True Stories
of Angels, Miracles,
and Healings

Arielle Ford

A PLUME BOOK

PLUME
Published by the Penguin Group
Penguin Putnam, Inc., 375 Hudson Street,
New York, New York 10014, U.S.A.
Penguin Books Ltd, 27 Wrights Lane,
London W8 5TZ, England
Penguin Books Australia Ltd, Ringwood,
Victoria, Australia
Penguin Books Canada Ltd, 10 Alcorn Avenue,
Toronto, Ontario, Canada M4V 3B2
Penguin Books (N.Z.) Ltd, 182–190 Wairau Road,
Auckland 10, New Zealand

Penguin Books Ltd, Registered Offices:
Harmondsworth, Middlesex, England

First published by Plume, an imprint of Dutton Signet, a member of Penguin Putnam Inc.

First Printing, February, 1998
10 9 8 7 6 5 4 3 2 1

Ⓟ   REGISTERED TRADEMARK—MARCA REGISTRADA

Library of Congress Cataloging-in-Publication Data
Ford, Arielle.
   Hot chocolate for the mystical soul : 101 true stories of angels, miracles, and healings /
Arielle Ford.
      p.   cm.
   ISBN 0-452-27925-9
   1. Angels.   2. Miracles.   3. Healing—Religious aspects.   I. Title.
BL477.F67   1997
291.2'15—dc21   97-28997
                                                                          CIP

Printed in the United States of America
Set in Palatino
Designed by Leonard Telesca

To my grandmother,
Ada Posner,
for sharing your gypsy soul with me.

Contents

3: Romances of the Soul

4: Spiritual Healing

5: Help from Above

6: Vision

7: The Other Side

Acknowledgments

First and foremost I wish to thank God for my amazing life and for putting me on the planet during a time of such wonderment and magic. I have been truly blessed to spend my life among some of the world's greatest thinkers and teachers. Mystical adventures at every corner!

My deepest appreciation to Jack Canfield and Mark Victor Hansen for their inspiration and for paving the way. Without their encouragement, this book would not exist.

My love and gratitude to the following people:

Ling Lucas, my beautiful and dedicated agent, and Ed Vesneske, Jr., my talented editor.

The entire Chopra family, Deepak, Rita, Mallika, and Gautama, for your love, trust, and friendship.

Danielle Perez, my champion at Dutton, for "getting" my vision.

Brent BecVar, Marcia Ross, Divina Infusino, Clardy Malugen, Nancy DeHerrara, Kimberly Rubin, Stephen Block, Carolyn Rangel, Tina Constable, Patty Eddy, Bruno Esparza, Pearl Fisk, Heide Banks, Jocelyn Eberstein, Janet Mills, Jeremiah Sullivan, David Simon, Randy Thomas— my friends and associates who make my life so much easier.

Neale Donald Walsch for your love and much-appreciated support.

Marianne Williamson for seeing me, even when I couldn't see myself.

Debbie Ford, the best sister on any planet, Michael Ford, my magical brother, and my parents, Howard and Sheila Fuerst, for continuing to travel this path with me at full speed.

Without the ongoing support of my staff (past and present) at The Ford Group, I would have never found the time to do this. My deepest appreciation to Peg Booth, Laura Clark, Shelley Miller, Linda Gomez, Gus Garcia, Shelley Seddon, and Jennifer Hill.

Finally, to all the brave and generous souls in this book who have shared their personal mystical stories with me, thank you from the bottom of my heart. You are all very bright lights.

Foreword

Life is mystical. Life is metaphysical—beyond the physical. Beyond our "normalcy" of five senses, our universe is the mystically, metaphysically magic journey of the soul.

Arielle Ford is a mystical lady. She has gathered mystical stories together that will make your heart and soul sing. The ideas in these entertaining and enlightening stories will inspire you. They will expand your awareness, your perceptions, and your abilities. You will think in new, exciting, and different ways. You will be renewed through the tools, techniques, and strategies contained herein.

You will be drawn back to reading, rereading, and sharing the sheer brilliance of these stories—again and again.

Stories have life and being. We learned in writing and compiling our Chicken Soup for the Soul series that they can affect people's lives and futures profoundly.

Arielle's book will do the same in a different way. Her readers will be transported imaginatively—in countless ways, and to countless places in their consciousness that have always been there, but separated by the flimsiest of screens. Her book is the impetus that stimulates us to awaken to vast new potential and infinite possibilities.

Our minds are not endowed, they are overendowed with the capacity to explore mystical, magical, and magnificent possibilities of our and others' souls.

As we rush toward the millennium, we are experiencing the most prosperous and spiritual time in all of human history, with each individual investigating his or her depth and the treasure of their soul. Each of us wants to awaken the spiritual genius and power within. To do that we need coaching, stories or parables, and informational tools and maps that provide us with a directional compass in previously unexplored territory. Arielle's book does that and more. It will have you go places you didn't know were there, and think thoughts you didn't know you could think.

May your mystical soul be united with the mystical, magical tour you've been wanting and waiting for.

—Mark Victor Hansen

Introduction

This book is a collection of highly unusual, inspiring, and empowering stories of ordinary people who have had extraordinary, even mystical experiences. They include stories of wonder and bliss, stories of angels, miraculous occurrences, near-death experiences, divine interventions, healings, personal transformations, encounters with holy men and women, and fantastic coincidences. The people who had these experiences come from all walks of life. They are authors, doctors, dancers, musicians, teachers, bakers, actresses, lawyers, architects, students, government employees, radio DJs, publishers, and even socialites!

The stories in *Hot Chocolate for the Mystical Soul* are for those of us who love magic and mystery, and who know for certain that an unseen loving presence is watching over us. I like to think of them as fairy tales for adults (big kids!) . . . most with happy endings. Like fairy tales, many of these stories offer hidden bits of wisdom that will make your life richer and more satisfying. You will discover that there is a rhyme and reason to the universe, and that the events in our lives are not random.

Hot Chocolate for the Mystical Soul has been designed to nourish you both emotionally and spiritually—and if you actually drink a cup of hot chocolate while reading it, you'll get a sweet-tooth fix at the same time! With 101 stories, this book should last for many cozy nights of reading. (You can read them all in one sitting, but I suggest savoring them a few at a time.)

There are many ways you can read this book, but here's my favorite: make yourself a mug of hot chocolate (sugar-free Swiss Miss is my favorite!), snuggle into a comfortable chair, and read a few stories. Then call a friend and share the stories you've read with them.

Author Joan Borysenko has said that "America is a nation of closet mystics." I think she's right, and this book is proof that many of us are having mystical experiences with increasing regularity. It is time for us to share those experiences as we race toward the new millennium and our own personal spiritual evolution.

You may find that certain stories in this book trigger memories of experiences you have had in the past. If you have had a mystical experience that you'd like to share in a future edition of *Hot Chocolate for the Mystical Soul*, please send it to the address on page 363.

While compiling these stories during the past two years, I have had the privilege of learning about spiritual practices and organizations I had never heard about. Working on this book has opened my eyes to new paths and has given me a renewed connection to the Divine. It is my highest vision that this book serve as a catalyst for your own spiritual growth.

Arielle Ford
La Jolla, California

1

MYSTICAL PLACES, MAGICAL MOMENTS

The Day the Gods Were Thirsty

Mallika Chopra

Giggling to herself, Ananya whispered into my ear, "Give him another spoon. He's thirsty. Go on, just give him another spoon."

Colors whirled before my eyes. Arms nudged and poked. Sobs and salutations swirled. Incense tantalized my nose, holy mantras echoed in the distance, the sunlight reflected against plates of silver and gold that framed the shrine. Baffled, nervous, emotional, joyful, my hands shook as I made my offering. Silently, amidst the hysteria, I had my moment with God.

Outside, old men and women danced in jubilation. A young *sadhu* chanted hymns as a hunchbacked beggar woman with a malnourished baby in her arms cried uncontrollably, hailing praises to the sky. A frenzy of voices compared tales and techniques, while a crowd of scientists hypothesized explanations for this bizarre phenomenon that defied common sense. Today was a day of miracles, and even the skeptics had to admit that something magical was in the air.

Ananya took the spoon from my hand and filled it again with milk. Kneeling on the ground, she placed it next to the trunk of the marble statue of the elephant god, Ganesha. The milk, within a minute, disappeared before our eyes. The god literally drank it, sucking it slowly from the spoon. And, unaware of the gasps and cries around her, my four-year-old cousin, innocent and joyful, simply offered another spoonful to the thirsty god.

Later that day, CNN, the BBC, broadcasters throughout the world, announced the bizarre phenomenon that took place over the course of twenty-four hours in Indian households and temples throughout the world. Reports showed lines of people outside holy shrines, waiting to make their offering. In fact, all the gods were drinking. A line protruded from the flower shop at a five-star hotel, because the small stone statue in the corner of the store was thirsty for milk as well. Headlines the next day read, "MILK SHORTAGE IN DELHI DUE TO EXCESSIVE CONSUMPTION BY THE GODS."

To experience a miracle, as it is, may be unique. But to experience it with millions of other people is a gift from God. The day the gods were thirsty in India was a day of celebration and revelation. People danced in the streets, friends and relatives shared their visions, the elders knowingly and approvingly nodded their heads. Children were dismissed from school early, shops and restaurants closed. Communities gathered together at places of worship. There was laughter and excitement, and there was a reason to smile. There was a moment when all else ceased to exist, and we were reminded that we live in a world of mystery.

In a world of pollution, violence and crime, poverty and depression, we sometimes forget that there is magic in our universe. At times, when things look dark and dismal, we need hope. We need reassurance that our faith has meaning. The "milk miracle" gave people a reason to hope, a reason to believe and dream of something better. It let us know that something greater, something more meaningful, exists for us. It let us know that a spirit hears our call.

It reminded us that life itself is a gift of the divine. That there is so much in this world to love and praise. As Walt Whitman once wrote:

WHY, who makes much of a miracle?
As to me, I know of nothing else but miracles,
Whether I walk the streets of Manhattan,

Or dart my sight over the roofs of houses toward the sky,
Or wade with naked feet along the beach, just in the
    edge of the water,
Or stand under trees in the woods . . .

To me the sea is a continual miracle;
The fishes that swim—the rocks—the motion of the
    waves—the ships with men in them,
What stranger miracles are there?

In India the bizarre is somehow always expected and accepted. The morning the gods were thirsty, the city was hysterical, but a week later, explanations abounding, the excitement was almost forgotten. The extraordinary became the ordinary, and life continued as it had before.

However, one very important thing did happen: We were given a moment to breathe, to look around us and marvel at our world. We were given a moment of excitement and exasperation, magic and divinity, a place of wonder and amazement. We were reminded that human nature is about love and joy and belief. And we were given a day to laugh and play and dance.

Reunion

Charles Lewis Richards, Ph.D.

Mary was a successful young insurance representative in the San Diego area, happily married, and the mother of a four-year-old girl. Having been given up for adoption immediately after her birth, to a very loving couple who cared for and raised her well, Mary had many unanswered questions about her heritage. She had always wanted to meet her birth mother, and these feelings only became stronger after the birth of her own daughter.

The problem was that Mary had little, if any, information with which to begin her search. She was also concerned as to how the impact of actually meeting her biological parents might affect her, and all the families involved.

Through a friend, Mary had heard of my work as a psychotherapist specializing in non-hypnotic past life therapy. People often come to me with blocks, fears, and problems that they have been unsuccessful in getting relief from, using more traditional methods of psychotherapy. I also use conventional methods of therapy, but in the majority of cases past life therapy gets results that are quicker and much more complete.

However, Mary's request was unique. Sitting in my office, she said, "I know this might sound like an odd request, but I am wondering if you could take me back to my birth, to find out anything about my birth mother." I told Mary that it was indeed unusual to reexperience one's birth primarily to attain information, but that it couldn't hurt to try.

Knowing that the birth experience is often a traumatic one, I decided to ease her up to the moment, by starting with some incidents that happened to her mother while Mary was still in the womb. We began by going back to the time when her mother first realized she was pregnant, around the second month.

We find her mother sitting in her bedroom, feeling a little nauseous, fearing that she is pregnant. She is fifteen. She doesn't know what to do, only that it will not be a happy moment when she breaks the news to her parents. So she puts it off.

Mary and I then went to a later point during the pregnancy. It was around the fifth month, summertime.

We find Mary's mother and her boyfriend standing in the living room of her home, facing her mother, father, and grandmother. Mary's mother is petrified of telling her parents, but she knows she can't hide it any longer. Through her mother's eyes, Mary describes a tense scene. She sees the living room in detail: her seventeen-year-old father stands near the door as her mother tells her parents she is pregnant. They are not supportive. They insist that the two must get married, and make plans to drive them to a neighboring state where marriage is legal at their young ages.

Finally, I guided Mary to her birth.

She is just coming out of the womb. Mary describes the shock of cold air and bright lights as she is brought into the world. For the first time, she gets a look at her biological mother's face, and feels the warmth of her embrace as she is briefly given to her to hold. I have Mary focus closely on everything she can see and hear in the delivery room. She reads name tags on the doctor's and nurses' uniforms, and describes how they prep her after she is born. Then she hears her mother's name being spoken by the doctor: "Marsha." I have her repeat it several times for clarification. I ask her if she can tell me the last name, and she eventually says: "Marsha Powers."

Armed with the name of her biological mother, Mary began her search. During the subsequent weeks, she traced her birth mother to the Pacific Northwest, and made an initial phone contact. Her birth mother was surprised and delighted, telling Mary that she had been praying for this day. "It was really a fairy tale," Mary told me. "She said all the right things."

Soon after Mary booked a flight to see her birth mother in person. The moment of finally coming face to face with her was one of indescribable joy, a very deep and somehow spiritual experience that Mary could scarcely find words to express.

Mary described to Marsha the bedroom she had seen, where Marsha had first realized she was pregnant as a frightened and confused young woman. She described the living room, and the conversation in which she had delivered the news of her pregnancy to her parents and grandmother. Marsha confirmed every detail. Both of them were astounded by the accuracy of Mary's descriptions of these places she had never actually seen or even heard of.

Mary continued her search, finding her biological father, who also resides on the West Coast. She told me it was a wonderful reunion, during which he corroborated the scene in which Marsha told the family that she was pregnant. When Mary asked her father why he'd stood near the doorway of the living room while Marsha delivered the news, he explained that he had always felt like an outsider with her parents because of his Latin heritage.

Today Mary maintains contact with both of her biological parents. They're happy to know that their daughter has gone on to establish a family of her own.

A Promise Kept

Nancy Cooke de Herrera

It was the spring of 1963 when Helen Lutes called to tell me the good news. "Maharishi will be here tomorrow night. His plane from Canada will arrive about midnight. Why don't you go out to the airport with Charlie and me? We'll pick you up."

Charlie Lutes was the head of Maharishi Mahesh Yogi's worldwide organization, the Spiritual Regeneration Movement. We'd been close friends ever since I'd started practicing TM (Transcendental Meditation) the year before.

I had been hoping that Maharishi would hurry up and get

to Los Angeles for several reasons. First, I loved seeing him, and second, one of his longtime followers was ill and praying to see him before she died. Millie Hoops's cancer had returned several months earlier. We, her friends, were dismayed at the news, as most of us believed she'd been cured. During the special teaching course at Catalina in September, Maharishi had ordered Millie into complete silence.

"In this way you can marshal the entire energy of your body to help drive the cancer into remission." He also gave her instructions on a technique designed to strengthen her nervous system, and advised her, "When ill, go to a doctor for help from the outside and at the same time help yourself from within."

She had responded to this schedule and quickly seemed the picture of health again, gaining weight and energy. However, a few months after Maharishi left us to visit TM centers in Europe and Canada, Millie, weary of the silence and inactivity, got on the phone and slowly joined the social scene again. It didn't take long for the cancer to reappear.

One couldn't blame her—she was such an outgoing personality. She had been especially kind to me when I first started meditating. She called every other day urging me to be consistent with my meditation, knowing that as my energy level increased from the daily practice, I'd be tempted by more activity and have even less time for TM.

Hearing she was close to death, I'd visited her at the hospital just the week before. On entering her room I thought I heard Maharishi's voice saying, "Put your thoughts on God and on love." It was a tape, which she switched off immediately. I commented on how nice it was for her to have that tape, and asked what else he said.

She replied, "It's about God, but I'm not allowed to let anyone else hear it. Maharishi said it was for my ears only."

She confided, "This has been an incredible experience. Between meditating and listening to the tape, my day is full. All the rest, the shots, the doctors, all that seems unreal."

Millie looked so pretty propped up on her pillows. Her

blonde hair was freshly washed, and she appeared thin, but healthy and happy. It was impossible to think she was dying. However, her voice had an urgency when she asked if I'd heard from Maharishi.

"Do you know when he will return? He promised to be with me when I die."

I insisted she was not going to die.

She shook her head. "Yes, I am, and I'm not worried about it. I have no fear. We all have to die someday, and Maharishi promised he would be here to guide me across to the other side, where Guru Dev will be waiting."

Sadness engulfed me. I wished I could share her faith.

On my way out, I asked the nurses how much more time they thought she had left. They expressed amazement that she had survived this long. "She is riddled with cancer, but seems to experience little pain. She refuses painkillers despite the malignancy and the cobalt treatments."

The small inner circle, alerted by Helen, was at the airport to greet Maharishi. He looked so happy as he slowly descended the plane steps carrying a handful of flowers. We were thrilled to have him with us again. It was decided that he would go to the Olsen house in Efram Zimbalist's Rolls-Royce, and I would accompany him. It was a perfect opportunity to alert him to Millie's impending death, even though he said little about it.

It was after 1:00 A.M. by the time we settled on the floor of the Olsens' library around Maharishi, anticipating the intimate moments we enjoyed when "the family" came together. It had been a long, tiring trip, but our questions and enthusiasm soon roused Maharishi and he announced his success energetically.

"The Canadian center is growing fast. They have centers springing up here and there with good people coming forward." His fingers plucked the petals of a rose. "Their plan is to buy a small airplane for me to use. With it I can fly from there to there to there," waving his hand over an imaginary map in front of him. While going into detail about future plans, he suddenly grew silent.

We waited. Then, in a hush, he said, "I will leave you for a few minutes." He uncurled his legs, picked his way past us, and left the room. He seemed somber and preoccupied about something. Standing by the door, I saw him hike up his robes and run up the stairs. I had never seen him hurry before.

I mentioned this to Helena Olsen, but she thought nothing of it. "With Maharishi, you never know if it's a response to some spirit or merely a call of nature."

But it impressed me to see him hurry like that.

I looked at my watch: 1:50 A.M. For a moment I considered leaving, but a few minutes later Maharishi came down the steps. Smiling and looking over the gathering of his favorites, he returned to his seat and continued telling us about his plans to finally write his book. We were thrilled at the prospect. It was close to 3:00 A.M. by the time I got to bed, tired but happy.

The next day Helen called to tell me that Millie had died early that morning, quietly and without pain.

Sunk in my thoughts, I did not detect the note of excitement in her voice.

"How sad that she never got to see Maharishi again. That hope kept her alive for weeks."

"But that's just it! She did!" Her voice exploded through the phone.

"What do you mean? Maharishi did not have time to see her. He was with us."

"Nancy, this is what is extraordinary. Charlie was just down at the hospital with Dick Hoops to help with Millie's things. The nurses told him that just before Millie died, they saw a person in a long white gown come down the corridor out of the darkness. As the figure came closer, they realized it was a bearded man in white robes. He was carrying a bunch of red roses. He smiled as he passed the nurses station and walked right into Millie's room as though he'd been there before. Leaving her station, one of the nurses looked through the open door and saw him make a gesture over Millie's head. A few moments later, he turned and left the room. Shortly after, she died."

Her words struck me. "Maharishi had promised her he would be there to guide her across the river of death. That is why she had no fear."

"I know, that is why we were all praying he would arrive in time, that he wouldn't let her down."

Slowly Helen spelled it out. "Do you realize what happened, Nancy?" I waited.

"Millie died at 2:00 A.M. At that time we were all sitting in the library of the Olsens'. Do you remember when he left us to run upstairs?"

"Yes, but St. John's Hospital is at least a half hour's drive away."

"Exactly." I felt a chill as Helen continued, "Now do you believe in teleportation, the ability to be in two places at the same time? It is on the nurse's register that he was there!"

As my head buzzed with wonderment, my heart swelled with love for Maharishi. He had kept his promise to Millie!

A Message from Jerusalem

Nick Bunick

Contrary to the Scriptures, Paul of Tarsus and Jesus of Nazareth had a one-on-one, close, personal relationship. Paul was twenty-one years old when he met Jeshua (Jesus) in Jerusalem. Jesus was twenty-three, and accompanied by two brothers from the fishing town of Bethsaida, on the shores of the Sea of Galilee. Their names were Peter (Cephas) and Andrew.

It wasn't acknowledged that Jeshua and Paul knew each other because Paul was not a disciple—in ancient Greek, *discipulus*, a pupil. Paul was more educated and economically independent than the disciples. They tended to resent Paul's relationship with Jeshua, and Paul in turn did not respect these uneducated followers, who oftentimes didn't understand what Jeshua was preaching. Thus, it's no wonder that Paul's knowledge of Jeshua and his teachings, as expressed in his letters, was greater than that described in the Gospels. Paul verifies this in his letters, when he says, "We knew him in the flesh, and now we know him in spirit."

Through the memory of Paul, I heard the words of Jeshua. I saw his graceful movements and I received his love. Now I share his true Messages. On radio talk shows, on television and in symposiums, I have been asked, "What was Jesus really like?"

When Jesus was hungry, he ate; when he was thirsty, he drank; when he was tired, he slept. But, unlike any other human then or now, Jeshua came onto Earth already a perfect soul. His conscious mind and spiritual mind were one and the same. Unlike all of us, who have angels as our spiritual guides—and some of us, who have Jeshua as our spiritual guide—He had God as His spiritual guide.

Jeshua did not care about wealth or status, for He surely understood that the only true qualifier for happiness is to be at one with that part of God that is inside us all—that is, our immortal spirit and soul, which is a gift from God, our Father/Mother. It was that understanding that He tried to impart to His followers two thousand years ago.

Through the memory of Paul, I witnessed Jeshua's charismatic wisdom, His tremendous sense of humor, and His eloquent and extraordinary skills of communication. But even with all of this, Jeshua had to revert to miracles to win the hearts and minds of His followers: the healing of the sick, the raising of Lazarus from death, and His own resurrection. One of the most extraordinary scenes that I witnessed, through the memory of Paul, was Jeshua performing His first healing in the city of Jerusalem. Although Jeshua had said He would teach me how to heal others, nothing prepared me for the first time I actually witnessed His healing power. It happened at one of the wells away from the temple grounds.

A great crowd had gathered. Jeshua stood on the outer rim of the well, directing people who wanted healing. He told them to form two lines: one line for those who had become sick in the course of their lifetime, and the other line for those whose sickness and afflictions were from birth, or caused by accident.

Many people were there who were not sick, and it amused the onlookers to see some of those who had brought on their own sickness unwilling to admit it. Neighbors and acquaintances tried to tell these people, "You should be over in the other group. You weren't born with that!" But they would edge over into the other line, unwilling to admit how greed, anger, jealousy, and intolerance had festered within, causing disease in themselves and unhappiness to those who were close to them. They did not realize that this inability to admit this in themselves would prevent them from being healed.

Large groups of onlookers stood on either side of the lines, watching all that was going on, listening to Jeshua preach that they must have incredible faith in their love of God and God's ability, as well as in their own ability from God within themselves, to be able to bring healing to themselves. He talked to them for a long time, almost an hour, under the partly cloudy skies. It was midafternoon.

I stood in one of the side groups at the front, not more than ten feet from Jeshua, studying all that was happening before me. Jeshua's loose-fitting brown robe rippled back and forth as He gestured. Then He stepped down from the well and approached the line of those who had brought illness to themselves. With deliberation, He placed

His right hand on the forehead of the first person in line, and His left hand on the shoulder.

Praying out loud, He asks the man to forgive himself and for God to forgive him, telling the man that he will not sin again and thus bring harm to himself. He tells the man, "It is up to you. You must first acknowledge and then forgive. But you cannot forgive unless you first acknowledge."

The man does acknowledge, and is healed of the stomach disease from which he had been suffering. The man shouts to all around him that he is healed. The crowd is amazed by what they see. Excitement travels throughout the two groups of observers. Those in line crane their necks to see what is happening, when their turn is to come.

I am deeply moved as I witness healing after healing. Watching Him heal people, I understand that I am coming to terms with Jeshua—with who Jeshua is. And I am coming to terms with myself. I realize profoundly that Jeshua is the one it was predicted would come to be the Savior of the people. This day I am forever changed.

So powerful was this scene that we have received a number of letters from individuals who experienced their own physical healing while reading this particular chapter in my book, *The Messengers*. What was true two thousand years ago is true today. The message is constant, the message is perpetual. God dwells within each one of us. The magnitude of understanding and accepting that truth can change each one of us the way it changed Paul that day in Jerusalem.

Some say that Jeshua died for us, and surely He did. But I say to you, more importantly, He lived for us, and was for us a gift from God. I am so grateful that through the persistence of the angels, I am able to share with others Jeshua's life and His Messages.

The Edge

Andrea Cagan

Standing at the edge, I could feel the almost unbearable heat penetrating my shoes. Poisonous gases were forcing their way through holes in the volcanic ash, destroying all life they came in contact with—as if they were so determined, the Earth herself could not hold them back.

It was mid-morning. The volcano had erupted on the Big Island of Hawaii—in fact, was erupting as I stood there. Burning lava flowed into the sea, new land taking shape before my eyes. I was watching creation, standing on newly formed earth, earth that hadn't been there yesterday.

I had passed countless signs along my way: "DANGER! NO ENTRY!" I saw them, had considered them, felt the fear they were meant to instill, but my feet had kept walking, fear and all. I was compelled to keep progressing toward the heat, toward the gases so thick and sulfurous that I could see them rising into the atmosphere—hovering above a boiling liquid mass the hottest, wettest shade of red I had ever seen or imagined in my life or in my dreams. I had been inexorably drawn right here, to the edge, where red-hot lava had bubbled and spilled its way down an immense mountain to meet the cool blue sea. Death was so close by, I could smell it in the atmosphere, and I knew that being alive was my personal choice.

I was not alone. My girlfriend Katrina and I had come walking here together. After we'd scaled a massively swollen bulge in the newly formed ground, the warning signs had stopped, as if they weren't needed any longer. Officials passed us in neon orange jackets that looked drab compared to the hot lava pouring forth. Since we were the only civilians who had ventured this close, the officials gazed at us disapprovingly, but they didn't stop us. It was as if we had been sufficiently warned, and once we had come this far, the risk was our own.

I stood as close to the edge as was humanly possible, watching the seeping reddish stuff ooze and blister, spread out into brand new surfaces, extend and define its own boundaries. Who would claim ownership of this fantastic display of the power of God? What person would drive a stake into the virgin ground and try to give it a name? Who would foolishly think they had control over the Earth herself?

Watching the lava claim parts of the sea, I asked myself: Does water overwhelm fire, or is it the other way around? The world itself seemed to be shifting before my eyes, and there was nothing to do about it but simply watch. I felt frightened and hollow when I realized that I had always assumed that the edge was the edge. But as I watched this edge extend and consume everything in its path, I realized that it all keeps moving and changing. Nothing is ever what we think it is, not even the edge.

The lava passed dangerously close to my right foot. The nerve endings in my toes tingled, anticipating the searing heat that could destroy my foot, my leg, my entire body. My breathing had become shallow. Fear had overtaken my chest, pressing in on it, crushing my ability to reason. The oozing gases were so strong, the mere act of breathing had become something I needed to think about. It was crucial that I stay connected to my breath . . .

The deeper I breathed, the calmer I became . . . until I was shocked to discover that I wanted to jump, not into the water, but straight into the lava. Into the creative core of the Earth. All fear had left me. I could have done it, had my legs only begun to move: I had to hold them in place, keep them from pitching me forward. It was not that I wanted to die. I didn't. I was happy in my life and suicide was not a part of my equation, never had been. Yet the compulsion to heave myself into the fire was overwhelming.

My body shifted forward, trying out the limits of how far I could go. I peered into the fire, and it was not alien. It was a part of me, a life force so strong and compelling I wanted to merge with it, to fly into the belly of it, to be consumed by the heat, to be the hot, seeping, sexual, oozing fire.

"Don't do this," my inner voice warned me. But why was it better to stand on this side? Both sides contained mystery, light and darkness and infinite possibilities. Each contained its own version of the edge.

But where would it all end? I looked around. Land continued to form out of the fire. The edge was expanding and moving further and further from me—showing me that standing still was the same as retreating. So, in actuality, standing still was impossible. I was either moving forward or moving backward, because the very earth beneath my feet was moving. No matter what I did or didn't do, I was a part of the movement, woven into the creation and destruction of the Earth herself, even if I thought I was standing there doing nothing.

Katrina touched my arm. I looked at her. She was feeling it, too. Were we candidates to fly across the edge together, the Hawaiian version of *Thelma and Louise*?

We turned our backs to the seduction, breathless. We had felt the pull, the draw to our inevitable future. It would happen one day, but not like this. This was too mad, too dramatic, too surreal, and ultimately too meaningless. Leaping to our death? Ridiculous. And yet—the molten syrup sizzled behind us, beckoning.

I was tired of laboring for breath. I began to walk away and Katrina followed. At first it was like wading through thick pudding, straining against the tide, trying to resist the inexplicable urge to be at the center of the cyclone. But resist it we did, heading back across the charcoal-colored porous ground.

Wherever I placed one foot, then the other, had once been the edge—the fine line between here and there, between this world and the other. Even the flattest, most nondescript parts of this newly formed ground had, for an instant, been as sharp as a razor. Now they were simply part of the whole, reasonably safe and solid.

As we left the sacred territory and got closer to the mainstream of life, officials in orange showed up once again, eyeing us irritably, as if we were now once again their concern. I had left no man's land, where gases ruled the atmosphere and fire ruled the sea. Now these people though that *they* ruled—and I looked like a dissident, someone who had broken their rules and could not be trusted. Their stern faces were masked by an efficient demeanor that spoke of important work to be done. But I saw the fear peeking through, the understanding of the mortality of it all, of having been in the awesome face of creation. They had seen how little control they had over anything. They knew how small they were in the scheme of things, but it was as if they didn't want anyone else to know.

They said nothing as we passed, since we were now walking in what they considered the proper direction. At least we were moving away from danger—or so they thought.

Where is safety, if every moment of life contains its own version of the edge? Now we were returning to the confines of society, where decisions on mortality were no longer left up to the individual, a world where there were laws against dying. Perhaps fear served its purpose here. Perhaps it was an illusion to keep us on the path, to keep us safe, to keep us connected to the necessary lessons of life and maintain us on our journey. Or perhaps it was simply one of God's stunning and mysterious ways to keep us on His time, not our own, to keep us from getting too close to the edge.

Gettysburg

Paul V. Johnson

I had come to Gettysburg College to attend a program sponsored by the Spiritual Frontiers Fellowship, which had invited me. I was in advertising and public relations at the time, and I was there purely to gather information that might help me promote the foundation. I had no other expectations, except perhaps of a few days away from my normal routine.

A number of "sensitives" attending claimed they were having unusual experiences on this campus, which was situated on land that had seen heavy fighting in the battle of Gettysburg. I was skeptical, to say the least, and decided to set up a challenge for one of them, a medium named Phyllis. She was probably the most vocal, speaking of experiences that I felt were not only incredible, but a bit weird. So I said to her, "If this is happening as you say, then show me." Not one to back down, Phyllis said she'd take me out to the battlefield.

On the evening of July 21, 1971, we headed off in her car. First we took a quick trip through the cemetery across from the battlefield, and she commented on the number of spirits lingering by various gravesites. I saw nothing, but it did spook me, to say the least.

Then we went onto the battlefield itself. After considerable searching, she selected the site of the monument to

Major General Winfield Hancock. We settled on the base of this huge monument, which had a flat seating surface. She gave me a number of instructions—a quick course in mediumship, really—and then we went into a meditation sequence.

As we sat there on East Cemetery Ridge at dusk, the aura of the battlefield was awesome. Its location, just across the street from the National Cemetery where President Lincoln gave his famous address, added to its eeriness. The Hancock statue itself, with the general astride his horse, was dauntingly massive. To be there at dusk with only one other person was indeed a bit frightening.

Suddenly the silence was broken by a rifle shot. The bullet seemed to pass by the left side of my head and ricochet off an adjacent tree. It about scared me out of my wits: I thought someone was shooting at us, perhaps for trespassing.

However, Phyllis assured me it was "paranormal," and nothing to worry about. I stayed in place, albeit uneasily. Then the battle noise came into focus, and I became part of a spiritual dimension that was totally unexpected, and completely engrossing.

Phyllis began to describe what was taking place around us, and kept asking me, "Can't you see what's going on?" No, I couldn't—nothing but the memorial grounds slipping into the dark of night.

But there was no question about it: All around me I began to hear rifle shots, the roar of cannons, horses, wagons moving, and the horrifying shouts and cries of human rage and pain. The sounds were everywhere, all-encompassing, real—although coming so thick and fast I had little time to recognize all that was happening.

Then Phyllis said a small contingent of soldiers was heading toward us. They were wounded, and she explained that they were being attracted by our "light." As she said that, I began to feel something like a blanket of cobwebs completely covering me and moving on through me.

That must have been about all my nervous system would allow. Shortly thereafter, the sounds began to die down. I gradually returned to a more normal state of consciousness, at which point I quickly suggested we leave. I was terrified—yet transfixed with excitement.

I now *knew*, beyond doubt: There *is* something beyond this plane. Those moments on the battlefield had changed my life, instantaneously, and forever. But that is another story . . .

Close Encounters of the Alaskan Kind

Gina Kelly Russo

It all happened about seven years ago, when I was coming back from my first and last Alaskan bed-and-breakfast fishing expedition. I was working as the promotions director at the NBC affiliate, KTUU-Anchorage, at the time, and had been given a weekend at this groovy retreat on the water for all the hard work I had done on a bus advertisement campaign.

I'd invited my girlfriend Stephanie to accompany me. When I first asked her if she wanted to go fishing, she had immediately said no. I didn't really think she'd say yes, as she was a "Chanel Girl" from Newport Beach stuck in Anchorage, Alaska. This was not her kind of trip. I was prepared to set off alone when she called me back to say she was ready to go.

We had a wacky weekend of fishing. We didn't even have to bait the hook. I immediately caught a twenty-nine-pound king salmon, and then spent the rest of the time sleeping in the bow of the rugged little fishing boat. Stephanie fished until she was blue in the face, and didn't quit until she broke a nail. We spent three glorious days breathing fresh air on the Kenai Peninsula, removed from all responsibility.

We started our journey back to reality late Sunday afternoon, which meant we wouldn't get back to Anchorage until about eleven. As we were nearing Anchorage, the northern lights started to put on one of the most spectacular shows either of us had ever seen. If you're not familiar with the northern lights, also called the aurora borealis, it's a phenomenon caused by the electromagnetic fields close to the North Pole. The northern lights are most often greenish in color, and look like ribbons of light performing an electrical dance in the sky. Alaskans are known to call each other, no matter what the hour, to make sure everyone sees this rare display of nature.

As we drove closer to home, Stephanie and I became mesmerized by the lights. They seemed to be leaping and swirling all around us. We both found ourselves with our heads out the windows, gazing up into space. This would have been fine, except I was supposed to be driving. So we finally pulled off the road about fifteen miles south of Anchorage to give this cosmic wonder our undivided attention.

I put a blanket on the hood of my Isuzu Trooper and we both lay there listening to George Winston's "December," staring at the ribbons of energy that now seemed to be coming down around us in a brilliant circle. By now we could *hear* the northern lights. It sounded like the whirring of a gigantic windstorm, with no wind.

We held each other's hands tightly. We couldn't speak. We were in a trance. The phenomenon seemed to be calling to us, inviting us to dissolve into the energy. The lights turned red and blue and green and white and continued making a circle around us that looked like the bottom of a spaceship.

Suddenly a twig snapped behind the car, and we flew off the hood. We frantically climbed into the truck, locked the doors, turned off the music, and assessed what we thought had just happened. We spoke in half-sentences, unequivocally knowing that we had just had the same unspeakable experience.

We drove on in silence, eyes straight ahead. Within a matter of moments, we were filled with an overwhelming desire to stare back into the sky, as if something, somewhere, beckoned to us. Seven more miles down the road I pulled the truck over into an area called Potter's Marsh. The northern lights had disappeared as we came around the mountains. We quickly got out of the car as our attention was once again drawn to the heavens.

This time, our eyes fixed on a new bizarre occurrence. Every time I looked at a star, it would attach itself by a "string" to the next star, creating a chain of stars. The stars then seemed to pull like a snake through the sky. I could hardly speak at this point, but I managed to ask Stephanie if she was having the same experience.

She whispered a breathy "yeah" and started to walk away from me and the truck. I screamed, "Don't!"—and Stephanie kept walking, just saying, "It's okay," with a smile in her voice.

At that same moment, whatever I had been staring at in space seemed to come screaming through the universe right toward us. It took only an instant, and appeared to be red. Then something hit the back of the truck with a huge thud.

We both frantically tried to climb back into the Trooper from the driver's side. I pushed Stephanie over the armrest, climbed in, and floored the gas pedal before I'd shut the door. I drove straight up a swampy embankment without even using the four-wheel drive.

I had my chest pressed against the steering wheel for the next long eight miles back to Anchorage. Stephanie was sitting backward in her seat. Both of us were crying hysterically.

We got off at the first exit, jumped out at the first gas station, and examined the car under the floodlights. There was nothing: no dent, nothing in the back of the truck. Nothing except the haunting memory of the seductive lights, and the unmistakable sound and impact of something from another world hitting the car, but leaving no evidence.

We drove back to Stephanie's parents' house with our eyes glued to the asphalt. We retreated to her room, pulled the drapes closed, and never talked about it again.

The Miracle Bouquet

Doreen Virtue, Ph.D.

The day before my birthday, my husband Michael and I took an afternoon walk along the Southern California beach near our home. Usually our walks are filled with lively discussions. This particular day, however, Michael and I walked in more of a silent meditation. We were together physically, holding hands, yet were each peacefully absorbed in our own thoughts.

We reached a large stone jetty known as "The Wedge." I love to sit on the quartz stones and meditate, drinking in the sound of pounding surf and the warm embrace of the afternoon sun. But recently, extra-high surf at The Wedge had marred my meditations. I hadn't felt able to let go. A part of my consciousness was always focused on my physical surroundings, making sure I was safe from the fifteen-foot waves that could suddenly change course and wash me off the rocks.

This day, Michael sweetly offered to watch the surf while I meditated, freeing me to lose all awareness of my surroundings. We walked next to the jetty, looking for two comfortable rocks to sit on. We carefully inspected our seating options, seeking a location near enough to the water to hear the pounding surf, yet far enough away to afford us safety. Finally we selected two flat quartz stones.

Eyes closed, I deeply inhaled the misty salt air as the spray cooled my warm skin. Trusting Michael to watch for high surf, I rapidly let myself go into a deep meditation. I visualized my chakras and pictured white Christ energy cleansing and purifying each one. As I did this, my heart swelled with bliss. I felt so much love right then, a deep love for all of life. I was conscious of the connection of every being. I was one with everyone and everything in a powerful state of love. I came out of this glorious meditation stretching my arms with gratitude for the beautiful truth of life. Opening my eyes, I saw Michael peacefully sitting next to me cross-legged. He noticed my stirring and smiled. "You ready to head back now?"

I nodded and started to push myself off the rock. As I turned to climb down, a bright pink object against the gray rock caught my eye. *That wasn't there before*, I thought. Then I gasped as I realized what I was looking at. There next to me was a bouquet of lilac orchids and deep pink rosebuds, tied with a bright pink satin ribbon.

The bouquet hadn't been there when we'd sat down: We'd inspected the rock too carefully to have missed seeing such a colorful object. Michael hadn't brought the bouquet: All he was wearing was shorts and a tank top, with no place to hide a bouquet. Besides, these flowers were fresh, not crumpled as they would have been had they been squirreled away under his thin cotton shirt.

I picked up the bouquet and excitedly showed the flowers to Michael. Just then my inner voice loudly said, "Happy Birthday, Doreen!"

My miracle bouquet was a birthday gift from the universe, celebrating my meditation of love and my anniversary of being on this earth plane. Today I keep the dried bouquet in my office, as a reminder that a consciousness of oneness and love calls forth beautiful miracles in the most surprising ways.

A Dolphin's Love

Arielle Ford

It was an intensely bright summer day and I was fulfilling a lifelong fantasy: swimming with dolphins! Having grown up in south Florida by the warm, soothing waters of the Atlantic, I had long dreamed of dolphins. My favorite TV show as a kid had been *Flipper*, and I'd prayed that someday I would swim side by side with dolphins and become part of their world, if just for a few moments.

Well, my dream had finally come true—and not only was I in the water with a dolphin, but she really seemed to like me. We had created our own little game. She would roll on her back while I scratched her silken tummy with my flippers. Then she would offer me her dorsal fin and take me on a ride around the lagoon. I lost track of time while my dolphin friend and I frolicked in the water.

At one point I found myself staring into her beautiful blue eyes and was amazed at what I saw. Not only was she looking directly at me, but I could feel waves of unconditional love radiating into me. As she continued to look at me, I realized that I had never been loved so completely and so unconditionally as I was in that moment. It was an unforgettable moment of pure bliss. I had always suspected that dolphins were special ambassadors on this planet, and now I knew for certain that they were ambassadors of love.

My encounter with that dolphin truly changed my life and opened my heart. I hope that someday I will be evolved enough to look at someone and radiate love to them the way that dolphin loved me.

Reunited by the Pyramids

Richard Greene

At the age of four, Chiara already had a strong, definite interest in Egypt. My wife Dee and I were very intrigued by this, since it seemed a little unusual for someone so young. Then the invitation came.

A travel company that was interested in my work was holding their annual seminar in Cairo. They wanted me to conduct two weekend seminars for them, and would send me and my family on a cruise down the Nile for the entire week in between. Chiara was very excited.

Then Elizabeth, the company's representative in Cairo, called. She said that she and her five-year-old daughter, Sabrina, would meet us at the Pyramids on the way from the airport to the hotel in town.

Chiara was even more excited about the prospect of meeting up with Sabrina than she was about going in the first place. Dee and I thought nothing of it. "Of course, another little kid to play with. How nice for Chiara."

We landed at the Cairo airport and jumped into the car waiting to take us to the Pyramids. The entire way there, Chiara kept asking, "Is Sabrina going to meet us there, Mommy? Is Sabrina going to be with Elizabeth, Daddy?"

"Yes, honey."

The first view of the Pyramids made all of us gasp. Rising out of the heat and the completely barren desert were those stark, spectacular, ageless geometric forms.

"Are we there yet? Are we where Sabrina is yet?"

"In a few minutes, sweetheart," we responded to our excited little four-year-old.

We reached the parking lot, the Pyramids now huge in front of us, and pulled up near Elizabeth's waiting car. As soon as we opened the door, Chiara ran to the other car, where Sabrina sat waiting in the back seat, and jumped in.

Then Dee, Elizabeth, our driver, and I all watched with our jaws literally hanging open as Sabrina and Chiara—a four- and five-year-old who had never seen each other, never even spoken to each other—threw themselves into a wild embrace. The kind of embrace that brings tears to your eyes. The kind of embrace you see when relatives separated by wars and years of circumstance finally meet at an airport terminal or a train station.

And then an even stranger thing happened. Chiara and Sabrina came out of their embrace, looked at one another, and almost simultaneously said something they could not *possibly* have said . . .

"Oh, Chiara, I'm so glad to see you again!"

"Oh, Sabrina, I'm so glad to see you again!"

Again? Elizabeth looked at me, I looked at Dee, Dee looked at Elizabeth. Did we hear the word "again"?

"Girls," Elizabeth asked, "have you been together before?"

With a confidence and a maturity far surpassing their years, Chiara and Sabrina turned away from each other, faced the three startled adults, and said, "Uh-huh!"

And that was all they would say.

The Cosmic Hobo

Karena Delite

In the spring of 1992, my friend Debbie and I were driving home after an exhilarating afternoon jog along the Intra-coastal Waterway in West Palm Beach, Florida. We shared stories and laughter as Debbie drove the normal route home. As usual, we passed through an older, somewhat rundown part of town to reach our neighborhood just on the other side of the railroad tracks.

As Debbie slowed down for the railroad crossing, my head turned almost involuntarily to my right, and I saw a hobo walking toward us along the railroad tracks. He was less than thirty feet away, walking leisurely. He wore a cap, and over his left shoulder he carried a red sack that swayed to and fro with each step. For some reason, I was mesmerized by him. I just stared as he slowly approached us. Although I squinted to see his face, he was looking down at his feet as he walked, and I could barely make out the line of his left cheek.

No words passed between Debbie and me, but I realized that she must have been watching him, too. She had completely stopped the car. As he continued walking toward us, my eyes never left the hobo. His stride was animated. His clothing, right down to that bright red sack, was almost like a costume. He could have been a character right out of a play. He was the perfect hobo.

Despite the colorful image he made, it wasn't so much his appearance that intrigued me. It was more the way I felt inside as I watched him. There was wonder in my heart, a kind of sweet curiosity. I was delighted, grateful, and humble, all at the same time. I felt a sense of expectation all around me and inside of me, almost like the way I'd felt as a child when I first awakened on Christmas morning. I had entered a space of timelessness. My whole being seemed to pause for a moment, my awareness fully focused on the hobo.

I remembered watching fireworks on the Fourth of July, the way I felt as I breathlessly sighed "Ahhh" after the most fantastic ones. I was full of awe.

I don't know exactly how long I watched him, but when the hobo was within ten yards of our car, he suddenly lifted his head. Our eyes met. In that instant, an amazing thing happened. His face lit up as if someone had aimed a bright spotlight on it, and his eyes blazed lovingly into mine. It lasted only a few seconds, but the memory of the hobo's spectacularly lit face and beaming blue eyes is something I'll never forget. I had never beheld such a beautiful sight. My body felt light, and a rush of energy ran like chills up my spine.

As he came in line with the front of our car, my head turned slowly to follow him. When he was almost directly in front of us, he glanced at both Debbie and me, face still shining, and tugged gently at the brim of his black cap, nodding slightly as if to say, "Greetings." It felt like a blessing.

I nodded back to him and smiled, then watched as he continued walking down the railroad tracks away from us. I watched while he became a small spot on the horizon, moving farther and father away until . . . *poof*, he disappeared.

At that moment, Debbie and I turned to each other and simultaneously said, "That was an angel!" We drove the rest of the way home in silence, as if talking might disturb the sanctity of the miracle we had just shared.

Months later, when I told a friend about the experience, he asked me how I knew that the hobo was an angel.

I simply answered, "He was to me."

Of that, I will always be certain.

"I Know You!"

Richard Greene

It was a beautiful autumn Sunday atop the mountains over-looking what was Zagreb, Yugoslavia. The weekend work-shop of twenty-five English-speaking Yugoslavian doctors, lawyers, and others had been a particularly good one. We'd gone deep, very deep, into understanding how we communicated with our friends, co-workers, lovers, children, and ourselves. Because of the warm, intimate atmosphere of the retreat, many who had been tight, reserved and quiet on Friday night were opening up like lotus petals during our exercises on this last day. But none like Alexander.

It was about three o'clock, just hours before we were to say goodbye and head back down the mountain. As one of the last group exercises, designed to generate an experience of real person-to-person intimacy, I told the group, "Okay, now everyone pick a partner. Then stand face to face and, without talking, just look into your partner's eyes and see what you see."

Alexander, a very well-known medical doctor in Zagreb with a thick beard, rushed over to me and said, "Please, Richard, may I do this exercise with you?"

Generally, I don't participate in exercises with my students, choosing instead to circle the room and supervise. But there was something urgent in Alexander's voice, so I said, "Of course."

With music gently playing in the background, Alexander and I stood and looked into each other's eyes. No more than fifteen seconds after we'd begun, there were tears slowly running down his cheeks. I continued to look into his eyes. The tears began running faster. He couldn't control himself.

"I must tell you, Richard, I know you. I know you. I really know you!" As the tears came even faster, his body began to shake. "I know you," he repeated.

Then, without any warning, he threw his arms around me and began to sob and wail unlike anything I'd ever heard before. If there's a place deeper than one's soul, that is where these sounds seemed to be coming from.

The rest of the class stopped cold. The atmosphere of the room was completely dominated by this large man bear-hugging their teacher and repeating the words, "I know you, I know you, I know you."

After five full minutes of this intense crying and shaking and shouting, Alexander relaxed his grip on me, pulled away gently, looked once more into my eyes and said softly, one last time, "I know you, Richard."

After he'd had the time to collect himself, I asked him the question everyone was thinking: "Do you know what that was about?"

He didn't hesitate. "No, not a clue."

He was not alone. I remembered feeling a very nice connection with Alexander when I first saw him on Friday, but had thought nothing of it until now. I had no clue myself about the origins of his intense reaction. In about thirty minutes we would stumble, almost magically, on the answer.

The class began again. Inspired by the depth of feeling we had all just experienced, I began to talk about the nature of emotion. During the course of this discussion I happened to mention that astrologers believe that people born under the water signs of Pisces, Cancer and Scorpio are more emotional than those born under the other nine signs. I mentioned, very offhand, that I am a Pisces.

Alexander blurted out, "So am I!"

Hardly a reason to get excited, I thought. One-twelfth of the world is, too.

"February or March?" I asked him.

"February."

"What day?"

"The twenty-fifth."

A chill ran through my body. "Me too."

I turned to the rest of the class. "Now, this is beginning to get interesting." The fact that there wasn't a sound or even a breath in the room told me they agreed.

I talked a little about birth dates and coincidences, but since Alexander looked to be at least five years older than I was, I hadn't thought to go further. Then all of a sudden the question jumped out of me.

"What year?"

"Nineteen fifty-four. And you . . . ?"

I started to shake a little as a I announced, "Ladies and gentlemen, Alexander and I were born on exactly the same day. How many of you think that might have something to do with what we all just witnessed?" Every hand rose.

"Okay, Alexander, what time were you born?"

"Six-forty in the morning."

I let out a sigh. Thank God it wasn't the same time—that would be far too weird. And then it hit me.

"Where were you born?"

"Zagreb."

My face flushed bright red. I looked into his eyes as I said, "Ladies and gentlemen, you are looking at two human beings who were born a continent, four thousand miles and six times zones apart—at the same precise moment in time! Can there be any doubt that this is why Dr. Alexander Soltsyn felt, in the deepest part of his heart, that he knew me?"

After the workshop was over, Alexander and I agreed that we had to make the hour-long drive down the hill together. As we talked, we found similarities in almost every area of our lives. He had chosen to become a doctor, become disillusioned with conventional medicine, and helped pioneer the holistic medical movement in his country. I became a lawyer, became disillusioned, and helped bring alternative conflict resolution and communication techniques to people around the world.

Alexander had one child. So did I. Alexander was a vegetarian. So was I. Alexander went to India in 1986. So did I. And on and on.

The vivid image of two close friends leaving the spirit world at precisely the same moment to inhabit bodies about to be born on Earth—one in a hospital in Zagreb, Yugoslavia, the other in a hospital in Petersburg, Virginia, USA—had come to both of us as our stories unfolded. Though neither one of us remembered this actually happening, we both thought of it as we looked again into each other's eyes.

And this time, we both smiled.

The Miracle Maker from India

Julia Loomans

When I was four years old and living in Wisconsin, my parents became interested in the teachings of a holy man from India named Sai Baba. Although they studied a number of spiritual teachings, I noticed there was something distinctly different in the air whenever Sai Baba was mentioned.

When we began attending gatherings to study Baba's teachings, I often joined in. Although I was usually thoroughly bored at religious services, I loved the lively, festive atmosphere at the Sai Baba Center. Prayers were read, songs were sung, and amazing stories were told about the miracles people were experiencing in the presence of this ageless Hindu with warm brown eyes and halo-shaped hair.

Sai Baba's teachings were universal, emphasizing the unity among the major religious paths of the world. Although I was the youngest one at the meetings, I felt a connection, and loved to take part in the inquiries. Occasionally I would pose a question or, to the delight of the adults, come up with an answer to someone else's question. I didn't know a single word of Hindi when I started, but I learned the *bhajans* (chants) almost effortlessly, frequently singing them at home as I played with my toys. I put a picture of Sai Baba in my bedroom, right next to a few of my other favorite teachers, like Jesus, Buddha, Big Bird and Mickey Mouse! The photo had an uncanny presence to it.

No matter what angle I looked at it from, I could feel Sai Baba's eyes looking straight into the very center of me.

A woman named Angie who ran the Sai Baba Center told a story one night that proved to be of great importance to me. She began by explaining that she had gone to India a year before to meet Sai Baba. Although several thousand people were visiting him each day from around the world, she had the rare opportunity to speak with him, which she felt was a life-changing event. During their brief encounter, Baba placed a medal in her hand and simply told her to "give this to the child." Since she didn't have any children of her own, she wondered who it was intended for.

"I have held this precious medallion for over a year," she said, "waiting for this special child to arrive." She was silent for a time, and then suddenly Angie turned to me. "I feel moved to give this medal to you, Julia, because in my heart, I feel you are the child Sai Baba spoke of."

My mouth dropped open in awe as she placed the shining medal in my small hand. I was filled with joy as I examined it. On one side there was a picture of Sai Baba, on the other a Hindu symbol for peace and prosperity. Although I was very young, I knew how very special it was to receive such a gift. I wore the pendant with honor.

That same night, my father, Lou, had a lucid dream that he and I were traveling abroad together on a plane. I appeared to be about twelve years old, and he sensed that we were going somewhere of great importance.

The next morning, we received a call from Angie, who enthusiastically told us what had occurred at the center during the night. There was a small wooden meditation table that was always covered with a small sprinkling of *vibutti*, a gray, sweet-smelling ash. It was said that Sai Baba would often manifest this "holy ash" out of thin air and pour it into the hands of visiting devotees at his ashram in India. It was considered a great blessing, since people often experienced a healing when they received the holy ash.

She said that occasionally, when something of mystical significance happened at the ashram, an overflow of *vibutti* would appear out of nowhere. When Angie opened the center that day, she was amazed to discover a heaping pile of the holy ash on top of the table, overflowing onto the floor. "Sai Baba must be happy that you received the medal, Julia," she said, laughing, as I listened half in disbelief. When I went to see for myself, she gave me some of the ash to keep in a small container, and told me to rub a little on my hands or forehead when I said my prayers.

Over the years, it seemed that no matter how much I'd use the ash or give away, the supply never ran out. This was mystifying, but not uncommon among those who used the ash. I remember giving some to a relative with a high fever and telling her to put it on her forehead every few hours. Although she had been sick for days, in just hours her fever broke. Sometimes, when I put some on my hands or face before falling asleep, I would wake up in the middle of the night feeling the presence of Sai Baba peacefully watching over me as I slept. When my grade school friends came over, I would tell them that it was "magic powder," capable of curing anything from a skinned knee to a difficult little brother!

A few years later, my father became friends with a man named Ram while attending medical school. Ram was from India, and had a few stories of his own about Sai Baba. By this time my dad had great respect for Sai Baba and had read most of what was written about him. When he was invited to attend Ram's wedding in India, he knew that it was time to visit Sai Baba as well. He fell in love with the country and the culture, but most significant to him was his visit with Sai Baba, which changed the direction of his life. When he met Sai Baba face to face, he handed him an envelope with a photograph of me inside and broke into tears. For the first time, he said, he could see our father–daughter relationship from an ageless, timeless perspective. He came home with a notable aliveness, and a desire to return to the ashram in the next few years with me.

During my twelfth year, my dad had a chance to take a month off, and seized the opportunity by booking two round-trip flights to India. Before long, we were on a plane and headed for Madras! Just as he had seen in the dream years before, we were traveling together to meet Sai Baba in person.

When I first laid eyes on the man from a distance, I was astounded to see a bluish-white glow surrounding his head and shoulders. I realized then that perhaps halos are more than just a symbolic image! The next small miracle was watching him produce *vibutti*. Although there were very large crowds each day, my dad and I were determined to get a close-range view of the process.

One day, as he passed through the crowd, Sai Baba walked straight to us. He put his hand directly over us, palm down, and moved it in a circle—and a shower of the holy ash poured out of his hand. I look up and saw six to nine glowing circular lights on the palm of his hand, like a shower head pouring ash. As he walked away, he gave us a big grin, as if to say, "See, I am for real!"

As an M.D., my father takes an open but scientific approach to such things, and yet to this day he speaks with utter astonishment about watching Baba make *vibutti*. My dad is now committed to using his healing powers to help cure infectious diseases in India. He feels it is part of his destiny to enrich the lives of others, as Sai Baba uplifted and inspired him.

Meeting Sai Baba helped me to realize that miraculous things are within my reach. I now know that I came here to make a difference, and that every human being is living proof that miracles do exist.

I think it ought to be a requirement that all young people encounter a miracle maker like Sai Baba before they graduate from high school. It would offer them an opportunity to see and believe in something extraordinary . . . and those who grow up believing in the invisible learn to do the impossible!

The Wailing Wall

Judith Orloff, M.D.

A few years ago I visited the Wailing Wall in Jerusalem, a place so holy that people of many religions make pilgrimages there from all over the world. For the Jewish people, this wall is especially sacred. It's all that remains of the ancestral temple that was destroyed in A.D. 70, when the Jews were forced into exile. Traditionally, Jews have journeyed there to shed tears and mourn the original loss of their homeland. The wall is not merely a historical marker, however; many Jews regard it as a physical touchstone to a greater sanctity.

As I slowly approached the women's side of the wall, I felt I was being drawn into the vortex of a tornado. At least a hundred women, heads covered with shawls in muted colors, where wailing at the top of their lungs. I felt besieged by their outpouring of grief. I wanted to run from it, yet I just stood there. As usual when overloaded, my first response was to go numb. Mechanically, I lifted my arm and placed my neatly folded prayer into a crack between two mammoth golden-brown stones, as was the custom. Then, as if a switch had been flipped, my feelings returned, but magnified, larger than life. Like a hypnotic incantation, the moaning and wailing of the other women lured me in. I hadn't intended to cry, but soon tears filled my eyes. I was startled; I'd been feeling fine. I was sure I had nothing to cry about.

Uncontrollably, my body began to tremble as a wave of sadness hit me. So many personal losses came back at once: memories of smaller disappointments, my grandfather's death, relationships I'd worked so hard on that failed. And my weeping didn't stop there. Gathering momentum, I cried not only for myself but for my family and friends, for all the troubles and injustices in the world that came to mind. Finally, I cried just to cry. In a tremendous release, I completely let loose. It was a cleansing, purifying catharsis, as the despair washed through me and became something more. My cries and the wailing of every woman at the wall blended together with all that had come before us, merging into a single sound. I was immersed in a whirlpool of grief, not just my own, but a larger grief that seemed to be arising from the heart of the collective.

As if coming out of a trance, I noticed the sky growing dark. I could hear the evening prayers of the Muslims echoing mournfully throughout the city from a central mosque nearby. I looked up at a clock tower, stunned to see that two hours had passed when I'd only planned to stay a few minutes. The old city of Jerusalem glistened, the last rays of sunlight reflecting off the winding cobblestone streets. I walked briskly back to my hotel. Exhausted, I couldn't wait to jump into a steaming hot bath. But I was also exuberant: Beneath all that grief at the wall, I'd felt a collective oneness, an ecstatic and merciful unifying force. At that point, I'd only been meditating a year and had gotten just glimpses of it. But now there it was—right before me, glorious as could be.

It took many months for what happened to fully sink in. Yes, I was somehow catapulted into a profound feeling of connection. But how did I get there? I needed to know. Slowing everything down, examining it in stages, I came to appreciate more than ever that the Wailing Wall itself was sitting on a powder keg of energy—amplified over the centuries by every person who'd ever come to grieve. Even those who don't think of themselves as psychic can't help but feel its pull. I'd no idea how tremendous it would be and within minutes had been launched into a hyperalert psychic state. First, without intending to, I began to cry. But that was just the starting point, one layer that soon melded into another. Surrendering to my sadness, I let it carry me as it grew in intensity, until its very force lifted me from my own emotions to an experience of collective grief. I could never in a million years have willed this to happen. And then, not resisting the frenzy of this collective grief, I felt it evolve into a sublime oneness. I knew we all were of a single heart, the ancient memory of love binding us through time.

Love has a way of moving us beyond the artificial boundaries we've created. It's the uniting ingredient, no matter what path we choose, transcending religious differences. Just because we adhere to a particular faith doesn't have to limit us from appreciating the good in them all. Without love, we are spiritually adrift. The world can appear impoverished, fraught with an endless series of insoluble problems. Separation from love is the primary cause of our pain. With love, we have the courage to take our difficulties in stride and turn them into demonstrations of faith.

The Noble Truth of Suffering

Ara Ketenjian

Dawn had not yet broken on Varanasi, Uttar Pradesh, India, the oldest continuously inhabited city in the world. I made my way among the sleeping bodies of pilgrims and rickshaw drivers, through the narrow streets leading to the

Ganges River. The city stood like a fortress atop a wide row of stone steps, leading down to where long-hulled wooden rowboats haphazardly caressed each other, waiting for their tourist cargo.

Entering my boat, I began my slow journey upstream. The water was a mesmerizing kaleidoscope of shimmering colors. Reflections of the soft blue sky were criss-crossed by the bathing worshippers' brilliant saris in orange and rasp-berry, gold and green. We passed small merchant rowboats filled with trinkets and imitation brass relics and came to the cremation grounds.

A dead body, bundled in a luminous yellow-sequined sheet, lay propped up on a short bamboo ladder awaiting its turn. Some garlands of orange flowers that had once adorned the dead had floated to the edge of the river, and were being eaten by a black cow. Two dogs were scaveng-ing the grounds for scraps.

I found myself at the foot of the burning corpse of a woman. The fire had started at the middle of her trunk, and smoke, seeping upward along her chest and neck, was ris-ing from underneath the brown cloth that covered her face. The whole experience felt unreal, and I had to remind my-self that this was not an effigy.

Here was a woman who once had lived, whose children were even now watching her burning body. She had loved them, nursed them, raised them. Now I wonder what else was burning, along with her body. What yearnings, what longings, what memories?

For a moment, I imagined that it was my mother burn-ing there: those were her smoldering thighs; that was her face obscured by smoke. I remembered how I had always yearned for my mother's love, but how I had felt aban-doned by her.

I was two years old when I was diagnosed with tubercu-losis. My family transported me to my uncle's hospital, some two hours away from home, and deposited me in a crib with metal bars taller than I was, where I stayed for six months. I was imprisoned. I wanted out. But every time I rattled my cage or tried to climb out, my six-foot-two-inch uncle would subdue me with a beating, or by pulling on my ears. To my infantile mind, I was the victim of a mother who had abandoned me. I could never bring myself, after that, to believe my mother truly loved me. I felt close to her, yet distant; concerned, yet dispassionate.

As I kept gazing at the burning corpse, I had a vision.

I saw my young mother emerge from the burning body. She was holding me in her arms: I knew, somehow, that I was barely ten months old. I could see that her whole body, her whole essence, was love. She loved me . . . truly, deeply, effortlessly.

How could I have missed it? How could I have thought otherwise? Gradually, my mind wandered to earlier times. I found myself thinking about the time when I was still in her womb. Although it had the quality of a reverie, it felt like an authentic memory. I saw myself as happy, contented, and serene. I loved the buoyant feeling of the amniotic fluid. All my senses were gently catered to. I was in need of nothing. I was in paradise.

Then, one unforgettable day, after hours of being squeezed and pushed, I was forcefully ejected into an alien and painful environment, accosted by bright lights, loud noises, cold, biting air. Now I had to cry to be fed, cry to be cleaned. My senses were dazzled by a fusillade of stimuli. I had been traumatized, introduced to pain, hunger, thirst, isolation. And the likeliest explanation was that I had been expelled by my mother. From that day on, I had never forgiven my mother for her cruel act.

Suddenly I was completely overtaken by a heightened state of clarity that opened all the pores of my awareness. In that moment, I comprehended the profound statement of the Buddha, that "Life is suffering."

Previously, I had agreed that life was tinged with suffering, that struggle was a necessary ingredient to survival. But surely, there must have been some who had never known the acrid taste of depression, poverty, and hunger.

There must have been some who had been spared the cruel sword of inner turmoil. Suffering could not be universal. No, it was *I* who, through psychological hurt, neglect, and malconditioning, had fashioned for myself a life sprinkled with fear, anxiety, and worry.

But the vision made me realize otherwise. Clearly, the very act of birth, and hence life itself, could occur only with an experience and awareness that I had identified with suffering. Without birth there could be no life—but birth and suffering could not be separated, or even exist without one another. My mother was not to blame for my pain. In fact, it had been an act of love for her to endure the agony of birthing; to give me life, a future, a dream; to nurse me, cuddle me, and sing for me.

I was filled with a deep, genuine compassion toward my mother. For the first time in memory, I loved her—truly, simply, loved her. Unable to contain it any longer, I burst into tears, which poured out in spasms of forgiveness, of belonging, of oneness.

In that moment of reconciliation, I got my first glimpse of the true nature of suffering as part and parcel of the human condition. Through the pain that it had caused, my focus had been riveted on *my* role in creating my own psychological torment. But *life itself*, through birth, had infused suffering as part of my condition. Suddenly I saw the answer. It was existence before life that was joyous, loving, and serene—while life itself was suffering.

My task was to experience existence, the empty sky against which my suffering had exploded like fireworks that disintegrate into vanishing sparks. The light and noise of suffering had captured my attention and made it seem real. But, ultimately, only the sky remained.

The secret lay in knowing and becoming the backdrop against which suffering had appeared. For therein lay the true understanding of existence. Therein was freedom. Therein was to be found the end of suffering: Nirvana.

A Family Regathering

Michael Peter Langevin

It was 1974, and I'd been traveling in Peru for about a month. Now my time there was drawing to an end, and as I stood on an Andean mountain looking out over endless, glorious valleys, I was suddenly moved to scream at the top of my lungs: "Okay, Peru, I am leaving! But I will be back one day for more of your life-changing plans for me. I know we have work to do together!"

I was twenty-two. I didn't realize I'd made a date with destiny.

Fifteen years later, I asked the most wonderful, most intense, most challenging woman I had ever met to marry me.

Deborah accepted, on the condition that we adopt a child. She felt we should adopt a child who had little hope of a "good life," and offer him the great love we shared. Neither of us felt the need to have biological children, and there were so many children who'd been born without the advantages we had known.

Our wedding was idyllic, our honeymoon otherworldly. Soon after, we started looking into adoption.

We didn't feel ready to adopt a teenager or special-needs child as our first. And at that time, it seemed that every agency in the U.S. was discouraging interracial adoptions—effectively making young, adoptable children a rarity, at least for us. So our search continued.

We learned that interracial adoptions were easier and faster outside the States. The cost of travel and fees varied from country to country, and Deborah and I agreed that Guatemala and El Salvador were just barely affordable—but the waiting time in each country seemed to be years. Discouraged, we went to another agency, where they told us Peru had many children waiting for immediate placement. Unfortunately, the costs were way beyond our means.

That night, the pictures of the children waiting in the orphanages haunted me. I prayed for help.

A few days later there was the big earthquake of 1990, and our house was damaged: not unlivable, just noticeably damaged. This set in motion a series of events which soon provided us with most of the money for a Peruvian adoption.

We called the agency and they put us in touch with a social worker in Peru. We sent her our legal papers, and within a week she called saying she had a two-year-old boy we could adopt, if we could come to Peru that week. We quickly made our arrangements, and off we flew to a new life.

We landed in Peru in the early evening. The social worker and her husband met us at the Lima airport and got us through customs. They drove us to our hotel and checked us in, then took us to a local seafood restaurant, where we were exposed to memorable Peruvian culinary delights and proceeded to get very drunk on strong Peruvian beer. They told us adoption stories, and much about life in Peru. They were warm people with whom we quickly felt comfortable. At the same time, they were obviously checking us out, to see if we met their criteria.

We found out the next morning that they felt we were suitable. The social worker woke us early with the news that we had to go right to the Hall of Justice to sign papers for the little boy.

The Hall of Justice in Lima is a grim place. Most people who work there are extremely underpaid and overworked. Many resent rich Americans flying in to adopt Peruvian children, so they tend to make the process slow and painful, and fill it with confusing bureaucratic roadblocks. We filled out the papers, and waited for hours for them to be processed.

While we waited, convicts and orphans paraded by, being processed in and out of institutions. One baby was carried by four different times, crying so loud she gave me a headache. Finally, we were called for further processing.

In a small office, three clerks asked us a multitude of questions and slowly typed our answers. One of the clerks was holding the loudly crying baby, feeding her Coca-Cola from a spoon and a Peruvian candy bar.

The social worker talked at length to the clerk holding the baby, and then came over to us. "That little girl was found abandoned on the side of the road," she told us. "She has been in the police orphanage for the maximum waiting time. No one knows anything about the child or how it got there. It was to be transferred to the state orphanage today, but they are overflowing with babies, there is absolutely no room. This clerk is taking her home because there is no other place for her, but she has no money for food and has to work tomorrow. If you want two children and will sign the papers, the clerks will see that this second adoption processes quickly."

We went deeper into shock. Not one, but two children?

Deborah and I attempted to discuss it rationally. We had said that eventually we would like a girl as a second child. We couldn't really afford the extra adoption costs now, but it would be less expensive than coming back in a year or two.

My wife asked, "What do you feel, Michael?"—meaning in a deeper, spiritual sense. I examined the baby.

She was not too cute, almost ugly for a baby. Her eyes looked somehow wrong. They lacked luster, and didn't follow my hand when I waved it over her face. She seemed as if she might be blind, or have birth defects or brain damage. She was clearly sick and suffering from malnutrition, with an overextended stomach. There were bugs visible in her hair and scratches and bites on her face. She hadn't stopped crying and screaming except to eat the chocolate and drink the Coca-Cola.

I turned to my wife and said, "I feel it could be very difficult. However, I also feel we wouldn't be asked if it wasn't destined to be this way."

My wife hesitated, then said, "Well, okay. If you feel that way, then we will adopt a daughter today as well as the son we had planned on."

The social worker and clerks were a little surprised that we were willing to make such a big decision on the spur of the moment—as were we. But they handed my wife the child and began the paperwork, which would take another hour. Could we take the child someplace and try to quiet her?

We walked around the halls of the Hall of Justice in Lima, Peru, on our second day in the country, with a baby that was to be our daughter. Many lawyers and clerks asked us, not so nicely, to quiet our baby or leave. Our baby! What a moment.

My wife eventually handed her to me. I rocked her and sang her songs my mother had sung to me as a child. She finally fell asleep in my arms.

Moments after we finally got her to sleep, the social worker found us. "Come on, quickly," she yelled. "We are to meet with the judge." Our daughter awoke and began to scream some more.

The judge seemed relieved that we were taking the second child. She seemed to like us. She asked many more questions, then signed the first-stage release papers. We were the guardians, with temporary custody, of this baby and the boy. We were to go pick him up at once.

The social worker got a cab and we proceeded to the orphanage, a huge, worn, gray institution with hundreds of children and too few caretakers. The conditions were depressing. The children owned nothing. They slept three and four to a bed. They shared clothes, with different shirts and pants distributed each morning, but no socks and shoes. There was little running water, sporadic electricity, not enough food. There were no toys beyond a few soccer balls. Worst of all, there was no medicine.

We were brought to a sparsely furnished office, where

some dedicated, exhausted child care workers attempted to tell us about Henry. We gathered that he had been found a year earlier, walking alone down a dirt road in one of the shantytowns that surround Lima. However, beyond this we learned very little, because our new daughter screamed the whole time. We attempted to ask questions over the screaming, but our Spanish was too slow and not advanced enough, and theirs too fast. The social worker was asking about other children and didn't translate very much.

We gave them the lice medicine we'd been asked to bring, and the clothes our new son was to wear—they couldn't spare any of theirs. Frustrated, we kept trying to find out as much more as we could about our new son as we waited to meet him. Finally, the door opened.

There stood a scared little boy in the clothes we had brought. They were way to small. His hair was cut in patches. He, too, was suffering from malnutrition. He had an extended stomach, and bug bites, scars and scratches marked his face, arms and legs.

This is my son! I thought as I knelt to hug him. He burst into tears and screams of fear at my touch. The social worker assured us it would be fine. No, he had no belongings to take. We were just to take him and leave. We were now his guardians.

All five of us bundled into the cab to return to our hotel. The children sat on our laps, holding a screaming match the whole ride across Lima. When we arrived, the social worker helped us feed the children. They both ate and ate; they were starving.

As they finished eating, our Peruvian lawyer arrived to meet them, and the social worker left. Our lawyer told us the children should be washed immediately because they could be carrying all forms of germs and viruses. Seeing our confused state, she offered to assist. So she, in her expensive business suit, and we, totally exhausted and deep in shock, proceeded to wash the children.

Back at the courtroom, we had named our new daughter Sophia, for the goddess of wisdom. She was about eight months old, so she was unaware of the orphanage-assigned name of Zila, which we kept as her middle name. Our new son was already answering to Henry; we gave him Miguel as his middle name.

Washing Sophia was difficult. She twisted and turned, fought and screamed, succeeding in drenching us all. Henry, however, made her seem easy. He refused to take off his new clothes, fearing he would never see them again. He fought us tooth and nail as we stripped and washed him. He was strong and a fighter, and it was a battle royal. They both had warrior's spirits to have even survived under those circumstances until we arrived.

After his bath, we were all totally exhausted and completely soaked. Henry's new pajamas fit better than his day clothes. We gave them both toys we had brought. They ate again, and then quickly fell asleep. The lawyer wished us the best of luck and left.

We called room service for dinner and a couple of Peruvian beers. My wife and I ate and drank, watched our new children sleep, and tried to help each other adjust to what had just taken place. We were now a family—not yet legally so, but we believed we would soon be.

A son and a daughter: They were sick but strong, descendants of the Incas. Who were they? Who would they become? What would life be like from now on? On and on we talked.

The evening passed, and my wife eventually went to sleep. I just couldn't, even though I was beyond exhaustion. I went down to the hotel bar for one last beer.

Sipping my beer, I walked out to the courtyard. I looked up at the glorious southern sky, and the promise I had screamed to Peru sixteen years before came back to me in a flash.

I swear I then heard an elder Quechuan voice in my head say, "Now you belong to the family of the Incas. Your future, your destiny, is linked to the mysteries and magic of the Incas. Give these children your best, and make them proud of their heritage. You have been chosen."

My spine tingled. I looked around. I was all alone in the courtyard. Was it just my overactive, exhausted mind?

I whispered into the cool night air, "I will do my very best. I pray and beg for all the help you can provide. And thank you for the greatest gifts you could have ever shared with me."

Returning to our room, I kissed each child and my wife, wrote for a little bit in my journal, and went to sleep. It seemed I had just fallen asleep when I was awakened by my new daughter screaming. I jumped up, as did my wife. We were both at the bed in a flash. What was wrong? We changed her diaper, rocked her some, and gave her a bottle. She quickly fell back asleep. Henry slept through it all. We returned to bed.

This time I dreamt of the Andes mountains as they were before the Europeans came.

I was in an Inca holy valley, inhabited by priests and priestesses, shamans and prophets. They knew what the future held, and were working to guarantee that spiritual power and knowledge would survive and be available to all the planet when the dark decades had passed and the spiritual vibrations of the planet and humanity were ready to enter a new era of existence. In this valley, I lived with my present-day wife and children. We were a family then also. We were workers of magic, and in this dream we performed a ceremony to ensure that we would reincarnate and come together as a strong unit when the Earth was in need. The ceremony was other-dimensional. I dreamt of shapes I could smell, and sounds I could see. I dreamt that we danced and shared the most intimate energies with cosmic god beings. They found our request worthy and granted our wish, but said it would not be made easy. We would have to remember our purpose on our own in that future time, and convince each other to perform our chosen roles. But we would be given knowledge of two worlds, and we would have each other's love and support. I felt a transcendent, shamanic, orgasmic energy run through me and I shivered, waking myself up.

My son was crying quietly. I got up and picked him up onto my lap and rocked him. He smiled, and after a while fell back asleep.

I sat there with my new son in my lap and thought of my dream. Was it just a dream? Was I filling in the details as I wished? It was so intense and unusual and otherworldly. I wondered if it could be based on reality.

I decided it just might be, and that I was going to let myself belief that it was. I wouldn't share it with my family until I felt the time was best, but I would use it as my guiding vision. I was not just a new father. I was an ancient Inca shaman who had reincarnated with my family, to help rediscover the lost wisdom that would help unfold a new evolution, a new reality, for Earth in the twenty-first century. I said a prayer to the ancient goddess being who had helped us. I asked that she help us to achieve our goals in this life, and help me to teach my children to be all they could become.

Sophia and Henry are now seven and eight. They are both excellent students, fluent in Spanish and English. Healthy and beautiful, they are great athletes. They have many friends, and are two of the greatest people I have ever known.

Even if my dream that night wasn't the truth; even if my children grow up with no taste for magic; even if the twenty-first century is just more of the past two thousand years, with no major dimensional shifts that we help usher in ... I will always know that my life is blessed. Raising Sophia and Henry has been the most intensely demanding experience of my very adventure-filled life. It has given me a deeper understanding of who I am, what pure love is, and what it can accomplish. For that is the most powerful transformative magic: pure, unselfish love.

A Moment of Clarity

Jerry Snider

Though the mystical experience can be profound, it can just as easily be dismissed. Second-guessing that magical flash of illumination drags it from sacred time into real time, where, like a shimmering pebble removed from a stream, it loses its sparkle and sheen. So when the muse of magic presents herself to you, don't look for explanations or proof; don't expect her to enter your world, but make the effort to enter hers.

The four or five genuine moments of grace that I have experienced in the course of my forty-five years have shared one thing in common: the feeling of two worlds coming together, overlapping for a moment, and then moving on. When it happens, the experience is palpable, but if you blink, the moment will be gone.

My first such moment occurred when I was fifteen years old. The experience was dramatic, and I can honestly say it changed my life. But in retrospect, the moment itself has moved on; its magic lives not in the memory of the moment, but in the effect that moment had.

The year was 1967. The youth of this country were caught up in a gale of cultural crosswinds. These winds of change were exciting but exhausting and, to those of us still floundering around in puberty, totally confusing. Too young to join the parade, we watched from the sidelines as the "youth culture" put its stamp on society. We watched the flower children take their stand in San Francisco; we saw our older brothers drafted and shipped off to Vietnam, many of them never to return. From politics to culture to spirituality, everything seemed to be changing, and those of us who were to inherit this changed world had little recourse but to watch it unfold around us, sometimes in spite of us.

One of the few movements that offered easy access to those old enough to care but too young to have much of an influence was the Jesus movement. Growing up in a small middle-class town in the Midwest, I don't remember many spiritual alternatives to Christianity. Though Buddhism and Wicca may have been flowering on the West Coast, and Islam was making an impact in the inner cities, Christianity was the only game in my landlocked town of ten thousand.

To put it bluntly, what I had seen of it through local church services was, in a word, boring. In a world threatening to break apart with change, Sunday School stressed only the need to conform. While the birthright of spirituality is passion, the religion I was taught concerned itself only with passivity. Then came the Jesus movement, whose reinterpretation of Jesus as a social rebel suddenly sparked life back into what to many appeared a dead religion, and promised a spirituality applicable to the times.

And so it was that once a week I joined with friends in often heated discussions of biblical passages and their meanings. These informal discussions were nothing like the church services I had attended; they were full of angst and anger, and I often felt flushed and overwhelmed by the passion they stirred in me.

After all these years, I cannot honestly tell you *what* we discussed, but I vividly recall the emotions fired by these meetings, and they were seldom pleasant. When I think back to the image I have of a bunch of adolescent, apoplectic religious scholars using the Scriptures to beat each other over the head, I can't help but laugh, but at the time it was serious business. We took Jesus at His word when He said, "I come not to bring peace, but a sword."

The last of these meetings I attended was the most difficult. I remember feeling like I wanted to explode—and to
keep from doing so, I rushed outside. Not only was I angry,
but I was ashamed at losing my composure in front of my
friends. I was quite certain that they would no longer want
to have anything to do with me, and, frankly, I wasn't sure I
wanted anything more to do with them.

Compared with the oppressive heat of the house, outside was cool and refreshing. The sun was just beginning to
set, and the sky was ablaze with color.

And then something changed, something impossible to
describe except to say that for a moment, two worlds
touched. One nigh, huge cloud passed over the sun, drain-
ing the color from the sky. As it passed and the color again
returned, every bit of anger was gone, every touch of
shame was released, and instead of confusion, an amazing
sense of certainty flooded my being. In that moment, God
spoke to me, not in a voice, but in a clear, clean message
that I did not have to hear, because it spoke to every cell of
my body.

There were no words, but now, thirty years later, perhaps I can put into words what I learned on that cool, clean
fall evening: Forget religion; it is a thing of the mind. Live
your life with integrity. Make each moment count, and regard every living thing as an expression of the Divine. That
is spirituality, and that is what you will answer for. All the
rest is personal expression, like the food you like or the
clothes you wear.

The message was simple and obvious, but were it not for
the profound experience that accompanied it, I know I
would not have listened. And had I not listened, my life
would have turned out much different than it did, for that
mystical moment released me from my own personality.

My adult life has been directed toward the spiritual
quest. I have followed the spiritual impulse to every con-
ceivable corner of its expression, and I have been able to do
so because of the truth that was presented to me that eve-

ning thirty years ago, when one cloud passed over the sun and another passed out of my life.

Were it not for that moment of exquisite lucidity, I would have invested my interest in spirituality with the need for an answer. Because of that one mystical moment, I have escaped the prison we construct by confusing interest with answers.

The world still fights in deadly earnest over beliefs, and the number of martyrs of all faiths continues to climb. And for what? I mean no disrespect when I tell you it is for nothing. People hate and die over beliefs, while the truth of their own lives becomes lost in the fracas.

All I know now is that beliefs are important, but not as important as a life well lived. It's as simple and as challenging as that.

2

DIVINE GUIDANCE AND INNER DIRECTION

Do It Yourself!

Rick Gomez

About four years ago I was a guest at the "Hotel California," otherwise known as CCI: California Correctional Institution. I had ended up in this awful place out of my own stupidity, but it still seemed like nothing was going my way. I've heard a lot of people say that out of every bad experience comes something good. I didn't think things could get much worse.

They seemed to, though, after I went from being a pretty trim guy to a husky 212-pound slob. I could barely look at myself in the mirror. But in prison, there really isn't a whole hell of a lot to do, so I decided to get myself in shape.

I put my plan into action right away, started running hard and eating healthy. But I decided not to weigh myself. I'd just keep at it for one month and see what happened.

Every day the same routine, until finally a month had passed. Excited to see some results, I darted over to the chow hall and jumped on the scale. What I saw made me more disgusted than ever. I had gained two pounds!

This was just plain unfair. "God," I complained, "you're tore up! You can't even let me lose a lousy couple pounds. You're tore up!"

Still griping, I angrily headed toward the bathroom. No one was in there but me, and I said it once more. "God, you're tore up!"

Then, for no reason at all, I reached in my pocket, felt

something there, and pulled it out. It was a gold business card, with exquisite handwriting on it in black ink. The words seemed to leap off the card at me:

If I answered all of your
prayers I'd be your slave
Not Your God!

I went, "Whoa!"

Could God have actually just "talked" to me? If so, why me? I'd never shown a whole lot of faith in him. The words rang in my head, over and over.

Still not believing this could be happening, I took the card to the only people who could have placed it in my pocket. I checked with the most likely person first, our laundry guy, Shaggy. I questioned my mother about the card. I asked the Bible study leader, Captain Frank, if he had seen any other cards like it floating around. Like everyone else, he answered no, and added that it was a revelation.

I stuck the card in a book for safekeeping. My attitude took a 180, and I began to believe.

The following month I weighed myself, and I had lost five pounds. My weight continued to drop each month. When it came time for me to leave, I weighed in at a lean, mean 170.

But not just my excess body weight was gone. So was my excessive blaming and begging God. And, just as mysteriously as it had appeared, the card disappeared, too. I guess it had served its purpose.

People shouldn't go through life asking God for every little thing. That isn't what He is there for. If you want something bad enough . . . do it yourself. If you have faith in yourself, God will be right there with you!

A Burden Light as a Feather

Robert Gass

The canyonlands wilderness of Utah is one of my places of vision and power. I go to the desert, with its primal sandstone turrets, obelisks, and spires and pristine beauty, for clarity and solitude.

I was on a ten-day solo retreat, staying in a remote cabin at a ranch that offered such spiritual haven. I spent the first days emptying myself of the stress and speed of modern daily life. As I became quiet, I put out prayers for guidance about direction in my work and life. In one of my meditations, I heard that I was to write a book on energy and work with individual leaders as a guide and coach.

The next day, I'd left the ranch to hike in a nearby canyon, and climbed partway up one of the red sandstone walls. I was feeling very agitated about my "assignment" and spontaneously started talking out loud to God.

"Okay, God, what about this book and this work? You know, I don't need to do this stuff anymore. I really get that I don't need to do important things in the world to be happy; in fact I'd be quite happy doing very little for the next while. If this is important and serves you, I'll do it. Otherwise, I don't know. Please give me some kind of sign if this really matters to you. Some kind of physical sign so that I'll know this is really mine to do."

All of a sudden, it started raining. Concerned about the rock becoming slippery, I descended rapidly, forgot about the conversation, the sign, and God, and started walking back to the ranch. About fifteen minutes later, I turned around. There was a rainbow. One end went directly into the rock I had been standing on.

Rather than finding this reassuring, I became far more agitated. "That's a sign. Definitely a sign . . . Well, maybe not. Rainbows do happen . . . But that's the promise God gave to Moses. It's the classic sign of the covenant of God and man . . . So now you think you're Moses? Sign, *schmine*, it's a rainbow."

I debated the point all the way to my cabin.

Beginning to feel desperate, I talked to God again.

"Okay, I know this is asking a lot. I asked for a sign, and there was a rainbow coming right out of the rock where I stood. I should be feeling grateful, but I feel scared and confused. I have doubt. Maybe doubt isn't handled by signs. But if it serves, I would ask for one more sign. A sign so clear and unmistakable that even my doubting fears will be stilled. I ask that a feather come to me in some unmistakably magical way. I also understand that I may not get this sign. Maybe I need to live with doubt, and that's okay."

At that point, I released it. I felt a letting-go inside: Even if the sign did not come, I was prepared to accept my assignment as best I understood it.

That morning, a group of women had come to the ranch for a ceremony. They had heard from the ranch owner that I was in the retreat cabin. My musical recordings were an important part of their group life, and they sent a delegation to ask if I might be willing to come and sing a few songs at their ceremonial fire that evening.

I suppose I should have felt honored, but I was a little grumpy. *I'm supposed to be on retreat,* I thought to myself. I was going to say no, but I remembered my request to God. I felt, in this moment, that that spirit was in the form of these women, and I smiled and accepted.

That evening, we gathered around the fire for prayers, songs, and dancing. The evening was finished. I was packing up my guitar when a woman stepped up to me. She looked me in the eye and said, "Here, this is for you. I heard I was supposed to give it to you." In her hand was the feather of a red-tailed hawk.

As my hand touched the feather, I heard the voice of my doubting self try to come up with a counterargument. And there was none. For once, my inner skeptic was speechless.

The feather sits on my altar as a reminder of God's will.

An Author's Angel

Diana Loomans

A good book is a sacred treasure, inspiring new realms of thinking and serving as a friend and guide in the great adventure of life. Because of the power of the printed word, I've always held authors in high esteem, but it wasn't until I was an adult that my own callings to become an author began to stir.

I was a college teacher and speaker with a growing sense that it was time for me to publish my ideas and share them with the world. I'd been filling journals for years, but somehow the concept of writing a book still seemed "larger than life." It seemed that it was part of my life purpose . . . but I didn't have the foggiest notion as to how to go about becoming an author.

I started out writing children's stories with the help of my young daughter, Julia. After receiving wonderful feedback from family and friends, I sensed that it was time to publish some of them. So I began to read up on the subject . . . and the more I researched, the more discouraged I became. I learned that only about one in twenty thousand children's manuscripts submitted to publishers are actually selected for publication.

Finally, I decided to do away with the research and rely on my intuition for further direction. I decided to record my own audiotape, describing my ideal publishers in vivid detail. I included such statements as, "When my publishers see the work and the impact that it will have on the world, their eyes will fill with tears." Although it seemed a little far-fetched, it certainly couldn't do any harm. I entitled the tape "Divine Authorship."

For several weeks I listened to the tape every night before drifting off to sleep. What followed within a few short weeks was nothing short of a miracle!

First, all in the same day, three separate acquaintances advised me to attend an upcoming booksellers' event. The next day, I was browsing in a local bookstore when a book literally fell off the shelf onto the floor in front of me: *Do What You Love, the Money Will Follow*. As I paged through the book, the store manager approached me and began to talk about the same booksellers' event I'd just heard about! When I told her about my desire to publish my work, she surprised me by saying, "I happen to have an extra ticket to the convention, and an extra bed in my hotel room. Would you like to go?"

My attention definitely aroused, I went home and called the airlines to check flight costs. After adding up the expenses, I decided it was best to put the idea on the shelf and attend the following year.

That evening, I went with Julia to the premier showing of a new movie, *Field of Dreams*. I was deeply moved by the inspiring message that the main character heard repeatedly about his dream: "If you build it, they will come." That night, it became clear that I had to follow suit and find a way to attend this upcoming event.

The next morning my daughter wandered into my room, still half-asleep, and said, "Mom, please go to the conference. If you don't go, you'll never know what might have happened!" An hour later, my travel agent called to offer me a special half-fare flight. "I don't know why," she said, "but I feel that I'm supposed to give this special to you, instead of the client I was saving it for."

A week later I was off to Washington, D.C., to mingle with over forty thousand people in several large convention halls that seemed to go on for miles. For two days I roamed the aisles and met plenty of interesting people, but it didn't feel like I was making any real progress. By the end of the third day I was exhausted, with blistered feet and a bout of the flu. I stayed in my hotel room the following day, taking shelter under the covers, wondering what on earth had possessed me to make this last-minute dash across the country! What was I doing here, anyway?

I called Julia to tell her I was planning to return home a day early, and chalk it off as a learning experience. I felt a mix of discouragement and gratitude as my daughter reminded me, "Remember, Mom, if you build it, they will come. Don't give up, you still have one more day!" That night I prayed for faith and direction, and decided to stick it out for the final day.

The next morning, I woke with an amazing sense of enthusiasm and purpose. The first woman I met at breakfast steered me to a publishing company that was just starting to add children's books to their list. Since this was the second time the name had come up, I was intrigued and decided to track down their booth.

I found a stately looking gentleman with snow-white hair and a vibrant face. It was Hal Kramer, the president of the company, in the midst of what appeared to be an important meeting. I waited a while to get a word with him, and then decided that it wasn't such a good idea after all.

I was walking away with a forlorn look on my face when a cheery young man playing a flute called out from his booth, "Excuse me, you look like you could use a friend . . ." I told him my story and showed him my ideas. "It just so happens that I know Mr. Kramer," he said, grinning. "You know, the two of you might be just perfect for each other! If

I were you, I'd interrupt his meeting and ask him for a few minutes of his time when he's through."

With that, I turned back and walked right up to Hal Kramer, who was studying an official-looking document with a few of his colleagues. "Excuse me, Mr. Kramer," I said with startling confidence, "I would very much appreciate a minute of your time when you're through with your meeting."

"I'll only have a few minutes," he said tentatively. "We're packing up, and my wife and I will be flying home in a few hours."

"That's all I need."

As I waited, I scanned the display of inspirational books that Mr. Kramer had published over the years. I was amazed to discover that he'd published the book I brought with me on my trip to keep my spirits up if I became discouraged.

When Mr. Kramer finally had a free moment, I placed the proposals for two of my books on the table and briefly explained my work. He looked them over carefully, and after a long pause he said, "Your work is very special. Perhaps it's time to get it out into the world."

He motioned to his wife and business partner, inviting her to take a look. Within moments, her eyes filled with tears—just as I'd predicted on my tape!—she looked at me and said, "This looks like the kind of material we've been waiting for. Can we take you to lunch?"

We were whisked off by taxi to a plush hotel restaurant in the heart of downtown Washington. By the end of our luncheon, Mr. Kramer said, "In my forty years of publishing, there have only been a few authors that I was absolutely sure about when I met them. You are one of them. I would like to publish both of these books. I'll send you a contract within three days. Will that be an acceptable waiting period?" I nodded speechlessly as he continued, "As a matter of fact, I have a hunch I'll be publishing several of your books. . . . I have a feeling there's a lot more in you!"

We finished with handshakes, hugs, and ear-to-ear grins

all around. I walked out into the midday sunshine feeling dazed and elated. My new publishers fit the description I had put on my tape to a tee!

As I waited for a taxi, a spry, elderly gentleman with deep crevices etched into his kind face approached me from out of the blue. He reached out for my hands and said, "Well, young lady, you have such a beautiful glow about you. You look like someone who has just found her ideal publishers!"

How did he know, I wondered. Was it the hustle-bustle activity of that week between authors and booksellers that spurred him to make such a statement? In a flood of excitement, I proceeded to give him a condensed version of the entire story, rattling off half-sentences and talking in circles. He smiled serenely, patting my arm and nodding in quiet affirmation. As I finished, a taxi pulled up and the gentle old man embraced me warmly. "My dear," he said quietly into my ear, "let me assure you that your publishers are as fortunate to have found you as you are to have found them. There are no coincidences, you know." He gave me one last soulful look and squeezed both of my hands. "I'm very happy for you, and for the world . . . and this is only the beginning."

Thanking him for his words of encouragement, I got into the taxi. What a day this had been! And to think I might have missed it altogether had I flown home early. I was filled with gratitude and awe, recognizing this as a moment of grace. I couldn't wait to celebrate the news with family and friends, and to thank my precious daughter for her unwavering faith in me.

As the taxi began to drive away, I had an urge to turn around and wave to the kind man who had been the first to congratulate me on my newfound success. But—just as I had somehow suspected—he was no longer there, nor anywhere in the vicinity. I felt the hairs on the back of my neck begin to rise.

I waved to him from a deep place in my heart, and

thanked him for "showing up" to help me cross the line into my new world.

My life would never be the same. Shortly thereafter, I signed my first two book contracts, followed by another six books (with my daughter as co-author of two of the books), with more to come.

I meet aspiring authors often these days. Their burning desire to share their treasures with the world takes me back to my own first days, when I had the same fire in my eyes and longing in my heart. I'm often asked for advice on how to go about getting published. Sometimes I want to jump up and down and say, "follow your hunches, make time for your dreams, believe in yourself, ask for what you want . . . and never give up!" Instead, my answer is a simple one: If you build it, they will come!

A Window Washer, a Woman with a Baby, and a Gift

Bruce Stephen Holms

Every once in a while, one of my guests on *Timeless Voyager Radio* (a syndicated show that explores the unknown areas of human experience) tells a story that has a strong impact on me. That was certainly the case with the following.

About seventeen years before the two of us spoke, Morris Fonte was working as a window washer. He was on his way to lunch when he was flagged down by a lady holding a baby in front of one of New York's many cathedrals. He was immediately struck by the fact that she was wearing only a long silk dress and a shawl, on a very cold March afternoon.

He was worrying about the health of the baby in such cold when the woman said, "Morris, you have forgotten your God. Come pray with me."

"Why do I have to pray?" inquired Morris.

The woman answered that it was her duty to bring him back to God. They started to talk about God, religion, and things of that nature. They'd been speaking for about half an hour when she said that she represented God in his life. When she went on to say that she had a message for him from God, Morris felt that the conversation had gone too far. He was beginning to think that the woman, although well meaning, was probably crazy. She should be preaching in one of the city's parks, but not in front of a church. So he excused himself, and went about his business of washing windows.

At the end of the day, he walked past the same church, and there she was. It was as if she had been waiting there all day in the cold, just for him. She called out to him.

"Morris, you have forgotten your God! Come pray with me. I have come to give you a message," she went on, "and a gift from God."

"Why are you doing this?" asked Morris. "This is a lot of baloney! God doesn't just send down gifts to people."

"You must come back to the church. Show your worthiness and the gift will be yours."

What bothered Morris the most was not what the woman was saying, but the fact that she was standing out in the cold with that little baby in her arms. The baby was beautiful, the woman was beautiful—it was as if neither one of them belonged in this world. She looked Israeli or Arabic, and talked to him with incredible love and understanding.

After about fifteen minutes of this type of conversation, however, they parted again. It was cold, and Morris couldn't justify to himself standing in front of a church talking to a "nut."

From that point on, every time he passed the church she would be standing there, calling out to him, insisting that God had sent her to give him this gift.

"You shouldn't talk this way," he would tell her. "You could be locked up . . . especially in front of a church! If a priest hears what you're saying, we'll both be in trouble. We could be arrested!"

But no matter what he said to her, there she was, every time he passed the church. After three weeks of this, Morris decided to invite her for coffee at the corner shop. It was so cold that day that he just wanted to relax and have their usual conversation in a warm place, without worrying about getting arrested.

"What's your name?" Morris asked after they'd settled at a table. "I should at least know that, especially since you somehow know mine!"

"I am the Blessed Virgin Mary, and I have come to give you a gift. I am to bring you back to the church, help you pray, and make you worthy of the gift that God is going to give you."

Morris stood up from the table in shock. This was too much! He walked outside for a moment. After he'd regained his composure, he went back in to confront this woman once and for all.

She greeted him by saying, "I am the Blessed Virgin Mary, and I live in the hearts of all in the world."

Morris blurted out, "You're nuts! I'm going home!" Walking out of the coffee shop, he decided he would never talk to her again . . . even if it meant going out of his way to avoid the church where she'd stationed herself.

After walking aimlessly for about thirty minutes, he arrived home. He opened his apartment door, and there the woman was, sitting in his favorite chair.

Once again she greeted him, saying, "I have come home, and I want to tell you who I am and about the gift I am going to give you! It is coming from God, and it is a gift you have to help people with. It is a gift that I am going to teach you how to use."

Morris yelled. "Lady, I don't know how you got in here, but breaking and entering is against the law! If you don't leave I am going to call the police."

"I can go through walls, Morris. I can go wherever I wish to."

"No . . . no . . . no . . . !"

"I am Spirit!"

"Okay, prove you are what you say you are," Morris said, almost in a whisper.

She was sitting in the chair. But when he turned around she was in the hallway. And when he turned around again she was by the chair. At that point, Morris passed out.

A few moments later he picked himself up from the floor. Apparently oblivious to his condition, the woman again said she was the Blessed Virgin Mary. She had come to give him the gift of extrasensory perception.

"Use it in a mannerly fashion," she told him, "and do not hurt anyone with it. Use it to help people." Then she began to teach him how it worked.

Later, they went back to the coffee shop. As Morris started to talk to the waitress, he found he was able to tell her about herself, her future, her past, her dreams—it was amazing.

Then Mary went away for a while, but she came back to the apartment later that night—with Jesus.

Jesus said to Morris, "This is the gift that my mother has given to you. You must listen to her and use it exactly as she has taught you."

Morris Fonte has since appeared on many radio and television shows. He is known worldwide, and through the yeas he has helped thousands of people with his gift of ESP. Whenever Morris is asked about his unique abilities, he always answers, "Prayer, fasting, meditation, and going to church daily is what strengthens the gift."

The Mouse

David Simon

I awoke early Sunday morning, eager to drive to the garden center to purchase cuttings for my vegetable garden, only to discover that my keys were missing. I looked in every pocket, under each bed, compulsively searched every room and drawer in the house, to no avail. Perplexed and frustrated, I spent the rest of the day continuously scanning my surroundings, waiting for my keys to mysteriously manifest from the black hole that had consumed them.

By evening, I was resigned to the fact that they'd disappeared into "lost object heaven," along with countless single socks, expensive pens, and my scuba diving card. I was looking up the phone number of my car dealership, thinking I'd get my ignition key replaced in the morning, when my son called out, "Dad, there's a mouse in my room!" I ran in to catch a glimpse of a tiny gray field mouse as it ducked under a chest of drawers. Apparently it had entered the house through a back door that had been left open during the warm spring day.

We spent the next two hours trying to snare our little intruder. This proved no easy task. The nimble critter repeatedly outwitted our efforts to corral him into the cardboard trap we'd constructed. As he scurried under the bed, then dashed behind the desk, his ingenuity and sense of timing were impressive. Finally we managed to trap him under the box. But as we attempted to slide a cover onto it, he squeezed through the narrow space and found a new hiding place in my son's closet.

Since this was obviously one smart and resourceful mouse, we rigged up an elaborate scheme to capture our unintended guest. Cutting a hole in the corner of the corrugated cardboard container, we securely taped a large plastic garbage bag to cover the opening. We then tied my son's wooden snake to the end of a wooden rod, and carefully positioned the box so it blocked the entrance to the closet.

Although we were sorry to contribute to the tiny creature's panicked state, we concluded that we would have to in order to liberate our friend. We dangled the snake over the mouse and he instantly bolted for the door. Running into the box, he immediately found the hole cut in the corner and scurried into the plastic bag.

By the time we'd captured him, the sun had long set, so I picked up a flashlight as I carried the bag out of the house. I hiked about a hundred yards to the edge of a canyon that lay beyond my property, and carefully placed the bag on the ground with the top open. Shining the beam of the flashlight on the opening, I waited for our furry friend to emerge. He timidly poked his nose out, then gingerly exited. Squinting in the light, he sat on his hindquarters for a few moments, looking at me with an expression of curiosity and relief. A moment later he scurried away into the darkness.

This is when the magic occurred. There, at the exact spot where the mouse had paid his farewell to me, sat my ring of keys. I had apparently dropped them while clearing some dead branches the day before. By some miraculous coincidence, I had released the mouse at the precise spot.

Now every once in a while my son asks me if I remember the little mouse who found my keys. He thinks Mother Nature rewarded me for liberating one of her meek and gentle beings.

Second Chances

Linda Tisch Sivertsen

My husband Mark and I were renting a beautiful duplex in Los Angeles. One day the owner, who lived next door, came over and caught a beautiful female stray cat we had been feeding. I pleaded with him, cried and screamed at him, but to no avail: He could no longer stand the "annoyance." To my disbelief and horror, he drove her to a local grocery story and dropped her in the parking lot.

Then Mark and I met her three kittens. Each day we would watch as they climbed into our outdoor garage cans in search of food. It was heartbreaking, so we started feeding them on our patio. We noticed that two of the kittens would beat up the runt when he tried to eat; he had scars all over his face from being scratched. We named him Luke, inspired by Paul Newman's performance in *Cool Hand Luke*, because he so bravely took the abuse.

Mark set up a trap, and the first day we were only able to catch Luke. "Lukey," as I called him, was terrified of us. Poor thing, he had lost his mother and now his freedom. Panic-stricken, he shook and cowered behind our bathroom toilet. When we tried to get near him, he would hiss and flail his skinny legs in revolt. Funny how such a little muffin could fight so hard. During the first night we kept Luke safely in the bathroom with plenty of food, water and towels.

Mark and I went to bed. Soon Luke began to cry in his itty-bitty voice. Then a most distressing thing happened. Luke's sister and brother, still free outside, came to the bathroom window and started crying back to him. He answered their cries with howling little meows of his own, clearly mourning the separation.

I removed the comforter from our bed and went into the bathroom. Luke was still huddled behind the toilet, hair standing on end. I wanted him to know that he wasn't alone, so I laid down on the tiles and spent the night on the floor. The minute I closed my eyes his crying ceased. By the second night, still on the tile floor, Luke came and lay down beside me. Gradually he curled up against my belly, and hours later his baby paws were clawing my hair. His purring lulled me to sleep. From that night on, I think I became Mom.

Since that time, Luke has always been adaptable and loyal. He has survived nine moves: coyotes in the Hollywood hills, hungry owls in Ojai, a cramped apartment in Beverly Hills, and speeding cars in the flats. Luke has always answered our calls and been an integral and cherished member of our clan.

Something happened, though, with the growth of our family, so slowly that I hardly noticed. First we got a dog. Then we had a baby. Shortly afterward we got another dog. Luke began to hide a lot, from the shrieking toddler running at him with pinching fingers, from the frolicsome mutts using him as a play toy.

As most new parents understand, time to yourself becomes rare once a baby is born. When I could finally sit down to read, Luke would lay on the book. I'd pull out my writing, and he'd chew on my pen. I'd lay down for a quick, much-needed nap, and he would wake me with those needle-like claws. So I did what I'd never thought I had in me: I began to shoo him away. Luke would meow for loving and I'd tell him, "Not now."

Then came the Northridge earthquake. The night before, as I sat working at my computer, Lukey jumped up on the table and started to walk across my keyboard. Involved in what I was doing, I gave him a gentle nudge onto the carpet. He meowed for attention; I ignored him. Eventually he gave up and went outside. Hours later, the quake hit with massive force. Our dogs would not leave our side, and our son sat glued to us for hours. All of us gathered under a big door frame in our living room, but Luke was nowhere to be found.

For days afterward we experienced frightening aftershocks. The ground moved like Jell-O. No place felt safe. I knew Luke was scared to death, wherever he was. I went door to door, and found that everyone in our neighborhood had lost their cats. We all took comfort thinking they were gathered at a "cat convention" somewhere. By day four, every cat on the street had come home except ours. Each day I walked our street calling Luke's name. Nothing.

I kept telling my husband that Luke was hiding under a house somewhere. I could see him there, vividly, each time I prayed about it. I saw that he was too traumatized to come home, and that we were going to have to find him. Mark thought I was being silly and negative. He had complete faith that if Luke was alive he would find his way home. "Cats don't get lost," Mark would say. I'd disagree, and we would argue.

At night we'd walk the dogs and I'd call for Luke. Mark would tease me by mimicking my high cat-calling voice. I knew, and he later admitted, that this was his way of attempting to detach from his hurt.

Five nights had passed. I couldn't sleep, knowing that there was something more I needed to do for our cat. I gathered the family and dogs together for our usual search, continually praying to God in my mind. Mark made clown faces behind my back, assuming it was foolish to think a cat would not know his way around his own territory. I thought my husband was acting like a bratty boy, but noticed that he had kept following me, so part of him wanted to believe my search had merit.

All of a sudden, I knew where to go. I could feel Luke on a street we hadn't checked yet. "Follow me, he's over there," I said, trying not to run too fast. Mark followed slowly behind with our son.

"Lukey, Lukey, Lukey kitty . . ."

I heard a faint meow and screamed to Mark, "Did you hear that? It's him!"

"How do you know it's not another cat?"

"I know it's him, I just know."

In the darkness I faintly saw a cat emerge from under a house two doors away. I called his name again, and Luke ran in the direction of my voice without hesitation. Our dogs scampered to greet him, sniffing and tackling their lost pal. I dropped to the grass and began to sob, relieved that I was being given a second chance to be a good mother to him, overwhelmed by the instructions I had received in the form of intuition.

Luke was so afraid that he wouldn't let us pick him up. We called the dogs and began the walk home. Sure enough, yard by yard, Luke followed. Whenever a car drove by, he'd bolt for shelter, but within minutes he'd emerge and continue on with us. It was a long walk to our street. When we were within five houses of our garden, Luke sprinted all-out toward home. We ran behind him, cheering and laughing cries of celebration.

Mark told me right away that he was sorry he had doubted my intuition. Since that night, we have both found plenty of time for our beautiful friend. I pet Luke whenever he wanders by, and talk to him frequently throughout the day. I notice that this doesn't take any time away from my schedule; I merely had to refocus my attention. I never let him go by without telling him how much I love him, or taking a moment to look into his mysterious yellow eyes. He loves the attention, and has become much more of a homebody.

This experience has helped us to give the dogs more quality time, too, conscious of the fact that they will not always be around. We value all of the people and things in our life more deeply now. I never again want to take anyone's love for granted.

Earthquakes have a profound effect of getting people to look at their priorities. Maybe that's why we have them.

A Ray of Light

Jyoti Dar

It was a particularly hot and sultry evening. The rain earlier in the day had made for an extremely humid atmosphere, though it had in fact brought down the temperature. I've always wondered why the climate in India—especially Agra, where my father's home is—more often than not is most uncomfortable. Other than the few winter months from December until February, when the air is crisp and cool, the climate remains extremely hot and dry.

My parents had both passed away, and I had returned to Agra to pack up the house and get the property ready for sale. Even though it was held in a Hindu joint family trust, in which my cousins from my father's side also had a share, they were not interested in participating. Despite my cousins' residing in India, they felt it was just too inconvenient to visit, and had not even been to the house in over fifteen years.

Since I lived in the United States, I found it relaxing to spend time where the lifestyle moved at a slower pace. My ancestors had built the original house, and four generations had resided here. Built in 1872, it had no modern facilities, especially in the way of plumbing. It had also been closed up for more than fifteen years, as my grandfather had lived there alone. His children had been employed elsewhere, and with modern lifestyles the joint family system had just no longer been practical. I was unhappy about the prospect of selling the property, but it badly needed renovation, which would have been expensive.

I therefore undertook the task of having all twenty-five rooms cleaned thoroughly. I had come with two servants who had been with the family for some years.

As the servants and I made our separate ways through the rooms, clearing our way through the cobwebs, I suddenly heard a shout from one of them. When I arrived, he told me he refused to go into one of the back rooms. "I think there are ghosts in there," he said, stepping further back.

"What nonsense," I said. However, he refused to go in. "I shall go in first," I volunteered, "and then you can follow." The other servant, who had joined us, also agreed to go in only after I went in first.

I felt a bit apprehensive myself. The air in the room was thick with dust. Cobwebs hung from ceiling to floor, shimmering in a ray of light that came from the only window, located up near the ceiling. I took a deep breath and entered the room. It was an eerie sensation, being in there, and I closed my eyes for a minute to clear my mind of any scary thoughts.

Suddenly a ray of light, shining on my arm, reflected a peculiar pattern on the far wall. I made my way through the dust and cobwebs to the spot where the light fell. On the wall, I noticed a few bricks that were uneven and protruding. I grabbed one of the bricks and pulled: it came away in my hand, revealing a sort of crevice that had cloth stuck inside it.

I called out to my servants to stay where they were, and that I would be out shortly. A strong sensation urged me to pull out the cloth. I tugged and pulled, and slowly the cloth started to come out.

Suddenly a big clump came out of the wall, and landed on the floor with a thump. I carefully unwrapped the cloth—and found myself staring at four gold bars.

I quickly wrapped them back up, left the room, and told the servants we would continue to clean the area later. "There was a ghost in there that has frightened her," one of them muttered. I agreed, and told them we would lock the room and finish cleaning the rest of the house.

Later in the evening, when the servants had retired for the night, I took out the packet and looked at the gold bars. Wrapped around them was a certificate, issued in 1920 by the British government, stating that the gold was in payment for services rendered to the British armed forces. Our family of leather manufacturers had provided leather clothing as well as footwear to the British army.

As children we had always been told by our grandfather that there was gold hidden in the house. For years we had believed this—but after many failed attempts to locate the gold, we had given up, attributing his stories to his confusing reality with superstition. Now I felt as if the ancestors had led me to the treasure, to maintain and keep the house in the possession of our family.

This was five years ago. Since then, the property has been upgraded and turned into a guest house for tourists. As Agra is the site of the Taj Mahal, one of the wonders of the world, there are frequent visitors to the area, many of whom like the idea of staying in a home reminiscent of a bygone era. The house has been upgraded with modern facilities, but still maintains its old charm, and we have recouped all the expenses that went into the renovations.

It was indeed a mystical experience to feel the bond with my ancestors—as they showed me a wonderful solution to what had been a terrible conflict in my mind.

Plant a Seed

Heide Banks

As much as I hate to admit it, there've been times when it's taken a good hard knock on the head for me to go ahead and make a move in my life. One of the hardest I ever hope to suffer was quite literal: delivered by an off-duty ambulance driver who decided to change lanes without looking, taking me and my teeny sports car off the road with him.

I walked away from the accident without a single broken bone. But something was wrong, frighteningly wrong. The doctors diagnosed it as an internal brain injury. I called it the start of tough times.

The doctors assured me that my brain would eventually heal on its own. For now, the best thing, really the only thing I could do, was take it slow. And they saw to it that I did, by taking away my driver's license and insisting that I stop all work. I ended up staying home for the next few years.

At the time of the accident I was a marketing and production executive. It was somewhat challenging and fulfilling, but always, somewhere in the back of my mind, and definitely in my heart, I'd known it wasn't my life's pursuit. What that was, I hadn't yet discovered.

Now, with my cash reserves steadily dwindling and no possibility of work, I still woke each morning with the best of intentions to get my life back together somehow. But for month after endless month, I was so exhausted by noon that I'd end up spending the remainder of the day staring blindly into space—wondering, increasingly, how much more I could possibly endure.

Until I woke up one morning feeling like the old me.

By that time I'd been out of work for over two years. I *needed* to work . . . but I couldn't go back: Most of the doors that had once been wide open for me were now closed tight. I told myself that if I'd ever wanted to make that dramatic career move, now was the time.

But what was my heart's desire?

I don't know how many times I asked myself that question. Then I remembered an incident that had happened almost seven years before.

In the midst of relocating—a career move—from New York to California, flying cross-country, I had a stopover in the Dallas airport. As I rushed to change planes, an airport maintenance worker called out, "Hey, writer lady, you dropped something."

I'd known instantly that he was talking to me. But why did he think I was a writer? My immediate thought was that I'd dropped a pen from my purse, but I looked down to see my scarf lying on the floor. I picked it up, puzzled, and approached him.

"Why do you think I'm a writer?"

He replied, quite matter-of-factly, "Because you are, young lady, because you are." Then he turned and walked away.

For years, I'd occasionally found myself thinking about that exchange. Now it took on new meaning. I even admitted to myself that more than anything, I wanted to be an author and share as much as I could about how I had learned to make my life work. But with so little money in the bank, how could I possibly consider a career move like this?

Fortunately for me, I'd been reading a book called *God Is Your Partner*, by John-Roger, on the power and miracle of tithing. Tithing, the book explained—giving back to God ten percent of whatever material abundance came your way—was a means of acknowledging that *all* abundance comes from one source: God. It was a way of accepting and offering recompense to God as your partner in this life. This concept was nothing new to me, but what I read next really caught my attention.

The book went on to introduce the concept of "seeding" as a similar route to financial prosperity. If you want to grow a garden, you plant a seed. If you want to have more money, a successful relationship, or a new career, these are things you can seed for.

I was hooked. The book said that classes were being held on incorporating these ancient biblical principles into one's life. Within a week I was enrolled. During this class, I decided to plant my first seed for my new career as a writer. I asked the class facilitator what amount would make a good "seed." That, I was told, was up to me: I would have to look inside myself for the answer.

Given how little money I had at the time, it was with a fair amount of trepidation that I closed my eyes and asked inwardly what amount would work. The number "100" flashed before my eyes. I thought, "Well, I could definitely handle that." Immediately, though, a voice within said, "But if you want this to happen quickly, consider a larger seed."

Now I was troubled. Anything above a hundred dollars represented a substantial risk for me. Besides, I reasoned, being a fledgling writer wasn't exactly a lucrative career! Even if a miracle did happen and I sold something, it could still take months and probably years before I saw any money.

"Remember, Heide," the voice went on, "this is not about how the world usually works. This is about making God your partner. Are you willing to trust and do that?"

Once again I asked how much would I need to seed to make this career transition happen quickly. The number "1,000" now appeared—not exactly the dollar amount I was hoping to see! I left the class that night very out of balance. How could I possibly write a check for a thousand dollars when I had no idea where my next money would be coming from?

I tried to ignore the figure, but as the days went by it kept popping back into my mind. The more fear I had about writing the check, the greater the anxiety I felt about becoming an author at all. By the third day I could stand the anxiety no longer, and decided to take the leap of faith: I mailed the check off. At the very least, I had made a decision.

From that point on, I began to look for signs of just how good a partner God was going to be. Not that I sat around. I kept myself busy by writing a book proposal, contacting book agents, and learning everything I could about what it takes to be a writer. As book ideas would pop into my head, I'd write them down. I began to meet people involved in the publishing industry. I even flew to New York to attend a publishing conference. With each passing day, I felt more like a writer.

I knew the seed was working: My fears were being calmed, and this allowed me to keep taking steps. But, quite honestly, I was still looking for a miracle. I wanted to know for certain, without doubt, that God was my new partner, and was keeping up His end of the bargain. In the back of my mind, I was waiting each day for the call to come: "Congratulations, we love your idea! Here's a check for fifty thousand dollars!"

But it didn't happen that way. In fact, I was met by rejection after rejection. Still, I remained confident that the seeding was going to work. I didn't know how, when, or where, but God was going to produce some great results, and soon.

A few months after the New York trip, I received a call from a friend I hadn't spoken with in about four years. By the tone of his voice, it seemed he was as surprised to be making the call as I was to be hearing from him. A magazine writer by profession, he'd been approached by a publisher to write a book, but felt he couldn't do it on his own—and for some reason, my name had popped into his head as the perfect writing partner.

Stunned, I had to ask, "How did you know that I want to write?"

Just like the airport maintenance worker years earlier, he had no explanation. He just knew.

We got together a few weeks later and agreed to write the book together. But once we sat down to actually begin the project, my partner began to lose interest. Realizing just how large an undertaking this book would be, he felt he had no other option but to drop out of the project.

Incredibly disappointed, I was left to call the publisher. It was then that the real miracle occurred. Mustering up all my courage, and trusting that God was in fact my partner, I asked if they would consider letting me, a first-time author, write the book all on my own. Fortunately, I had already begun work on the book. They asked me to send off a few sample chapters.

Within a few weeks, we had a new deal, with me as the sole author. That book, *It Works for Me!: Celebrity Stories of Alternative Healing*, is my first published book.

Now if anyone were to call out, "Hey, writer lady," I wouldn't hesitate to turn around. I'd know exactly who they were talking to.

And as for seeding: It continues to work for me.

Ask and You Shall Receive

Chérie Carter-Scott, Ph.D.

I'd always wanted to be an actress, and Mother had always been dead set against it. She wanted—asked—me to become a teacher. So, to please her, I did: got credentialed and started substituting at the local high schools.

I liked teaching, even though the discipline issues and constant politics were very stressful. I'd been doing it for about two years, when my mother died.

Not long after, a director friend asked me to return to New York to do Shakespeare in Central Park—and get my Equity card. I jumped. And sitting on that plane with my ten-speed bike, suitcase, and hundred dollars, I felt that I'd fulfilled my contract with my mother. I was free to pursue my dreams.

The Shakespeare was great. After the run ended I continued to get work, did soap operas and showcases, was doing well ... but I had a terrible feeling of emptiness. Somehow, I felt I didn't have the right metabolism to pursue this as a career.

Yes, I had become a teacher for my mother. But I'd become an actress for myself—and now it seemed I'd been wrong. I had no idea what I was supposed to be doing. I didn't know where to turn, either. Friends and family were offering lots of good advice and suggestions, but we weren't really connecting.

I decided to turn within, something I had never done before. I made lists of my happiest moments. I meditated. I told God, "I want to know what I am supposed to do with my life. I want to know why I am on Earth," and I prayed for answers.

Within a few weeks, I received a "message." It was like a flash of insight, but it was as if I was being addressed: "You are not an expert, you are a catalyst." I didn't know what to make of it, so I wrote it down and forgot about it. A few weeks later I received another: "You are to be involved with growth." I thought to myself, growth could mean plants, refinishing furniture, decorating houses. I didn't think much more about it, though, just wrote it down. Two weeks later, it happened again. "You have a special gift," this one went. "You must work with people."

All right, so I was supposed to be a catalytic agent who would work with people in their growth and development. I turned to God and said, "This isn't a job description! What am I to do with that?"

Three weeks later, I received a phone call from a friend who asked me if I would consult him about his business, a billing service for physicians. A little surprised, I told him I knew nothing about business and thanked him for calling. A week later he called again. I told him I was flattered, but was very busy looking at what I was going to do with my life. He let another week pass and called a third time with the same request. "Why me?" I asked, and he responded, "Because I trust you."

"But I know nothing!"

"That could come in handy."

All right, I told him, if he wanted to pay me to do something I knew nothing about, then I would accept.

The next week, I spent four days observing his office. I listened in on conversations, interviewed people, observed their systems and flow of work. Since I really wasn't an "expert," I was able to look with objective eyes. On the fifth day, the two of us met outside the office. When he asked for my observations I responded, "Before I tell you what I saw, I really want to know what it is that you want."

He proceeded to describe a multinational business that he could run from a hotel room anywhere in the world.

Then he said that he wanted to have a small family business, where people could roll up their shirtsleeves and pitch in together.

I simply commented on the discrepancy between the two images—and a lightbulb went on in his head. It was clear that he had to make a choice. After the choice would come the plan and the follow-through. He left our meeting as if he had seen an apparition.

After he left, I sat alone, thinking. Apparently I'd just said the right thing at the right time. And I thought: a catalytic agent, working with people in the areas of growth and development.

I've translated that since into consulting, teaching, even writing—always trying to say the right thing at the right time. The messages have gotten a little clearer.

I looked up and gave thanks. I had asked—and truly wanted to know—and I had received the answer that I longed for. I had found my purpose.

The "Artist" in Us All

Freddie Ravel

I first felt the power of music tugging at my soul somewhere around the age of four. To this day, I still find myself in awe of the infinite combinations of words, melodies, harmonies, and rhythms that make up what we call music. It all just amounts to a bunch of frequencies striking your eardrum, but when these frequencies vibrate in just the right way, something beyond words can happen. I equate it to spirit whispering musical messages in my ears.

Now, making a career in music is not for the squeamish. It requires relentless dedication—and it is with unbending devotion that I have spent the better part of my life traveling the world in my own little microcosms of bands and performing artists. It did not take long for me to think of myself as being part of a special "members only" type of club.

One day, upon leaving a club where I had just finished performing, an apparently homeless man ran up and begged me to let him clean the windows of my car. It was a cold winter day in downtown Los Angeles, and even though it was damp and misty, I obliged.

As I put my briefcase in the back seat, I studied this man. With a wrinkle in the brow of an otherwise young face, he pulled out a soiled rag and, leaking spray bottle in hand, began the task. I have never seen anyone clean anything with so much conviction; those windows were scrubbed as if his life depended on it. His dedication so thoroughly inspired me that I gave him a twenty-dollar bill, which he graciously accepted with a great sigh and a flood of tears. I asked him his name.

"Timmy Young," he hesitantly replied.

"What do you really do for a living?"

"Actually, I dance."

"What do you mean, you dance?"

His face brightening, striking a proud pose, he said, "I trained at the St. Louis Conservatory of Modern Dance. Over the years, I've appeared in all sorts of shows!" His face clouded. "Then I had a twist of fate, when my mother passed away. I came to L.A. to be with my aunt, but it turned out that her home was on the verge of slipping away from her. Without a base, I found myself in the streets . . . washing windows."

He was so calm and soft-spoken as he told the story that I knew it to be the truth. Suddenly I removed my vest and presented it to this broken yet kindred artist. As tears filled his eyes, he gently reached for my hand. After a warm handshake—followed by his beautiful double-spin there on the street, one that would have made Baryshnikov proud—we bade each other farewell.

As I got on the freeway I felt myself beginning to cry, and realized that the gift in this encounter was really from Timmy to me. You see, from that day on, I have looked at every human being in a new light.

I now know that we are all artists, filled with infinite gifts. Regardless of outer appearances, we all have something very magical to share and express: the artist in us all.

Sid the Horse

Sri Harold Klemp

Once a couple bought a horse they named Sid. Their plan was to train the horse, and when it reached a certain age, they would resell it. Of course, it never occurred to them to wonder what Sid thought of all this.

About a year later, the husband had an unusual dream in which he found himself entering a crowded bar. Seeing one unoccupied table, he went over and sat down. A man came over and introduced himself. "Hi," he said. "I'm Sid, your horse."

The dreamer thought this was the funniest thing he'd ever seen. "My horse in a dream, looking like a man," he said. "This is wild."

The only thing that bothered him about the dream was

that this man had a tooth missing, whereas his horse did not.

The dreamer and his horse got to talking. Sid said, "You know I love you and your wife. I'd like to stay with you. I've never had owners like you before who could Soul Travel and meet with me in the dream state so we could talk things over."

"Sid," he asked, "I notice you've been limping on one of your hind legs. Is something wrong?"

"I'm having a problem with that foot," said Sid. "It's just a minor thing, but if you can get a farrier to trim my hoof, I could walk better." And they continued talking.

When the man awoke and told his wife about the dream, they shared a good laugh over it. She thought the part about the missing tooth was really hilarious.

Later that morning as they walked to the stable, they saw a crowd around Sid's stall. The couple rushed over, concerned for the welfare of their horse.

The owners saw a little bit of blood on the door of the stall, but Sid seemed to be all right. The husband put a halter on the horse and led him outside. "If you plan to ride him, just don't put a bit in his mouth," one of the grooms advised him. "Your horse somehow got his mouth caught on the door lock, and his tooth broke off."

Husband and wife looked at each other. "The missing tooth in your dream," she said. Without another word, they leaned over to check the horse's hind foot. Just as Sid had said in the dream, his hoof needed trimming.

Blind Faith

Christen Brown

I use a working video studio to provide a series of Presence Workshops designed to help people gain confidence. The Presence Workshop starts at 9:00 A.M. on Saturdays and lasts until 5:00 P.M. One particular group was composed of eight women and four men. All looked like normal workshop participants except for a tall, stooped, bearded man who came tapping in with a cane. The workshop's eleven other participants faded into the background. A voice inside my head screamed, "My God, this is a *video* workshop and there's a blind man in here." I asked everyone to introduce themselves on camera for the first videotaped exercise. That's when I found out the man with the cane was from Santa Cruz. His name was Tom. I guessed he was about thirty. "I read about this in my Braille paper. Something told me to come here. So I got on a bus and came," he stated. Tom did not smile; there was a definite edge to him. "Perfect," I thought. "An *angry* blind guy!"

After everyone spoke, we played back the recorded statements to get a sense of how each individual felt about seeing himself or herself on the screen. Almost everyone responded with heavy self-criticism.

People who were guarded and uptight recognized it. People who were domineering knew it. Insecurity was obvious. When it was Tom's turn, I started a silent prayer, hoping there was a way to help this man.

We played the videotape, and I blocked off the picture on the television monitor. We used only our ears to hear his voice, relying on vibratory messages that usually only a blind person would "see." Sighted people, I realized, have a surplus of visual cues that distract them from voice tones.

Tom's "wall" was apparent.

"I sound kind of mean," he observed.

"Mean, Tom?"

"Yeah, mean."

"You've got an edge to your voice. You sound angry to me."

There was a moment's silence. "I'm angry because I'm blind, because I can't see."

"I can understand that. How long have you been blind?"

"A couple of months."

"How did it happen?"

"A car accident; it was instantaneous."

"You have every right to be angry! This is a lot to deal with. Have you been getting any help in Santa Cruz?"

"I have a therapist, and I'm in a counseling group," he replied.

Then I said something that just sort of rolled out of my mouth. "Tom, you are blind, but don't accept for a moment that you can't see."

"Is this a joke?" he shot back. "I'm one hundred percent nonsighted."

The anger was right there. We were on to it. But his anger was not going to solve his problem, so I switched to a more sympathetic tone: "It's so hard to let go of the anger and sadness. It feels so stuck and so bad. You're aching. I can feel your pain."

I said to the group, "Let's do an exercise now. Pair off in twos, pull your chairs to a quiet part of the room, and answer these questions for each other."

They pulled away and started to work on what each person perceived as his most "stuck" place. Could they find a way through it? What would life look like if they let go of their blocks? It was midafternoon. People were letting go.

They were working on themselves. The room was alive with presence.

I went to work on Tom. Now I felt confident that I understood his issues. "Okay, Tom, you can't see because to you seeing can only be done through the eyes, right?"

"Right," he said.

"It's not the same for me, Tom. In fact, my eyes are one of my least effective means of seeing. People can mask their faces. The voice, however, carries emotion, tone, and meaning. It's much harder to mask the voice. Lie detectors read the voice, not the face.

"Often, when people talk to me, I close my eyes to 'get' them; what I'm really doing is 'sensing' them. I don't believe for a minute that people are what they say or how they look. We're deeper than that. That's where you are now, Tom. Your blindness has cut through all the superficiality of life to the heart of the matter."

A glimmer of recognition showed on his face. "Things do seem simpler now," he said.

"Do something for me. When you hear the next person, Susan, try to 'see' her."

I turned the video back on. "She's in her twenties, attractive, not too tall. She's acting younger, more insecure than she needs to," Tom said.

People's mouths dropped open. Two women began to cry. Applause broke out. He had her down pat; he knew Susan.

Next, I asked him to "see" Dan. He read him to a tee: middle-aged, a bit overweight, and tough on himself. Tom said Dan needed to relax more, to lighten up.

Someone asked him *how* he did it.

"I don't know. They're there. I guess I just sort of see them." Most people understand that intuition can't be explained through the rational mind but that it is a sixth sense available to all of us.

My hunch was right. Tom's intuition was highly developed. He enjoyed the exercise. The real work, however, was getting him to move through his anger. He was standing tall now. He seemed to accept blindness as a condition of his life. We finished our work with the other participants. As we were closing, I asked Tom if there was anything good about being blind. He responded:

"I like pretending to get my cane caught in women's skirts and lifting them up. That's fun. I'm pretty intuitive about what's underneath."

The Little Book That Could

Patrice Karst

While other little girls played tea parties with their dolls, I would hold mine and wonder what her mission in life was, where she came from, and who she was, *really*. As far back as I can remember, I have felt a deep need to understand the mysteries of life and death, of who we are, where we are going—and, most importantly, who and what God really is, and how to get closer to Him. This and a passionate love of writing have been two constants in my life, along with a knowledge that there was something I was here on Earth to do, but I just couldn't seem to remember what.

My search led me around the world, from ashrams in India to hot springs in California, always knowing that God was my guide and that it was He, ultimately, I was praying to understand. Along the way I saw many miracles, things that challenged every belief structure with which I had been raised: saints who had marvelous abilities, people who knew things about me that were impossible for them to know, visitations from holy beings who would appear to instruct me in my half-awake sleep states.

By 1995, I was the single mother of an adorable four-year-old being named Elijah. On the morning of November 11 at 6:00 A.M., while Elijah was still asleep, I awoke simultaneously seeing and hearing the words "God Made Easy." My first thought was, "What a clever title for a book. If I was going to write a book called *God Made Easy*, what would I say?" Some ideas came, and I thought, "Well, maybe I'll write a book like that one day," and proceeded to try to go back to sleep.

It didn't work. An inner voice practically bellowed out, "Get up and write it now!" This wasn't particularly what I felt like doing. As a working mother I cherished my sleep, and I knew that I had a good hour and a half until my son would arise. Still, I reluctantly did as told.

What happened next was a most extraordinary experience. The words poured out of me faster than I could write them down. It was as if I were taking dictation from deep within my being: no thinking, no pausing, no rewriting. In just one hour it was done.

As I sat on my bed wondering what in God's name had just happened, reading what I written, I got goose bumps in places I didn't know you could get them! Either I was completely deluding myself, or I had just written a mass market book about God for the planet.

It was now seven o'clock, too early to call one of my friends for a reality check. My son was still peacefully asleep. The voice spoke again: "This is to be a book, and now your job is to get it published."

Three and a half weeks later I was sitting at a restaurant in Venice Beach, signing my first-ever publishing deal with De Vorss, a medium-sized publisher in Marina Del Rey, California. The word "elated" scarcely describes my frame of mind—but the story gets even more amazing.

Having accomplished my "task," it occurred to me that if I had taken it this far, then I sure as heck ought to do my best to make certain the book sold. I bought a copy of *1001 Ways to Market Your Book*. The first tip it offered was that you should try to get glowing endorsements from fellow authors (boy, did I love the sound of that: authors!) in the same genre as yours, to go on the back of your book. So I began the process of sending this little (64 pages) unknown book to some of the most famous speakers and writers on the spiritual/New Age circuit.

The results were amazing. The testimonials started pouring in from all over the country. People I'd always looked up to—Bernie Seigel, Gerald Jampolsky, Larry Dossey, Barbara De Angelis, Dannion Brinkley—loved my book!

One of the people I had sent the book to was Marianne Williamson, the bestselling author and inspirational speaker. When the envelope came back marked "wrong address," I almost gave up. After all, I now had more endorsements than I ever dreamed I would get—but something told me to continue to pursue this. Pursue I did, talking her assistant (who informed me that Marianne was not doing endorsements anymore) into giving me Marianne's New York address. I sent off my book and then completely forgot about it (like I said, it was a long shot).

Meanwhile, I had been praying that somehow the book could get into the hands of someone who could really get it out into the world in a big way. I had begun to realize that even though I had a publishing deal, the book was never going to have the kind of chances that a larger publishing house could give it.

I was at my day job when I was told I had a call. It was Marianne Williamson's literary agent, one of the best in New York. He told me that never in his life had he chased down an author, but he'd had a mysterious experience. While Marianne was in Egypt leading a spiritual tour, he had gone over to her apartment in Manhattan to collect her mail. He said *God Made Easy* "jumped into my hands, saying read me, read me, read me." I'll never forget his next words: "Honey, I think this book is going to be a bestseller, and I want to be a big part of your life!"

The next few weeks were a roller coaster of every emotion known to man. Fear, anxiety, disbelief, loneliness, excitement, hope, desire . . . you name it, I felt it. One night I was feeling very depressed. Al, now my agent, too, after making his incredible promises, hadn't called in about two weeks. It seemed like an eternity, and I had convinced myself that this was all just another big tease from the universe, yet another example of God letting me down. I was feeling oh-so-sorry for myself when I walked into my bathroom and, lo and behold, there shining out at me was a golden-white cross, glowing in the moonlight. I could almost hear it singing, "Oh, ye of little faith!"

I stared at it, incredulous. How could this be? How could a nice Jewish girl living in a mobile home park in Pacific Palisades be having a message from divinity? I cried in awe, I cried in humility. I cried at the brilliance—and I cried at how loved I felt.

The next day, Al called. He was holding an auction for my book with the top publishing houses in New York. A few days later, another call: Warner had bought *God Made Easy*. My prayer had been answered.

The rest has been an unfolding miracle. The cross continues to glow from the sun by day and the moon at night. There have been more unbelievable coincidences and showers of grace, one after the other. The doors have continued to open, guiding my little book out into the world.

At least once in my life, I heard God's call and paid attention. He gave me the great honor and privilege to share His message with people of all faiths. If I do nothing else in this lifetime, I feel complete: I brought a child into this world who loves God, and I brought a book into this world that tells of His wonders.

Audition of Faith

Shahin Kowarski

Standing outside the studio door, clutching the neck of my borrowed violin, I mumbled a silent prayer for courage and success. Inside I could hear David, one of the star student violinists at Indiana University: His playing was secure, flashy, flawless. For a moment I wanted to disappear around the corner and forget about the audition all together.

But attending this music festival had been my dream since freshman year. Friends who had participated spoke of living in a castle in Germany, eating gourmet food every day, playing in a superb orchestra of young musicians from around the world, and touring the great concert halls of Europe with the world's greatest conductors, like Leonard Bernstein and Sir Georg Solti. I could already hear the audiences shouting for encores . . .

The studio door opened and a short German man with a crooked nose called my name. I floated into the studio. In a heavy accent, he introduced himself as the concertmaster of the Hamburg Symphony Orchestra. Sensing his difficulty with English, I answered in German, which I had spoken since the age of eight. He was surprised, and suddenly became much more congenial. I don't know whether it was on the strength of my Mozart concerto or my German that he bypassed the procedural waiting period, but at the conclusion of my audition, he informed me immediately of my acceptance into the festival.

I wanted to dance, to scream, to hug the man—but I composed myself. I thanked him politely and walked to the door with forced control. As soon as it closed behind me, I bolted to the nearest pay phone and screamed the good news to my mother.

But as I hung up the receiver and walked back to my locker, a sobering impression seized my consciousness: The thought came to me, very clearly, that I should not and would not attend the festival that summer.

I pushed the thought away. But, having received such promptings before, I knew I shouldn't ignore it. Then again, this was too much! I'd anticipated this moment for three years. If God didn't want me to attend the Festival, why did He help me win the audition against such tremendous odds?

For the next three months I flexed my muscles before God and tried to create a situation that He, in His everlasting kindness, could not possibly destroy. I announced my summer plans, becoming the envy of the music school. I sent letters to friends far and wide, including one to dear old Aunt Sarah in London, telling her I would be performing with Leonard Bernstein in Royal Albert Hall. The course was set, anticipation was high among my circle of friends throughout the world: Surely God wouldn't disappoint so many good people!

Yet, in quiet moments when I would contemplate what to pack, or daydream of my upcoming stay in a German castle ... that sobering thought returned. Throwing its shadow over my plans, it challenged my will—and my faith.

The contract arrived in May, requiring my immediate signature and confirmation of acceptance. I turned to the last page ... and, with my pen literally poised over the dotted line, the conflict within me raged so tumultuously that I simply could not bring myself to sign my name.

I needed a sign. So I put the following proposal before God: I was willing to accept a "no," but I wanted to hear it with my own ears. No more of this feeling stuff. I designated Mr. French, Head of Instrumental Rental at the music school, as His mouthpiece. At the time, I was playing on one of the school's violins, and I needed Mr. French's permission to take it out of the country.

The next day, I knocked on Mr. French's door. Resolved to accept the outcome, I made my request . . . and God said, "No."

I walked back home, disappointed but relieved. I now had a valid reason to decline. And so the letters went out once again, to the festival, to Aunt Sarah, to all my friends: "Can't go. No violin."

I went home that summer, confident that He who had taken away would also recompense my loss. June and July passed without incident. In August I returned to Indiana for summer school, and contracted pneumonia and tuberculosis simultaneously.

Lying in bed, looking up at the cracks in the ceiling, I felt like a fool for following what I now called "the voice of doubt." I should have gone to the Festival—and I could have! Even after declining, messages had poured in from the Festival's organizers and from friends around the world, offering to lend me a violin for the summer. Even my family had found my decision irrational. But I'd held my resolve—and now here I was, utterly miserable.

September came and classes resumed. The few students who had attended the Festival returned with stories of the tour. I couldn't bear to listen to them. Soon enough, the routine of student life returned, and all thoughts about the Festival were obscured by exams, midterm papers and codeine-laced cough syrup. My condition was deteriorating.

It was mid-October when the letter came. By that time I was completely bedridden. The return address said "Aunt Sarah," but when I opened it I knew it was sent from God. "I'm sorry you do not have your own violin," the letter read, "and I'm sorry you could not attend the Festival. Enclosed is a check . . ." I looked in the envelope and pulled out a certified check for nearly $20,000!

How I received my precious 1860 Vuillaume violin (worth $40,000) for the exact dollar amount of the check is a separate miracle. But from the moment I opened its velvet-lined case, I knew that violin would be mine.

As for the Festival, my Vuillaume and I attended the following year. And when I was escorted to my private room in the tower of the castle, I unpacked my Vuillaume, placed it on the crisp, starched pillow of my feather bed, and took the first photograph of the most memorable summer of my life.

A Memory Come Alive

Kathi Diamant

I was nineteen the first time I heard her name. It was spring 1971 at the University of Georgia. In the midst of translating Franz Kafka's story "Metamorphosis," the German Literature professor interrupted class.

"Fraulein Diamant, are you related to Dora Diamant?"

My last name is unusual, and at that time I'd never met anyone, outside of family, with the same name. "It's possible," I answered hopefully. "Who is she?"

"Dora Diamant was Franz Kafka's last mistress," the professor explained. Kafka, we'd learned earlier, was one of the most important and misunderstood writers of the twentieth century. "Dora and Kafka were very much in love," Dr. Frederick continued. For the first time in his short life, Kafka was truly happy. But Kafka suffered from tuberculosis, and died in Dora's arms.

Dr. Frederick basked in the rare attention of the entire class. "And . . ." He paused, gripped the lectern and leaned forward, with a strange smile. He stared at me, and finally hissed, "and she burned his work!"

After class, I ran to the library. There were several references to Dora in Kafka's biographies. Dora was a Chasid and Zionist with dreams of emigrating to Palestine. She was young in 1923, when she met Kafka on the shores of the Baltic Sea: only nineteen—my age at the time, which only added to the thrill of thinking I might be related to her. By all reports, Dora was an extraordinary woman, full of intelligence and passionate intensity.

The problem with asking questions is that you have to be ready to hear the answers. My father's family was Jewish, and had come to the United States from somewhere in Europe a long time ago.

When I called my father to ask if we might be related to Dora, I was horrified to learn about letters that my grandparents received in the late 1930s from people named Diamant, asking for help in escaping Europe. The letters were never answered.

"Why not?" I demanded.

"We weren't sure who these people really were, how they had our address, or what they really wanted," Dad explained. "We couldn't get involved."

For the first time my father talked to me about the anti-Semitism he'd experienced growing up in New York City, about "restricted" schools, hotels and clubs. I didn't question him anymore. I returned the books to the library, and forgot about finding out if I was related to Dora Diamant.

The story might have ended there. But Dora refused to be forgotten. Over the next thirteen years, she infiltrated my life. "What would Dora do?" I would ask myself when confronted with a dilemma. "If I ever have a daughter, I will name her Dora," I announced. When I married, I kept the name Diamant, as Dora had done when she married several years after Kafka's death.

In 1984, everything changed when I joined a journal-writing group called "Live Your Dream." An elegant silver-haired grandmother, Joyce Chapman, brought together the first group of twelve women. We would try first to discover our dreams in life through journaling, and then set about making them come true. The trick, of course, was truly knowing what we wanted.

I was thirty-two years old, and had what I considered the best job in town. As the co-host of a popular morning TV talk show in San Diego, California, I was in the spotlight. Every day I met fascinating people, movers and shakers, movie stars, bestselling authors, sports heroes, and political leaders.

But through the journaling and other writing exercises, I realized that I was living a life based on appearance rather than substance, and that my five-year marriage had withered on the vine. At the end of the sixteen weeks of journaling, my new dream was to live a life with more magic, more meaning. I still wasn't sure what that meant, though, not entirely.

Within a month, Dora was back, haunting me. Strange, inexplicable coincidences occurred involving her, like clues leading me deeper into the mystery of our connection. Every turn I took seemed to point toward Dora.

As she kept being brought to mind, my questions about her multiplied. What happened to her after Kafka's death? Why did she burn his work? Did she survive the Holocaust? Why was I so obsessed?

Within a year, I found myself in Prague, at Kafka's grave. I seemed to relive his funeral, witnessing Dora's inconsolable grief. Another series of coincidences led me to the small sanatorium room outside Vienna where Kafka died in 1924. I traveled on to Jerusalem's Hebrew University, to see the Diamant Collection, a genealogy of over three hundred different Diamant families. Five years later, in London, I finally tracked down Mrs. Marianna Steiner, Kafka's niece and oldest living relative. Marianna was at Dora's beside when she died. She told me that Dora's last words were, "Do what you can."

What answers I found only prompted new questions. Although it was Kafka who asked Dora to burn any work of his she had in her possession upon his death—a detail my professor had left out—she didn't. She kept it ... but kept it "safe from publication." Why? Was it her way of granting him his wish?

Meanwhile, in 1988 I began writing newspaper articles based on my celebrity interviews. Two years later I became a full-time freelance writer—in order to tell Dora's story. Since then I've finished two drafts of a novel, a play and a screenplay, all about her love affair with Kafka and the results of my search for her.

Although it might be said that Dora was "responsible" for the loss of Kafka's missing papers, through me she may be responsible for their recovery. When the Nazis came to power in 1933, Dora's home in Berlin was ransacked and every scrap of paper stolen, including all the Kafka material. After the Berlin Wall came down in 1989, bunkers, basements and warehouses were found all over the former East Berlin, stacked to the ceilings with documents confiscated by the Gestapo. Gradually their contents were opened to researchers, and recently I received permission to begin the search for Kafka's lost work on behalf of the Kafka estate.

Dora did survive the Holocaust. She escaped first to Moscow and then, after a harrowing two-year journey to London, where she died in 1952, three months after I was born. As I lay gestating in my mother's womb in New York City, Dora lay dying in a coma in a London hospital. Who knows, I sometimes wonder, what connections may be made in the misty world between life and death?

Despite my searches through the archives in Jerusalem and elsewhere, I've never learned whether Dora and I are related—but it's ceased to be the point. We are connected. I am the person I am today because of Dora. And who knows where this story will end?

As Kafka once wrote, "I am a memory come alive."

3

ROMANCES
OF
THE
SOUL

Footprints of a Soulmate

Patrick L. Dorman, Jr.

Coming home from work one night in the spring of 1986, I had just passed downtown Miami and was heading into Coconut Grove through the bumper-to-bumper traffic typical of a Friday evening.

Suddenly I was transported by a striking vision—of myself playfully chasing a woman up a spiral staircase. Although I couldn't see her face, her legs and especially her feet were crystal clear.

I was then pulled back to the present moment, sitting in stalled traffic.

That image left an unmistakably clear impression on my consciousness. But I wouldn't come to appreciate its significance until some five years later; in fact, almost five years later to the day.

It's now 1991, and I'm working for a chiropractor, Don Osborne, in San Diego. I have heard numerous stories about his niece, Danielle, a model who lives in L.A. From the stories I'd heard, she sounded a little too pretentious for my taste.

It was a Monday morning when Don called me into his office to invite me to lunch. He told me that his massage therapist, who knew me fairly well, kept insisting that I needed to meet Danielle. At the time I was seeing a woman, but it wasn't serious. So I agreed to come to lunch on Friday.

When I walked into Don's home, I couldn't believe my eyes. Danielle was without a doubt the most beautiful woman I had ever seen. Her deeply penetrating blue eyes struck me first—and then I was suddenly possessed by a bizarre desire to see her bare feet!

We decided to walk to a neighborhood Thai restaurant. On the way, Danielle and I found ourselves talking deeply about life and spirituality. I couldn't believe the rapidly growing connection I felt with this woman, but most puzzling to me was how much I kept looking down at her feet. I started hoping she might kick her shoes off in the restaurant. No such luck.

I was completely mesmerized by her, and couldn't wait to see her for another date. We spoke on the phone several times, and I finally persuaded her to come to San Diego that following Thursday.

We spent a timeless day together, and sunset found us at the beach. *Good*, I thought to myself. *Now her shoes will definitely come off!*

When we got out of my car to walk to the shore, I looked down at her feet—and was instantly drawn back to my vision of five years before. It was Danielle's feet I had seen running ahead of me up those stairs. A wave of emotion rushed over me, along with a feeling of quiet certainty about who this woman was to me.

As I write this, we have been married for two years.

Redhead

Tom Youngholm

I'd always thought of myself as a typical kind of guy, meaning I exhibited most "guy" characteristics—including some of the shortcomings. A die-hard Chicago Cubs fan, I loved to watch and play all kinds of sports. And no "chick" movies for me. I was definitely more logical than emotional. In fact, I'd say I cried about as many times as the Cubs won the World Series. The only time I could truly emote was when I played the piano, and that was rarely.

Several years ago I saw the movie *Somewhere in Time*. I've never been so choked up by a movie in my life. The music, by John Barry and Rachmaninoff, stirred parts of me that I didn't know existed. I bought the CD and piano music. I felt driven, almost obsessed, to listen to and play the music every day.

One day when I was playing the score, my body began to move back and forth on its own. When I finished playing, I felt the urge to meditate while listening to the soundtrack.

I sat down, closed my eyes, and began to focus on my breath. As the music played, my body again began to sway gently.

Suddenly I was dancing with an elegant woman in a large 1800's-style ballroom. I could sense that this woman had long blonde hair and was about my height. The whole experience felt entirely real: It was occurring, although obviously not in the physical sense.

The music continued for some time, and so did the dancing. Only after I had completely forgotten that my body was actually sitting in a chair in my living room in San Diego in 1987 did the woman speak to me. She told me her name was Paula, and in that moment a warm, tingly sensation blanketed me. The energy began to swirl within me, and the pressure continued to increase, until I took a deep breath and exhaled.

The color pink flashed before my eyes, and in that moment a dam broke. I began to cry—no, it was more like sobbing: hard to breathe, you know, that uncontrollable stuff that "guys" think only women do. I had always associated crying with sadness and pain. This was different. It was a comfortableness, it was a reunion, it was the first time in my life I have ever felt unconditional love.

Paula told me that we were soulmates—that our energies complemented one another, and that when we were together, we were truly One. I questioned her: I thought one was supposed to find a soulmate here on Earth? She chuckled, and said most soulmates are not together in the same lifetime.

Then she told me I needed to let her go. I was having difficulty in relationships because I'd been looking for her in other women. On a superficial level, it was one reason why all the women I had dated were blonde. She said there are always many souls to join with.

As if on cue, the soundtrack came to a close. The violins diminished, and I felt her energy leave me.

As I lecture around the country, people inevitably tell me that as I speak about Paula, they see a pink glow around me. On three separate occasions someone has described a woman standing behind me. All gave the same description: a blonde woman wearing a long, flowing nineteenth-century dress. I just smile and give a knowing nod.

I've had many contacts with Paula since that initial visit.

Half-jokingly, half-seriously, I sometimes ask her to materialize, if only for one night. Her response is always the same: "Our time will come."

Then I feel her smile, and a warmth in my heart.

The guys kid me about my experiences, but I really don't mind.

It's hard to put into words. I just feel that I'm more than I used to be. More complete.

Incidentally, for the first time in years, I'm in love. It happened about two and a half years ago. Yes, she is my height, and elegant-looking—but she's a redhead.

I Knew My Wife in a Past Life

Daniel Tardent

My partner, Josse, and I have always enjoyed a very special relationship. When we met there was an instant feeling of recognition which has stayed with us. We enjoy a great sense of love and spiritual togetherness in our marriage.

However, about a year ago I erupted from my usual calm state into a series of explosions. I felt angry most of the time and struggled for control.

Like a volcano, I would fume for hours, until finally I could control it no longer. The worst part was Josse was the focal point of my anger. Everything she did annoyed me—for no reason. I would get so wild I wanted to pick up the nearest fragile thing and throw it. Sometimes I did just that.

As an ECKist I know anger is one of the five passions of the mind. We learn self-discipline through the spiritual exercises. Finding a larger perspective had always been easy for me before. In fact, I'd never really had to deal with anger much before.

I felt confused and upset—me, a previously calm and well-balanced person, suddenly out of control. I felt like two people: one who was slowly losing his mind, and the other who was calmly observing the destructive effects of anger on me and my loved ones.

I continued my spiritual exercises. I asked my inner guide, the Mahanta, for help. At first things just seemed to get worse.

Pretty soon, I stopped feeling anything. I had closed down. That evening, when I no longer cared, the Mahanta gave me two dreams.

The first notes in my dream journal for that night: "I've gone absolutely wild. Breaking things, screaming. Josse is around. I'm in a total rage." Later in the night I dreamed again: "I lie on the ground, badly wounded. Around me a swirling vortex of men and horses scramble for their lives. The red dust blows hot on my face as I slip into shock. The air is violent. I am a Sioux warrior in a fierce tribal battle."

I've had vivid past-life recollections before, but the experience always resembled watching a movie on a screen.

This time was different. I was caught in the movie! Nothing could have prepared me for the horror, pain, and fear I experienced in this dream: "A large white horse wheeled around me. My heart opened as I saw my tribal chief watching over me. I knew I was safe now, and I struggled to call out. But as his horse reared, the chief thrust his spear—with all his strength—into the place where my neck and shoulder met.

"The shock and pain of the impact were immense. I stared desperately at him as my world melted into hot blackness. In that moment his face changed and I was looking at Josse astride the big white horse.

"I left my body quickly and rage overcame me. The chief who I had loved and trusted with my life had betrayed and killed me!"

I woke up from the dream in a cold sweat. I could still feel the force of the impact of the spear in my neck. I wondered if I would ever be able to forgive Josse for betraying me in that lifetime.

My understanding of past-life healing had been very simplistic. Once you saw the cause of a situation, it would disappear, replaced with a great feeling of love and understanding. But I was full of sickness and anger. I told Josse about the Sioux dream, feeling my rage stir again.

As we talked, however, the light of Divine Spirit began to glow.

With it came a deeper insight into the truth of my dream: I had been very badly wounded in battle. Because of the intense fighting, there was no possibility of saving me. The terrible tortures I would suffer as a captive of the enemy tribe were well known. So my chief had done the most loving thing: he had killed me quickly and released me to freedom in the inner worlds.

Finally, I understood. The insight poured balm on an old, old wound.

As the weeks passed, my new understanding of what had happened in that lifetime slowly filtered into all levels of my being. I became less intense in my outlook on life. It was as though a heavy gray cloud had been lifted from me.

The wild mood swings vanished. I could trust life again. For the first time in many months I was happy.

The most wonderful gift was the new love I felt for Josse. Our bond of love as Sioux warriors filled me with awe. It was the love of two Souls committed to helping each other on the journey home to God—a love which continues to grow.

I learned many things through this experience. But the lesson that really stays with me is simply this: The Spiritual Exercises of ECK and the inner guide, the Mahanta, can help solve any problem.

The Turning Point

Freddie Ravel

I had waited all my life to meet the woman of my dreams and was getting to the point of thinking that it might never happen. One day I met her, and for the first time I felt that I had found a soulmate. In the days and weeks that followed, it became clear that there was tremendous harmony and love between us.

Life, however, is not perfect. Due to events in her childhood and other old patterns, she had a side of her that expressed great resistance to our relationship. I'm sure I had my own.

One particular evening, this resistance reached an all-time high, and we began to openly discuss these fears. Her reservations about our love so shook me that I thought I might lose this magical woman. I found myself weeping in her arms.

In the morning, as I awoke, feeling her beside me, I knew that I truly wanted her with me for the rest of my life. As she slept, I went to my study, and on a small notepad I let a stream of words flood through me.

Feeling a bit tentative, I presented them to her. She read, slowly and questioningly, and as the tears welled up in her eyes she pulled me close and said, "Honey, I woke up convinced that I would stop seeing you. But these words have melted all my resistance away. I love you so."

To this day, we continue to cherish and honor each other. Our love grows and deepens with each passing day.

These are the words that represented the turning point:

When feelings are strong and magic appears
It isn't so strange that there may be fears
For life is an ebb and love is a flow
The yin and the yang—it comes and it goes

Yet, there is an elixir with the strongest of cures
with "Love" on its label, it always endures
Like the light of the Sun and that of the Moon
Beyond time and space it heals all the wounds

Poured with great passion with my heart an open door
I offer you this drink that I have never served before

A Gift from God

Dharma Singh Khalsa and Kirti Kaur Khalsa

DHARMA

A person on a spiritual path caters to his or her soul by developing their sadhana, or regular spiritual practice. Mine is to rise in the hours before sunrise and meditate. I read Japji, the first of the five daily prayers of a Sikh, do a half hour of Kundalini yoga, and spend another hour chanting select celestial mantras. After that, I'm ready to have a great day.

But this day was different. After I'd dried off from my shower and dressed, I sat down to tune in by chanting the phrase "Ong namo guru dev namo," which means, "I bow

before my highest consciousness." After doing that, I usually say a few silent personal affirmations and prayers of
protection for myself, my family, and my patients. But today my thoughts were not my own.

As I entered into a pleasant, timeless state of mind, an
image appeared. I saw a vessel of pure white milk shatter
on a flat black surface. It was then swept away by a large
but otherwise ordinary household broom—to be replaced
by a beautiful silver chalice, as these words echoed in my
mind: "You have the most beautiful, perfect woman in the
world for you, now."

This sequence repeated three more times before it
stopped, and I moved on to my yoga and meditation. But
the next day it happened again, and the following day as
well. The fourth day, Saturday, nothing came, and Sunday
my mind again was quiet. But there was still an unusual
feeling hovering around.

That afternoon I got a call from a friend who said, "The
Siri Singh Sahib wants you to come to New Mexico." This is
the title carried by my spiritual teacher, Yogi Bhajan, indi-
cating he is the chief religious and administrative authority
of Sikhs in the Western hemisphere.

"What for?" I asked, rather curtly, for I'd only just returned from there.

"To meet your future wife."

After I'd regained my composure, I called Yogi Bhajan's
secretary to inquire about the woman I was supposed to
marry. "She's so sweet," she said. "She's Italian."

"Italian?" I stammered. "Does she speak English? What
does she look like? How old is she?"

The secretary simply replied, "Come as soon as you can."

I flew from Phoenix to Albuquerque through one of those
terrifying thunderstorms found only in New Mexico. I must
have chanted every mantra I ever knew, thinking, "I'm going
to die in a plane crash over a woman I don't even know." By
the time we landed I was so shaken that I asked a friend to
drive me the hour and a half to the ranch in Espanola. He

agreed, and we arrived at eleven at night, a mere four hours late for my first meeting with Kirti, my wife-to-be.

I was immediately ushered into the Siri Singh Sahib's cozy living room. I sank into the plush couch, but before I knew it I was on the edge of my seat, as Kirti entered, escorted by a few female friends.

I looked at her and felt good about everything. "It's going to be all right," I thought. Yogi Bhajan made some introductions, then looked at us and asked if we had any questions. I said, "No, it's okay with me."

But an alarmed look came over Kirti's face as she exclaimed, "Wait a minute, I don't even know this guy!" Her English was certainly fine.

Yet, on some level we did seem to connect. We went outside into the pleasant night air to talk, and the energy between us was strong and true. After about an hour of sharing our thoughts, we went into the Yogi's private temple to meditate together. That sealed our destiny.

We went back into the living room to sit at the feet of the master. "Do you have a spiritual relationship?" he asked.

"Yes, sir," we replied in unison.

"Then you have my blessing."

He leaned back in his chair and appeared to go far away. Kirti and I started jabbering about a few planning details, but the Yogi drifted deeper and deeper, finally saying dreamily, "That's not my problem."

We spent the rest of the short night apart, and the next morning I drove my new fiancée to the Albuquerque airport. Her time in America was up, and she was returning to her home and job as director of regulatory affairs for a multinational drug company in Rome. I was proud of my delightful, beautiful, twenty-nine-year-old blonde and blue-eyed bride-to-be.

KIRTI

It's not that I was looking for a husband. For some reason, at the last moment that summer, I changed my vacation plans. I was going to go to the South of France, but decided instead to go to the States to visit my best friend, also an Italian Sikh girl, living in New Mexico.

After I arrived in Espanola, I asked to have an audience with the Siri Singh Sahib. It took a few days, but finally I walked into his living room at the ranch.

As I came in, he looked at me in an unusual way and said, "You need to get married, and we have the perfect man in mind for you!" Then he turned to his secretary and said, "Get Dr. Dharma on the phone."

I remember closing my eyes to see if I was dreaming— three times. When I realized it wasn't a dream, I was shocked.

"I didn't ask for this appointment to get married!"

After talking around the issue for a few moments, Yogi Bhajan spoke to me very directly, saying, "It's time for you to work with a man." He turned around to give a few instructions to his secretary, then looked at me again and asked, in the sweetest, most nonthreatening voice, "Can you at least meet him?"

After what seemed like a long time, I said, "Okay, I'll meet him." I didn't know whether to laugh or cry.

DHARMA

My own arrival at the point where I was ready to meet Kirti wasn't straightforward, either. I could go back a while, over many events that led to that day, but three years previous will probably suffice.

It was less than twenty-four hours after I'd thoughtfully told a beautiful woman, whom I cared very much for, that I couldn't have a relationship with her because of the differences in our spiritual paths. I'd come to the ranch, and I found myself wandering into the Siri Singh Sahib's quarters, not quite sure why. He was having a rather lively discussion with his youngest son, Kulbir Singh.

"You need to do this and you need to do that," he shouted, "and you need to get married!" Then, without missing a beat he turned, pointed his index finger straight at me and said, his eyes brightly beaming, "And so do you!"

Although I was understandably quite surprised, I calmly sat down on the same couch I was to occupy three years later. Yogi Bhajan started to tell me all the attributes of the type of woman I should marry: her intelligence, her strong spirit, her sweetness. He was describing the ideal mate for me.

After giving me a few moments to let it sink in, he turned back to me and said, "I have someone in mind for you."

"I don't know if I'm happy about that or not," I said in a whisper.

"It doesn't matter. You'll make the rounds and fool around, but in the end, I'll have the final authority."

That was it. I was out as quickly as I'd come in.

The next morning I called his personal secretary and asked, "Who is it? Who does he have in mind?" His aide simply told me to be patient. One day, when the time was right, I'd get a phone call.

Sure enough, three years later almost to the day, the call came. Now I was at the airport bidding a fond farewell to my bride-to-be, as she got on a plane back to Italy. "Bride-to-be" . . . but when, and how? Would it all actually work out?

"Big hug," she said, smiling and waving as she disappeared into the plane.

We corresponded by fax, phone, and mail. We actually got to know one another quite well that way, and added to the depth of our first meeting.

More than a month later, I was back at the ranch at the feet of Yogi Bhajan. "Marry her, doctor," he said in a deep, booming voice. "She'll be like a tuxedo to you."

"I will, sir. I just have to figure out how and when."

"Tell her to come next week."

I called Kirti. I'll never forget what she said.

"I decided today I want to marry you."

"What did you say?" I replied softly, almost in disbelief. "I want to be your wife."

And so it came to pass. Our marriage was performed in the beautiful, golden-domed Sikh temple in Espanola, New Mexico, about a mile from where we'd first met eight weeks earlier.

After the ceremony, as we were standing outside on that lovely fall day greeting friends with wedding cake, the Siri Singh Sahib arrived, looking like a king. He wore a pink turban, which I subsequently discovered signifies good luck at a wedding.

We all seemed to meld together as he put his arms around the both of us in a strong embrace. I heard him say in my ear, so that perhaps only I could hear, "She is a gift to you from God."

Wishes Do Come True

Maxine Warsh

At forty, I was very content with my life. I had a relationship with a man who wanted no commitment emotionally, one best male friend who fulfilled the social, emotional, and companionship end, and a life free from monetary concerns. I was traveling and doing everything I wanted to do, when I wanted to do it.

Classes and seminars interested me, the more mystical the better. I had recently tried getting into a Kabbalah study group but had no luck—I was late for enrollment. One night, though, about three months later, my friend Manny

came over with a notice written in Hebrew announcing a
new Kabbalah class in a location that was nearly in my
back yard. Being neither particularly "religious" nor educated in Judaism, I was still completely open-minded to
this new mystical study.

The classes were fascinating, and the tools I learned for
self-improvement were working. After the first month of
classes, the Jewish holidays were nearing, and the Kabbalah Center was promoting a Jewish New Year celebration
in Somerset, New Jersey. I decided that I was ready for a
spiritual adventure. Besides, a weekend of this stuff could
be fun.

Upon arrival there was a luncheon reception. I was
standing in line when a man came up to me and told me I
was going to be overwhelmed by the experience I was
about to have. For some reason, I was infuriated. The nerve
of this man, to tell me what I was going to experience and
how I would feel! In a manner that was unlike me, I told
him I liked being overwhelmed, pointedly dismissing him.
He politely walked away.

Well, where do I begin to tell when and how I became
overwhelmed? Not only did I *not* enjoy or relate to what
was going on there, I wanted to leave almost immediately.
But I couldn't get a flight out, so I decided to make the best
of it. I went in and out of the services, observing them from
a detached point of view.

At some point near the end of the services, there was a
prayer that allowed you to make a wish. We were told that
if the wish was made in the right consciousness, it was
guaranteed to come true during the following year. *What
the hell*, I thought, *I'll go for it*. My wish was to "make someone as happy as I would like to be."

Soon after, the services were over, and I was elated. All I
could think about was going home. To pass the time, I took
a walk with a friend. We were discussing our experiences
when I spotted the man who'd told me I'd be overwhelmed. In a sweet but sarcastic way I asked him how his
weekend was. He politely began telling me, but I confess I

really didn't care. Eventually he asked me if I'd like to have a drink.

Well, while we were having that drink, we talked and talked and talked ... and I realized that I'd never felt so comfortable with anyone. He radiated kindness, and I intuitively felt I could trust him. I had no guards up, nor any desire for this to go anywhere. Hours passed, and we kept on talking and revealing ourselves to one another. We were about to part when he told me that all he wanted was to "make somebody as happy as he would like to be." My wish verbatim! Not only did this guy "know" me before he knew me, he actually mouthed the exact words that I had wished, only a few hours after I wished them.

After a six-month courtship between my home in Florida and his in Canada, we got married—something I never thought would happen to me. I never thought I'd meet a man so well suited to my personality and my soul.

Every day now, I see a miracle happening in my life— because my only care is making my husband as happy as I would like to be.

God, Who Should I Marry?

Dennis Calhoun

In college I met a woman I was sure I would marry. From the moment we met, it seemed as if we had always been together. But after we graduated, she got a job in Chicago, and I ended up working in Houston. We maintained a long-distance relationship.

One day during my spiritual exercise I told the Master I was ready to get married.

I explained that I wanted companionship. If the ECK (Divine Spirit) could work it out, and if it were for the good of the whole of life, well, that's what I wanted.

Time passed with no resolution to the situation. Finally my girlfriend and I decided to date other people. It just didn't seem likely that I could transfer to Chicago or that she would move to Chicago or that she would move to Houston. Shortly after that, I met a woman, Jaye, and we began dating.

Four months later my company announced they were opening an office in Chicago. I was going to be transferred! I thought, "This is perfect." I had let go of the situation, and the ECK had provided a way for me to move to Chicago and marry my college girlfriend.

Before I left Houston, Jaye shared her feelings with me. She believed we belonged together. She was certain I felt something for her, too—and I did. But in my mind, in my thoughts, I was headed for my old girlfriend in Chicago.

I moved to Chicago and became engaged. The relationship was peaceful and calm, as if we had been married before. But then all of a sudden, things began to fall apart. Somehow, it just didn't feel right to either of us to get married. Sadly, we broke off our engagement.

Once again I took the situation into contemplation. The answer I received was clear: Follow your heart. Go see Jaye.

I had followed my head, and that hadn't worked out. So I called Jaye. A wonderful feeling rushed into my heart. I knew I wanted to marry Jaye, but I still didn't understand why. I was making a big decision purely on the feeling in my heart.

About a month before we were to be married, Jaye and I went to New Orleans. As we walked, we discussed some wedding details. While in the French Quarter, we turned a corner and looked into a breathtaking courtyard.

In that one moment, I glimpsed an entire past-life experience.

I turned to Jaye in astonishment and saw that something had happened to her too. We began to talk and discovered we'd both had the same vision of a shared past life!

In this previous incarnation, I had been a young man in the southern United States of the late 1850s. In about 1859, I moved north to find a job to pay for medical school. I met a northern woman (my college sweetheart in this life), and we married. Her parents were very wealthy and put me through medical school.

Soon after, the Civil War broke out. I returned to the South to serve as a doctor for the Confederacy. During the time I was stationed in New Orleans, I met a woman (Jaye). We fell deeply in love. But I was married, and so we did not act on our love.

The war ended. I left New Orleans and returned to my wife in the North. Jaye and I lived out our lives without seeing each other again. I spent the rest of that life living comfortably with the woman I almost married in this life.

After the brief glimpse of this past life, I understood why my relationship with my college girlfriend had been so easy. We had been married before. I also understood why I thought we should be married again. The mind likes familiar and comfortable paths.

But I needed fresh experiences and growth in this life. My heart wanted to move on and fulfill the love I had left behind in New Orleans in that life. Jaye and I have been very happy together in our marriage.

Now if I hear two voices—one from my head and one from my heart—I know which is guidance from Divine Spirit. The heart is often more aligned with Soul, my true self. Thoughts are from the mind. The mind is a good servant, but a poor master.

I always tell my friends, "When in doubt, follow your heart!"

A Mystical Experience of Love

Harry W. Schwartz

For me, *life* is a mystical experience. I have always felt driven by an unseen force and never quite in control, my direction always a mystery, yet magical; hence, mystical. My balance has always come from an inner spirit . . . call it hope, call it luck, I call it spirit.

Perhaps the most mystical experience in my life stems from one of life's greatest mysteries of all: romance. Being a professional chef, and having a weight problem for all of my life—at times reaching 250 pounds on that darn scale—food is an integral part of my life. It is an integral part of me. Why should it not be the way to my love's heart?

My wife, Laurie, was born in the States but grew up in Mexico City and in Brussels, Belgium. Before moving from this country as a young child, she lived in Des Moines, Iowa, for a six-month period. Des Moines is forty-five miles from the town of Marshalltown, where I was born and raised. We had no idea of each other's existence at the time, but her family did meet some cousins of mine who live in Des Moines and they became friends. My cousins often visited Laurie's family in Mexico. My family had no idea, as they never mentioned Laurie's family to us. We all went our own separate ways.

As the years went on and time for college grew near, unbeknownst to me my cousins were coaxing Laurie's parents, who had recently moved to Ft. Lauderdale, Florida, to send Laurie to Grinnell College, where I had decided to go a year earlier. In their minds, Grinnell would be the perfect place for us to meet. We had not a clue. Laurie chose to go to Tufts University in Medford, Massachusetts. So much for my cousins' ability to make a match!

During my college years my family often went for vacations to Southern California on breaks. We always went to the same resort and in time found several families who had the same ritual. I made some friends who went to Tufts. Eventually I finished undergraduate work a year before these people, so my decision to do graduate studies at nearby Harvard seemed like a perfect social setup to me: I thought Harvard would be a good place from which to check out the undergrads. For the first time in my life I had slimmed down to a normal size, and was feeling my oats.

I immediately found myself attracted to the first female presented to me by my Tufts friends, a lovely New Yorker from Fifth Avenue who was something quite new to this Midwestern corn-fed farm boy. High heels, designer clothes and makeup—when I had been lucky to find someone at Grinnell who found it acceptable to shave the hair from under her arms.

Fifth Avenue and I dated for the entire fall of 1980. She fascinated me. She was confident, had great hair, her parents drove a Jag. Yes, quite a tidy little package. My life was going in the right direction. Uh-huh, yessirree Bob, I knew what was happ'nen.

After winter break, Fifth Avenue and I decided to meet quite a large group of Tufts socialites at Boston's number one disco. I was sipping a martini, thinking what a bore Fifth Avenue had become, when my eyes were drawn to a woman about to unveil herself by removing an ankle-length winter coat.

Underneath was a Spandex-wrapped, tanned, gorgeous creature with wild hair and fiery green eyes. It was like an out-of-body experience. No one else existed for that moment. She was not even looking at me, but I was fixated on her.

She was with some swim team star, and I was with Fifth Avenue. At one point, we brushed against each other on the way to the dance floor. The evening proceeded with me in a daze. I had to meet her.

The next day, I talked to one of the guys at Tufts and described her, begging him to fix me up. "But what about Fifth Avenue?" he asked, then added, "Come to think of it, you and Laurie would be great together." After a few more calls, he gave me her number. She had said it was okay for me to call. It seemed she and her stud muffin weren't getting along so well after all. Fifth Avenue threw a hissy fit, but quickly got over it, and Laurie and I were scheduling our first date.

Talk about mystical. Although the physical attraction was in high gear, love did not have a chance to develop in the first five minutes we were together. But a feeling came over me. I knew Laurie was for me, right then and there. I was being pulled to her by a force that was out of my control. I knew I had to be with her forever, because we had things we had to do and we could only do them together. It did not matter how much we were alike or how we differed.

I called her the morning after our date and asked her to marry me. Amazingly, she was not totally surprised, as I had expected her to be. She felt, however, that a couple of hours together might not have been enough for her to make this decision. I suggested we get together again for dinner, but this time I decided to prepare it myself.

Having loved to cook since a child, putting together a romantic dinner for two was no challenge. But putting together a dinner for two that was to fuel a decision that would last a lifetime was another matter. I went to work.

By the time I was to leave for Tufts to pick up Laurie, I had handmade spinach pasta hanging to dry from chopsticks wedged in my kitchen cupboards. There was a sweet veal basil sauce simmering slowly on the stove, my Caesar dressing ready to be tossed with some romaine, and an almond cheesecake chilling in the refrigerator. I was poised. I was creating fuel for the spirit that guided me. I was creating food for my direction.

We spoke very little over dinner, and even less as I took her home. There was not a whole lot of reason to talk. Laurie had been taken over by the same force. The mystery was no longer a mystery—but it was most definitely mystical.

The next morning, she called me and said yes. We began announcing it to our friends and family.

When my cousins who knew Laurie's family found out, they were stupefied. We had met all by ourselves, and been taken over by a force they had sensed for us a long time ago. Our wedding, five and a half months after our first date, was like a family reunion, as both sides had previous connections.

Seventeen years later, after bringing into the world one of the most beautiful creatures of our own, Laurie and I continue on our magical mystery tour. My life maintains its mystical path, but with a partner to whom I was drawn who now gives me my direction.

Butterfly and Tiger

Lisa M. Chan

"Stay out of China this summer," an astrologer advised me. "You will marry in May of 1990, but not your current boyfriend. You'll meet your husband traveling next fall."

Never having consulted anyone like this before, I didn't really know what to think. It sounded far-fetched. I soon forgot the whole thing.

With the Tienanmen Massacre of June 4th, 1989, my idealistic hopes for China, a country that had held a lifelong fascination for me, were shattered. I had no illusions about human rights in China, after studying and traveling there for almost ten years. But after weeks of watching the first televised demonstrations in Chinese history, it had seemed that change was inevitable. We all believed that there was new hope for the future. When those kids died, a raw, deeply hopeful part of me died, too.

The next day, I asked my Chinese boyfriend to join me in a march of remembrance through the streets of Hong Kong, with a million mourners, to protest the massacre. He replied that he needed to buy a microwave oven. So I went alone. I had stopped believing in the perfect mate, but his inability to respond to my grief and that of the entire world struck me as similar to the detached arrogance of the Chinese government.

Soon after, the China travel book I had just co-authored was taken off the presses. No American was going to travel to such a brutal place.

I returned to the States for an "empowerment training" to shake me from my depression, and to visit my family and friends. Within the course of a few days, my parents sat me down to watch *When Harry Met Sally*, *Crossing Delancy*, and *Moonstruck*—all movies about the trials of unmarried women in their thirties. Remembering the astrologer, I announced that I was to be married in May 1990 to a man I had yet to meet.

In New York City, my good friend, a Malaysian stock-broker, seemed just as concerned about my future as my parents. She insisted we do a conference call with her psychic in Malaysia. "You'll meet your husband within thirty days," said the psychic. "He already recognized your name as his wife's when he heard it one and a half years ago." Instead of feeling joy, I developed a paranoia about strange men who had access to my name: the UPS man, the mailman, the carryout delivery boy, the paper boy.

I attended the empowerment training, a smorgasbord of exercises designed to open people up to living their lives with awareness. In the evenings, I worked on a giant set of wings for a butterfly costume, gluing shiny bits of paper into a mosaic. I was going to a Halloween party in Washington, D.C. Privately, I envisioned myself emerging from a chrysalis with my new wings.

In L.A., a screenwriter had received an invitation to the same party. His friend promised that that woman with "the name" would be there. The screenwriter had repeated her name to himself many times since he'd first heard it a year and a half before; it comforted him. But he'd already purchased a plane ticket to visit his family in Illinois. He was disappointed about the party, but shrugged it off.

When he got to Illinois, his mother said, "Let's all get in the car and go visit your brother in Washington." Astonished, he jumped at the suggestion.

Three hours into the party and I still hadn't arrived. I had been to that address several times before, but still found myself hopelessly lost. Flustered by the time I finally arrived, I went in.

"I've been looking forward to meeting you for a long time," said a man with a velvet voice. He was dressed in Flying Tiger gear, garb I immediately recognized from pictures of the heroic World War II pilots stationed in one of my favorite Chinese cities, Kunming. I shook his hand. It was the thirtieth day.

From the moment of that handshake, a bubble of calm enveloped us—almost as if we had become the bubbles of the Perrier water we sipped, every exchange feeling clear and giddy. There was no subject we couldn't broach, no observation too mundane. The Butterfly and the Flying Tiger.

When we spoke on the phone three days later, after he had returned to L.A., he said, "You know we're going to marry, don't you?" I quickly agreed. But when I hung up, I think I fainted. Things like this don't happen so quickly!

A few days later, I started to get waves of intense pleasure shooting through my body as I went about my business in New York City. People on buses leaned over and asked, "Miss, are you all right?" He was sending me love from across the continent, and I was getting it! One night, as I sat in a bistro describing to a friend what was happening, three waitresses standing nearby simultaneously dropped their trays and burst into peals of laughter. "He missed," said my companion.

Within a week I flew to L.A., where we became engaged. We married in May 1990.

Saying Goodbye, Saying Hello

Frances Heussenstamm, Ph.D.

Five years, almost to the day, had passed since Karl's death, but I still had no closure.

I was taking part in a tour of Buddhist and Hindu shrines and temples in the northern part of India, as well as Nepal and Sikkim. On a previous visit to sacred spaces in South America, I had already discovered that I could tune into the sacred energy that was present where thousands had worshipped before, and shift peacefully into another state of consciousness. Now I was so comfortable in India that anything seemed possible ... spirit was so flamboyantly evident in every aspect of life there.

We'd been on the road more than a month when, leafing through a guidebook, I saw a description of the funerary city of Gaya. I felt a powerful, intuitive "pull" to go there, but there was no time to arrange for a side trip. I didn't know what the urgent feelings were about, but I grew restless and disturbed, vaguely uneasy. By the time we reached Varanasi—formerly Benares, the most sacred and holy city on the Ganges River, the city where Hindus long to spend their final days—I was feverish with desire for "something" to happen, though I didn't know what.

We quickly dumped our belongings in our hotel rooms. Then, in gathering darkness, we were whisked off to the bank of the river to visit the most revered of the *ghats*, or cremation platforms.

There was intense activity everywhere in the plaza above the river. It was filled with people. Everywhere there were torches, candles, flowers, musical instruments. There were vendors with incense, food, colorful little piles of spices and cosmetics, souvenir hawkers, and holy men, mixed with tourists from all over the world.

I halted before a great mound of flowers, some arranged, others heaped up pell-mell or overflowing their baskets, spilling into the street. They filled the night with a soft scent that intoxicated me. Through some compulsion, not knowing why, I bought a flowered *mala*—the Hindu ritual "rosary" or offering—from a beautifully arranged basketful of yellow, red, and white marigolds and carnations.

Our turbaned guide motioned us forward, and we found ourselves being led through twisting, narrow, pitch-dark alleys. An occasional candle or bare lightbulb dangling from a ceiling allowed us to peer directly into the houses and apartments that lined the alleys. Families were dining, or meals were being prepared; occupants dozed or bustled about, oblivious to our shy glances. We dodged cow pads and puddles, tripped over garbage and sleeping beggars, feeling the walls with our hands in the darkest places, stumbling forward to the accompaniment of reedy, eerie melodies. I was full of anxious anticipation. Where were we going?

We emerged onto the balcony of the *ghat*, which consisted of raised stone platforms and intermittent flights of stairs leading down to the river, the last few steps washed by the current. Below us, funerary fires were blazing. Hot, dense clouds of ashes, sparks, and smoke swirling around our heads made breathing difficult as we stared down, transfixed. There were piles of corpses. White cloth was wrapped around the bodies of men; gold or red saris—their wedding saris—enveloped the bodies of women.

I gazed into the center of one fire, at the stiff body of a man whose cremation was being tended by a *ghat* employee or priest. He was stirring the burning remains with a stout stick, occasionally beating the corpse to break it into faster-burning pieces. I was totally mesmerized, although I remember gagging, feeling sick, as I looked down in shock.

Without a thought, in a spontaneous, sweeping motion, I tossed the *mala* over the balcony down onto the pyre. As it fell into the fire-cloud, it burst into tiny sparks of light.

Feelings of longing, grief and loss flooded me. It was as if I were looking down on my own husband's cremation.

With that, I slipped into a kind of defensive trance— psychologists call it dissociation—for I had no other way to stem the avalanche of feelings. I remember nothing about how I got back to the hotel or put myself to bed.

The next morning when the phone rang with my wake-up call, I rose in a stupor and began to move very slowly, pulling on my clothes. Gradually gathering my wits, I picked up speed and hurriedly raced outside—but the bus with my group was nowhere in sight. The dawn would not wait for tour groups, and they'd already left to watch the sun rise over the Ganges.

I begged my way onto another bus, also loaded with American tourists, that was heading for the river. Surrounded by strangers, I felt embarrassed and self-concious. I looked out the window at a man and woman being pedaled at top speed by the sweating operator of a bicycle-rickshaw keeping pace with the bus. The most beautiful Hindu woman I'd ever seen looked up at me from the rickshaw seat: our eyes locked onto one another's, and I felt a flood of connection and sisterhood.

At that exact moment, our bus and the rickshaw collided, and the fragile rickshaw flipped over and crashed. The woman and her companion were thrown into the street. A huge crowd instantly swarmed around them, and as our bus ground to a stop I could see nothing but a mass of agitated Indians, all shouting and arguing at the same time. The driver dashed out, slamming the door behind him.

What had happened to her? I agonized, wringing my hands nervously while I broke out in a sweat. In a few minutes, the driver returned and announced harshly, "Everyone said it was the rickshaw driver's fault because he came too close to the bus." With that, the bus jerked into motion, and we lurched dizzily into heavy traffic again. There was no report on the fate of the rickshaw passengers: the driver refused to discuss it.

A sense of the preciousness of each moment of life came over me, a realization that beauty could disappear in an instant. Hadn't I just seen it happen? People's connections with one another could be severed in the blink of an eyelid. I was so moved with the truth of it, I couldn't even cry.

When we arrived at the river, only a few moments before dawn, I bought another *mala*. Softly descending the wide stairs to a boat where four oarsmen were waiting for our busload, I could see my own group far up the river in an identical dory. Amid hundreds of Hindus who were making morning prayers and ablutions, brushing teeth, bathing, immersing themselves in the sacred water, I climbed aboard and sat down . . . unnerved by the morning events and the spectacle around me.

A vendor stepped up to the side of the boat and proffered two identical memorial offerings: lighted wicks floating in oil in tiny clay cups, with fresh green leaves surrounding them. I reached into my pocket and found I had two rupees—exactly the price required.

A man's voice from behind inquired, "What are those for?"

Without looking up, I answered quietly, "One is for my parents who died. The other is for my husband." I heard him spontaneously sigh along with me.

When I floated those wreathed candles on the river and had thrown out the *mala*, watching it drift away into the deep, I felt as if a great door closed behind me and a new door swung open. Karl was dead. I was open to the future.

I turned to introduce myself to the man who'd spoken. His name was Phillippe. He told me that he, too, had lost someone: his wife and unborn child.

And this journey, so strangely full of images of death and mourning, now marked the beginning of another. Phillippe and I were together for the next four years.

As one door closes, another always opens.

4

SPIRITUAL HEALING

My Magic Heart

David G. Cooper

"Cardiac arrest CCU 6! Cardiac arrest CCU 6!"

Two days after my heart attack, I was sitting up in my bed in the Cardiac Care Unit, eating breakfast, when a total silence filled my body. Turning to look at the monitor over the head of my bed, there was no question as to what had happened: the EKG line was flat. I looked back at my oldest son, who was standing by the bed.

"Dad!" Kevin cried out. "What's happening?"

In a normal voice I replied, "My heart has stopped."

The silence within my body was overwhelming. It was similar to the silence in a room when the power goes off: For an instant, you are suddenly aware, from its absence, of all the background noise normally created by the electrically powered things around you. So too with the unexpected, total silence in my body.

Instantly my room was filled with nurses and equipment. Kevin was quickly ushered out into the corridor. Four nurses stood around my bed and, like a drill team, went into action. The first words I heard were, "I have no blood pressure." Then:

"I have no pulse."

"There's no heartbeat."

"The EKG is flat."

As I looked into their faces, a beautiful glow began to radiate from them, increasing in intensity until all I saw was four beautiful pairs of eyes surrounding my bed. They were warm and loving, and each sent a silent message: Have no fear . . . just trust.

Looking into the eyes to my left, I asked, "What's happened?"

"Your heart has stopped," the nurse quietly replied.

"What are we going to do about it?"

The nurse smiled and replied, "We're going to try to restart your heart for you."

Without thinking, my immediate response was, "That would be nice."

The words and events were so crystal clear, it was as if they were being etched into my memory so that they would never be forgotten. With all those beautiful eyes working over me, there was no fear.

The nurse on my left asked, "Do you mind if I hit you on the chest to try starting your heart again?"

What a strange request. Of course it was okay. "Please do."

She hit my chest with her open fist several times, but the silence in my body continued.

As the drama continued, my only pain came from my inner awareness of the tension of the four nurses as they struggled to restart my heart. Yet it was difficult for me to understand why they were so concerned. To me, the feeling of imminent death was one of complete relief, peace, and joy. It was like being wrapped in a warm cocoon of love.

Gradually I became aware of being able to view several things at the same moment. It was as if I was floating above the bed, watching what was taking place below me—while at the same time my main focus was from inside my body, looking out though my own eyes, watching the nurses around my bed.

As I looked at these two scenes, a third arose. I was observing my own funeral. My children and friends were sitting in front of my casket.

Then another: my three sons, Kevin, Jon, and Stephen, were tearfully re-entering our condo after the funeral and cleaning out my room. And at the same time, in another scene, my construction partner went into my office and began cleaning up the mess my death had left behind on my desk.

It was as if each scene in this multithought process was on a transparent screen in front of the previous one. Each screen confronted me no matter which way I looked. Each scene was complete with emotions, dialogue and, oddly, background music. The images seemed to fill the room, rather than being confined to my mind.

The nurse on my left continued to thump on my chest as the nurse on my right injected something into my arm. Voices echoed in my ears as each nurse gave her report.

"No blood pressure."

"No pulse."

"No heartbeat."

"The EKG is still flat."

The faces and bodies of the nurses were now indistinguishable from the golden glow that surrounded them. Their love and caring flowed forth, making me feel totally safe to be surrounded by such beautiful and loving beings.

"If my heart has stopped," I asked the nurse on my right, "why am I still breathing and talking? Watch this." I took three deep and loud breaths.

"I don't know."

After what seemed like a long time, through which I remained conscious, breathing and able to talk to the nurses, there was a shift within me. Speaking to the nurse on my right, I said, "You'd better hurry. The room is starting to spin. Things are beginning to close in on me real fast. It sounds like I'm talking from inside a hollow steel drum."

The emotional tension of the nurses became more evident to me, through a newly deep inner awareness. Then the room became filled with a mist. Sounds became tinny to my ears. Movements appeared as if they were in slow motion. It was like viewing and hearing several movies and soundtracks at the same time, all running at half-speed.

Out in the hall, I saw or sensed that another nurse was

heading toward CCU 6, pushing the "crash cart" with the electric paddles. *This looks just like the medical shows on TV. Will it hurt when they hit me? How high will I bounce?*

Through the mist, I saw tears streaming from the pair of eyes to my left. I quietly asked, "What's wrong?"

An emotion-filled voice replied, "We don't want you to die. We love you."

Warmth and understanding filled me. Without thinking, I replied, "All right, then. I won't."

As I took a loud and deep inhale, the top of my head seemed to burst open like a flower in bloom. Just above the opening in my crown was a brilliant crystal ball of white light—and a shaft of white light rising above the ball that appeared to extend to the point of infinity at the center of the universe.

On my exhale, the top of my head opened completely, and a bolt of white light shot down from the crystal ball, through my head, and into my heart. As the light entered my heart, I felt a beat.

The nurse on my left shouted, "I have a heartbeat!"

I smiled at her and asked, "Would you like another?"

The nurses all replied, "Yes!"

On my next inhale, there was the white crystal ball, just as on the last breath, glowing above the opening in the top of my head. And once again on the exhale, the light came down through my head and into my heart, and there was another heartbeat.

And I was intuitively aware of what had happened. I had disconnected from the infinite source of life. The crystal ball just above my head was my personal reservoir of life-force energy from the universe. My heart had stopped and the top of my head had closed, cutting off my connection. And my spirit body had been in the process of leaving the earth realm to follow the retracting source of life home, in my effort to stay connected to it. Now my spiritual and physical bodies were reconnected to the infinite source of life: God. I was not going to die.

With the excitement and amazement of a child on Christmas morning, I exclaimed, "Watch this." I kept rapidly breathing the light from the crystal ball into my heart, and with each breath there was a new beat. After several consecutive beats it felt as if my heart had reestablished its connection to the infinite source, and was beating normally again.

"I have a pulse."

"Blood pressure is normal."

"EKG is normal."

"The heartbeat has returned."

As if by magic, the four pairs of warm, loving eyes turned into four glowing, smiling faces. The concern that had been in their eyes was replaced with excitement, love, and puzzlement.

Yet the golden glow still radiated from their beings and continued to fill the entire room, wrapping me even more snugly in a warm cocoon of love.

To celebrate the moment, words sprang from my heart without my even thinking. "We made it. It was a good trip. Now, who's going to give me a big hug and welcome me back?"

The nurse on my right just shook her head, smiled, and said, "I don't believe this." She turned and left the room.

The nurse on my left, the one who had been crying, leaned over and gave me a tremendous hug and a kiss. Then she smiled and said, "We love you. Welcome back. You are beautiful!"

Looking around, I saw Kevin re-entering the room. His face showed intense fear combined with relief. One glimpse at him left no doubt that it had not been a dream.

My face and soul beamed like those of a child who has just discovered a deep secret: the healing power of my magic heart.

As the drama replayed itself in my mind, I realized these people really did care about me. They loved me even though they didn't know who I was, what I had done, whether I was important or not, or where I was going. And I didn't even know their names, nor could I remember what they looked like.

Then it suddenly hit me. Love, when it is truly unconditional, is far more than a word we share. The nurses' love had flowed forth without any expectations. Theirs was a pure love, a love that said, "We love you just because you are you, and if you die we will miss you even though we just met." The warmth of that love and the golden aura it created held the power of a miracle. And that energy was still present.

To experience the miracle of life created by the power of unconditional love was awesome. This moment would be with me the rest of my life.

With that thought, I gave Kevin a big hug.

Lying in the bed of the now quiet room, it became clear that there had been no mistakes in my life, for this was right where I was supposed to be. It became evident that all the events of my life were interrelated; each event had set the stage and prepared me for the next.

Each was another step toward learning to live a life based on unconditional love—and all of those steps allowed me to learn the lessons of CCU 6, the lessons of surrendering to life and keeping the doors to my magic heart open—for, with them open, the light of love will always shine on my path through life.

An Angel Named Levi

Becki Linderman

My firstborn, T.J., was a very difficult child almost from his first breath. He was curious, bright, a nonstop explorer. He was also colicky, easily frustrated, and very hyperactive. It took all my energy to mother him, so when my daughter was born almost three years later, I was in overdrive. T.J. challenged everything in his life: day care, preschool, our parenting, our family unit, and, most of all, being a sibling.

In first grade, T.J.'s IQ was tested and he scored very high, yet he was failing in school. His frustration level soared, and we watched him travel down a self-destructive path. In class he was banging his head so hard on the desk that the teacher was afraid he would knock himself out. T.J. was subsequently diagnosed with attention and focus problems, along with extreme hyperactivity. We had to do something.

All the experts believed that medication would help. At first the medicine seemed like a godsend, because he calmed down and functioned better. I thought I was seeing some semblance of my child return.

That began four and a half years of medication, counseling, doctor's appointments, psychologists, testing, behavior modification programs, seminars . . . all that goes along with treating a child who would quickly be labeled severely emotionally disturbed. In reality, although we'd hoped for further improvements, his walls kept building.

Even with all these interventions to help T.J., I could see that we were losing him. He didn't want to live anymore. Life was too difficult for this child, who challenged every intervention, every method of therapy, and shut out anyone who was trying to help. I was his only lifeline, and I was beginning to feel desperate.

All this culminated in T.J. being placed in an institution for almost one month when he was ten years old. A team of specialists was to do extensive psychological testing and brain scans, implement a strict behavior modification program, and provide in-depth counseling in the hope that they would find some way to help my child function.

The hardest thing I have ever done as a mother was to turn away from my crying child and walk away, leaving him behind those locked doors. I will never forget the heart-wrenching pain that I felt. No one loved this child like I did, no one was as connected to his soul.

The first time I spoke to him after leaving him there was over the phone, five days later. He begged me to come get him out. He was sobbing and exclaiming that he didn't belong there, he wasn't like the other children in there. When I told him that I couldn't get him out yet, he hung up on me and refused to talk to me again for several days. The one person in the world he trusted, and I couldn't be there or do anything.

When I picked T.J. up from the institution almost a month later, his counselor told me that they hadn't been able to reach T.J. He told me that T.J. was extremely manipulative and that he really needed extensive time in the institution. This was not feasible financially, and I would not have kept him in there anyway. The counselor told me that if T.J. did not change, he would probably end up in a juvenile facility somewhere.

The answer that I was looking for was not to be found. There were more medication changes, and two months after the institution, I was losing the battle. My son was lost in a fog of drugs, uncontrollable behavior, negativity, and pain.

Then a miracle happened. I met a woman I will call Dove, who talks with the angels. This woman, whom I had never met before, held me in her arms and poured unconditional love into my weakened soul as I sobbed and sobbed my pain away. She introduced me to my angel and also told me about T.J.'s angel.

Yes, they were with us, giving us strength. Their message to me was that I knew what was best for my son and that I needed to trust my instincts. That day, I found the strength to take my son's life back into my own hands.

With the help of the doctors, I weaned him off of all the medications. I was introduced to a nutrient-rich, wild-growing whole food supplement, and we started to work with T.J.'s body to find the answers we were looking for. We began to explore many alternative healing modalities, and I watched as T.J. became healthier and happier.

My instincts about my son were right on track. The sparkle in his eyes that had been gone for so long was beginning to ignite. The whole time, I knew our angels were right next to us, assisting when we needed.

The miracle that started to unfold with T.J. was phenomenal. He came to me one day and told me he had seen his angel, and he proceeded to describe in great detail what his angel looked like. We called T.J.'s angel Levi. T.J. also started to describe seeing colors and energy around people, plants, and objects. My son had finally begun to trust me again, and he knew that I would validate whatever he told me.

I was also beginning to see the amazing potential he had for knowing things and hearing things that were not considered within normal range. At times T.J. would check out of this reality. His eyes would glaze and his body would be on automatic pilot. He was somewhere else. When he came back, eyes sparkling, he would talk about floating above everything and looking down on what was happening. He would see these events very clearly. T.J. also started to describe seeing other beings and ghosts, each distinct in character and desire. My paradigm of reality was being blown wide open.

I had watched my son go from being in the pits of emotional hell to awakening. He woke up not only to this world but to other worlds that I am still learning about and trying to understand. He sees this world very clearly, but he is so closely connected to the other dimensions of reality that at times it has been difficult for him to want to stay here.

However, he now knows that he has an important mission here on Earth at this time, and has made the choice to stay here and see it unfold. I can't tell you how happy I am about this choice.

T.J. does and will continue to challenge the systems of belief that we humans have in place. That is part of who he is. Not only do I have my vibrant, healthy son back, but I myself have awakened to see the magnificent soul that he is, and to validate the gift that he is to humanity.

I asked him if he would like to share a message with everyone, and it was simply this: "Listen to the children. We, the children, are trying to get you to hear us!"

And So Life Appeared

Carol Willette Bachofner

I was going to die. Everything pointed to it.

It was November 1987. The holidays were coming, but I couldn't think happily about them or ahead to my birthday in January, because my doctors were questioning whether or not I'd make it to my own party.

That April, on my husband's birthday, I had been noti-
fied that I had cancer: a tumor on my left kidney. In a kind
of numb acceptance, I started chemotherapy and joined the
select group of people who live from treatment to treatment. Often I'd leave the hospital and, before we could
make the seven-mile ride home, have to stop to throw up
by the side of the road. Then I developed leukemia as a
by-product of the chemotherapy's assault on my immune
system. I lost pounds and pounds and became extremely,
devastatingly exhausted. My whole life was needles, vom-
iting, and sleep. I lost interest in everything, in life itself.

After a month or so of this, my doctor called and said
that my name had come up as a possible candidate for a
special, confidential treatment program. This program was
high-tech, controversial, and very dangerous. There was a
distinct possibility that I might even die of a "brain blow-
out," due to an uncontrollably high fever. I would have to
travel 240 miles round-trip, four days a week, for the treatments. I would have to sign papers putting myself in the
hands of people I'd never met.

But suddenly I was interested in something again, interested in staying alive. I took a deep breath, said a prayer,
and signed up.

Each treatment was an all-day affair, starting with the
donation phase. I'd arrive and donate body fluids: gallons
of blood, vats of urine.

Afterward came what I called the "peering" phase. I had
so many scans and x-rays, so much radiation, that it became a joke in our family that I could be used as a night
light: my "glow-in-the-dark" period.

Then came the injection phase. Hooked up to an IV, I
would get my dose of the "potion." All fifteen of us in the
program would lie in the same large room, hooked up,
watching TV or listening to music, or getting whatever
piped-in motivational message they had devised to cheer or
inspire us. I became clearly addicted to the Three Stooges
and Laurel and Hardy.

Then the twilight phase, wherein we waited a few hours

to see what, if any, negative effects might appear. My husband and I would play cribbage in the cafeteria, take walks, or read. I did a lot of cross-stitch embroidery. If all was well, I could go home until the next treatment day. The drives home were mostly quiet, as we both reflected on the happenings of our day and wondered what the next treatment might bring.

At the start of the treatments, they'd told me I had great hope of recovery: even total remission looked possible. In fact, I was the star patient. However, in November, things worsened, and even my doctor lost hope. Dr. Jack became depressed as my blood work took a serious dive.

Meanwhile, we'd been trying anything else that might help the treatments, including nutritional supplements, acupuncture, positive imagery, and, of course, prayer. As a lifelong Catholic, I believed in miracles. I had read about Lourdes, been to the shrine at St. Anne de Beaupré in Canada. As a Native American, although not raised in the culture, I had heard about and accepted as fact visions and mystical experiences. But I always thought miracles and mystical experiences were for others, not for me. I believed, but not for myself.

The day my belief system collided with reality, I was at the lowest point I'd ever been in my life. Out of the group's original fifteen, only five of us were still alive. And I was no longer the star patient.

I had completed that day's donation and peering phases and was meeting my husband for lunch. In spite of my four thousand-calorie-a-day diet, I weighed less than one hundred pounds at five feet eight. I looked like a broom handle with a head.

As the elevator started down to the lobby, it began making a strange clicking noise. Suddenly, with a jolt, it stopped. Annoyed, I immediately looked around for the emergency phone: no way was I going to spend lunchtime stuck alone in an elevator!

Then the door opened behind me. Turning, I was startled to see a swirling gray mist—and, visible through it, the biggest number seven I had ever seen. Out of the mist emerged a man. He looked like one of the many homeless people I'd seen in this city, but he was spotlessly clean. He stepped forward, handed me a little orange booklet, and said, "Tell your doctor he is doing everything right, and you will be just fine. He is not to give up on you or on himself."

Then he just vanished. The elevator door closed, and the elevator was moving again.

Over lunch I shared the experience with my husband. We started jokingly referring to the man as my "angel." We pored over the little booklet, which turned out to be one of those tracts handed out on the street. Neither one of us knew what to think of the whole thing.

Later that afternoon, during the injection phase, I shared what had happened with Dr. Jack. He grew thoughtful and asked if I was sure the number had been seven. The elevator could not possibly have opened on the seventh floor, because on that floor there was only a brick wall where an office backed up against the elevator. I knew what I had seen.

Early the next morning Dr. Jack called, very excited. Late the night before, in his hotel room, the same "angel" had appeared to him. He'd come through a locked door and had told Dr. Jack not to give up, that I would be fine. Then he gave my doctor the same booklet, and disappeared.

Everything changed after that. The treatments started to really work. My blood got stronger, and I felt less tired. My attitude changed. I felt certain I would make it. So did my doctor.

We both made changes in our personal lives, too. He got back together with his wife and put his family back into the number one slot on his priority list. I decided to live my life in a more authentic way, walking as I was talking.

By January, I was well on the way to total health. In 1993, I was pronounced cured. I later had some routine "female" surgery, and my surgeon took a close look at my insides: no tumors, no leukemia, no cancer of any kind. I am alive. Better than that, I am healed.

I haven't seen Dr. Jack for years, but I will never forget him or what we went through together. And I know he will never forget the angel, or the message and its meaning.

I live now with a new respect for all living things and for the beauty of creation. My husband and I are filled with gratitude. I know that the Creator sent a powerful message to me and to my doctor: We must live life in the realm of the positive. And I no longer just "believe" in miracles and in the mystical: I have proof.

A Healing Message

John F. Demartini

I met Mrs. Esperanza in 1984, at a seminar I conducted in Houston for the Cancer Prevention and Control Association entitled "The Healer from Within." At the end of the program, Mrs. Esperanza approached me at the podium, with a smile on her face and her arms and heart wide open, ready to hug. She told me that she'd found my presentation inspirational—and that she'd been healed through prayer and the message of an angel, and was looking for a doctor who understood such experiences. She asked for my card, and gave me another wonderful hug as she was leaving.

The next day, Mrs. Esperanza appeared at my clinic. I was delighted to see her: she had a special presence about her that was most open-hearted and gracious. As I wrote down her medical history, she told me about her miraculous healing from cancer.

Almost five years earlier, when she was sixty-four, she experienced a gradual onset of a bloody cough, difficulty breathing, fatigue and chest pain. At first she assumed it was a cold, then pneumonia; finally, after her symptoms showed no sign of improvement, she visited her doctor.

She was shocked to discover she had progressive lung cancer. She immediately felt overwhelmed, confused, despairing, and humiliated. She told me that, reviewing her life, she felt that somehow her cancer was due to her many unloving actions. She thought about her years of sorrow and frustration, her bouts of anger and blameful accusation—and, deep inside, felt there was a connection between her unwillingness to love and her present condition.

This was such a low time that just thinking about the cancer gave her a feeling that she was dying. Thoughts of suicide ran through her mind. She wanted to hide, just disappear, with no one knowing what had happened. Finally she realized that her thoughts were motivated by guilt and fear—and that if she was going to die, then maybe she could somehow clear her consciousness beforehand.

Her doctor recommended surgery: complete removal of her right lung. He told her there might be complications; given her age and deteriorated health, there was even a possibility that she wouldn't make it through the operation. This of course added to her despair, and made her even more determined to make peace with her children, grandchildren, and other loved ones.

The night before her scheduled surgery, she received many visits in her hospital room. She greeted each person with an embrace and a loving smile. She opened her heart to them, telling them that she deeply loved them and was thankful for their contributions to her life. Although her congestion, weakness, and the roughness of her voice made her words difficult to understand, the message from her heart came through clearly. She made peace with everyone

who came, and asked them to share her love and appreciation with those who couldn't.

After everyone had left, she lay in bed and began to
pray. She was more at peace, more grateful, than she could
remember ever being.

At about one o'clock in the morning, she was awakened
by an "angel of light." This angel in the form of a beautiful
young woman told her that everything was going to be
okay, that everything was fine now—that she was healed.

As she listened to this message, Mrs. Esperanza began to
weep in exaltation. After the angel disappeared, she lay
awake the rest of the night, inspired. Again, she reviewed
her life, but this time while envisioning a future. She saw
herself sharing her experience with others, for she felt that
she had been called by this angel to help others heal. She
couldn't wait for morning.

At seven, two nurses entered her room along with an
orderly who would accompany her down to surgery. Mrs.
Esperanza told them she wouldn't be needing the operation, and that she would like to check out of the hospital.
Alarmed, they immediately called her surgeon. After some
delay (and further confrontational discussion with the
nurses), the doctor arrived. He almost lost it when she told
him about the angel and repeated her request to leave. Angry, confused, he tried to talk her out of her foolishness—
but she insisted, telling him that she would be glad to come
back another day to be reevaluated. Now, though, she just
wanted to go home. There was nothing they could say to
dissuade her. Finally, a few hours later, she was released.

In the following weeks, she told me, her congestion
cleared up and the chest pains went away. She was bounding with energy she hadn't felt for years. And she felt that
she now had a purpose for living.

She began telling everyone she knew about her experience. Gathering her friends and family, she told them that
she was going to begin a healing ministry. Although some
of them wondered whether this was the wisest decision,
she knew it was her mission.

So, at sixty-four, she set to work, ministering to the sick and relating to anyone who would listen her message of hope. She began studying various aspects of healing, and opened a Center for Spiritual Healing where she incorporated everything she had learned—from Bible passages to herbs and foods. She continued to attend as many classes as she could, and this was how she had found me.

Mrs. Esperanza was truly an inspired woman, a woman whose life had been forever changed by the guiding message of an angel. Do I believe in angels? You bet I do. Have I had personal experiences with angels? I sure have. Can they bring us healing miracles? They certainly can.

So expect a miracle, and be ready for your message from an angel. A prayer full of love and gratitude prepares the way. May God bless you with such a guiding messenger of light.

How It Feels to Heal

Rick Wright

Upon returning from seeing some clients in my hands-on healing practice, I received a phone call from a dear friend. It had just been discovered that his fiancée had a brain tumor—one so large that the doctor could actually see it behind her eardrum while examining her. They were going to see a specialist that Friday, but they wanted to come for an energy healing session beforehand.

They came in on Wednesday. My friend waited in the other room while his beloved and I commenced the session.

I started in my usual manner, with a prayer in which I asked to be an instrument of spirit. I felt the familiar energy rushing down my head into my spine. Spinning through my heart chakra, up through my arms, and out my hands as I lay them on her head. Heat—rushing from me into her head.

I was filled with an overwhelming sense of peace and love. With memories of how I'd met both of them, how their love for one another had grown. Wondering if this tumor was the beginning of her transition out of this life. How it would affect him. My own sense of loss, if she left us. And an even greater rush of heat, love, and compassion for such a wonderful human being.

My hands were on fire, my body trembling from this rush of energy. She seemed so peaceful and calm. I was wishing, hoping, praying for a miracle of healing—for her to be okay, if that would be for the highest good. For her to be allowed to be married, to continue her life. Knowing it was not up to me, but up to something much greater. Feeling tremendous love and hope.

Finally, I could feel the energy cooling off, the session ending. And I suddenly felt, sadly, angrily, hopelessly, as though this had had no effect at all. I wondered why I had this gift if I couldn't help people who meant so much to me.

Not letting on about my concern and disappointment, I told her we would have to wait until Friday, to hear what the specialist had to say. I put on my best face with my friend—saying goodbye, feeling their gratitude, wishing I could do more. But one never knows how the energy moves.

Friday came and I received the call. I'd been expecting news that there was no change in her condition. But the doctor had found no trace of the tumor. It was completely gone.

I was shocked and grateful. Miracles do happen, no matter how hopeless we may feel.

Their wedding day was a delight. Their love continues to grow and prosper.

Christopher's Gift

Alexandra Light and S. A. Forest

Christopher was the black sheep of his very traditional, meat-and-potatoes, sports-oriented, middle-class family. He grew up in a section of Brooklyn where young men were supposed to be tough. But Christopher never fit in, not in his family or his neighborhood. Sensitive, creative, it was apparent even when he was very young (much to his family's dismay) that he was different from the other children.

"Chrissy the sissy," as the other kids called him, was interested in the arts—and that just didn't go down well in his part of Brooklyn. Things got worse when the other kids found out he was taking dancing lessons, and worse still when it was rumored that he was gay. His father was particularly hard on him, and his two older brothers and sister were not much kinder. But being the youngest, he always was favored by his mother. She didn't understand him either, just loved him unquestioningly, and Christopher felt very close to her.

When he was sixteen Christopher moved out and found a place to share and a job in Manhattan. All of his free time was devoted to studying dance. At eighteen he was accepted in the corps de ballet of a prominent dance company. At twenty he switched to modern dance, and was hired as one of the principal dancers in an up-and-coming company. Everyone said he had a promising career. But when he was twenty-three, he injured his knee and had to stop dancing. Two years later he moved to San Francisco.

From the time Christopher left home until he moved to San Francisco, he had made weekly visits to his mother, slipping in and out when the others were away. He hated the long subway ride to Brooklyn, and his old neighborhood depressed him, but he was a dutiful son and rarely missed a visit. Three years after he left home his father died; in the years that followed, the other children left home one by one. By the time he moved to San Francisco, his mother was living alone.

Now, whenever he went home, Christopher noticed that his old neighborhood was dramatically deteriorating. On each of his visits, Christopher would try to get his mother to move—as did his brothers and sister—but she wouldn't hear of it. This was her home. This was where she had raised her children. She had a wonderful park practically right outside her door. She knew all of the shopkeepers— although a great many had closed their stores and moved on. All her friends were there—although their ranks were thinning. Christopher was a very persuasive person, but nothing could get his mother to change her mind. She just wouldn't budge.

One day, Christopher got a phone call from his sister. He'd had little contact with his siblings, and from the urgency in her voice he immediately knew that something was wrong. His sister was beside herself. The neighborhood had taken a dramatic turn for the worse. Junkies had moved in. One of his mother's neighbors had been mugged and had to be hospitalized, and another had her apartment broken into. His mother's apartment building was being neglected and vandalized. The buzzer system and the lock on the front door were broken. His sister was truly afraid for their mother's life, but she didn't know what to do.

By now Christopher's mother was over eighty years old. She could barely hear, even with a hearing aid. But she was still a very independent, active person. She wouldn't dream of moving in with one of her children, and wouldn't even consider a nursing home. His sister had taken her to different facilities, and the only place their mother would agree to move to was a senior citizens' residence in Westchester, an upscale area about an hour from New York City. She'd fallen in love with the place the moment she saw it. The grounds were lovely, the staff friendly and caring. It was a short drive to her daughter's home, but she would have her own apartment and wouldn't have to give up her independence. She was ready to move in on the spot.

Unfortunately, space was limited, and there was a long waiting list: two years, one at the very least. Given the unsafe conditions in their mother's neighborhood, his sister was afraid she wouldn't last the year. But their mother would just not hear of moving anyplace else, even on a temporary basis.

When Christopher got the call he knew he had to fly to New York immediately. He didn't know what he was going to do, he just knew he had to go.

All during the flight he kept asking for guidance: "Please, God, tell me what to do." When he stepped off the plane, he had the answer, but it didn't make sense. He'd been told to gather everyone in the family together at his mother's home. He didn't see how that would help or change anything, but over the years he had begun to trust in His guidance.

Now, Christopher's brothers and sister barely spoke to one another, and there was so much bad blood between his aunts and uncles and cousins and nieces and nephews that getting them all together under the same roof seemed as impossible as bringing peace to the Middle East. Not only that, they were scattered all over the country. But Christopher was determined. By hook or by crook he managed to get each and every one of them to come to his mother's house in a week's time. He didn't tell anyone what it was about. All he would say was that it was a healing, a matter of life or death, and if they came they would witness a miracle. By noon the following Sunday, sixty-three anxious, hostile members of his family—many of whom he hadn't seen since he was a child—were packed into his mother's living room.

When Christopher stood up and silenced everyone, he had no idea what he was going to say or do. For the first few minutes, his mind was a total blank. He could feel himself begin to panic.

While he was waiting for inspiration, he just looked at everyone. Many of these people had been less than kind to him. But instead of harboring ill feelings, he felt his heart fill with love and compassion. He realized that their lives had not been easy. Suddenly he knew what to say.

First Christopher spoke about what a loving person his mother was, how she never said a bad word about anyone, how despite the family feuds each and every one of them had always been welcome in her home, how at any hour night or day there was always a full plate of food for anyone who dropped by.

Then he outlined the problem. He emphasized that he wasn't asking for solutions. No, that wasn't what this gathering was about. Christopher was a firm believer in the power of love, and he was asking everyone to put their differences and grievances aside, and join together to use the collective power of love to create a miracle. It didn't matter if they didn't believe in it, if they thought it was all a bunch of nonsense—all they had to do was get in touch with a warm feeling and open their hearts.

To help them, he asked anyone who wanted to to come up and talk about a loving experience they'd had with his mother. One after another, more than half of those in attendance got up and recounted a story. Even more would have spoken, but there were so many, and it was getting so late in the day, that Christopher finally called a halt to the sharing.

All during this time, even though she couldn't hear what anyone was saying, his mother had an incredible glow in her eyes. She might not have been able to make out the words, but she was getting the loving feelings that were being conveyed.

Before Christopher ended the healing with a silent prayer, he told everyone that they were the miracle they had come to witness. Their willingness to come to his mother's aid was a sign of the love in their hearts, and this love, their love, was the miracle. He said it was clear, from the loving looks on their faces, that the hatred and anger they'd brought with them had drained from their hearts. He said he'd always known that if they put aside their differences, they would simply love one another. That love was the reality, and conflict and separation the illusion. Christopher was as surprised as anyone by what he was saying.

When the prayer was over, relatives who hadn't spoken in thirty years were hugging and embracing and kissing each other. Children who normally taunted each other were playing peacefully together. There was hardly a dry eye in the room.

Still, Christopher couldn't see what good he had done. Sure, peace had been restored in the family, if only for the afternoon. But how was that going to get his mother out of her apartment? By the time he boarded the plane back to San Francisco the next day, he was ready to write the whole thing off as a waste of time.

Two weeks later his sister called to tell him that his mother had been accepted into the Westchester facility. She didn't understand how, but a space had opened up, and his mother's name had leapfrogged to the top of the list.

Christopher's mother lived there for the next ten years. Each time Christopher visited or spoke to her on the phone, she told him that these were the happiest years of her life.

During his last visit she took Christopher aside and told him that even if nobody acknowledged it, she knew he was the one who was really responsible for getting her off the waiting list and into the residence. She called him "my miracle worker." Two months later, on her ninety-first birthday, she died peacefully in her sleep.

A Death and a Healing

Chaz Burton

I was awakened that Sunday morning by a call from my sister Barb, who had just arrived at Dad's convalescent hospital for her weekly visit. As soon as I heard her voice through the receiver, a cold fear seized my heart.

"Chaz?"

"Barb . . . how ya doin'?" I replied cautiously. I could hear everything in her voice. The pause lasted only a couple of seconds, but my fear made it seem like forever.

"Not so good."

Barb and I had known, from our recent, separate visits and regular conversations, that Dad was drawing closer to death. Now he'd slipped into a semi-comatose state. I drove to the hospital in a trance, virtually oblivious to anything but the vivid image of my dad and sister in his hospital room.

When I arrived, all I could do was embrace Barb and cry with her for a while. Gradually I felt something deep within me relax and yield to her sorrowful, accepting presence. We turned our attention to Dad, holding his hand, stroking his head, and reading to him until Mom arrived.

But all the while, I kept wondering why I was not feeling sad, why I was not feeling pain when he grimaced, why

I was not crying at the sight of his emaciated body. It felt like I was straddled on a wall between two concurrent realities. On one side was what was actually unfolding before me; on the other was what my judging mind was dictating should happen and what I should be feeling. So I kept trying to do something, to say the right thing, to feel the right feelings.

It was not until later that night, when I returned to continue my vigil, that these judgments faded and I began to accept the grace that had been unfolding all the while. A singular, powerful process was forming out of what I had perceived as three separate stages in this ongoing drama: the visits to my dad over the last couple of months and the internal turmoil and clarification that had followed; the prayer that I had spoken the previous evening in the sweat lodge; and my presence in the room in that moment.

My visits in those last couple of months had convinced me that Dad was dying. Fully accepting that fact forced me to accept that if I wasn't willing to reach beyond my childhood wounds, the ones from my relationship with my dad, I could not give him the comfort and nurturing that he so desperately needed. If I didn't seize the opportunity at hand, there would never again be another.

Those wounds had prevented me from getting what I desperately needed from him. I felt a profound need to really connect with him, to connect with him heart-to-heart. I knew that those old wounds were long buried, and that I would have to reach deeper than I had ever reached. So I reached.

And along with the agony of the wounds came a melting forgiveness. I felt something in me soften and open. Over a period of a few months, both in my quiet meditations and in my time with Dad, I let go. And love came flooding in. It filled my heart and overflowed through my eyes that would tear as they took him in, my words that soothed him, and my hands that stroked his head. That had been the first stage, I now realized.

The previous evening I had participated in a traditional Native American sweat lodge ceremony with some men friends. In this sacred atmosphere, another stage unfolded.

Native American sweats are highly ritualized and are focused around honoring the ancestors and the Ancestor Spirits. We entered the sweat lodge evoking the Ancestor Spirits by speaking the word *"Witakawasi"* ("all my relations"). As the moist heat, darkness, and silence enveloped us, we were given the opportunity to honor whatever or whomever we felt compelled to bring into the space, through words and consciousness. In the glow of the fiery "Grandfathers"—the rocks that heated the lodge and symbolized the Ancestor Spirits—men were calling forth and offering blessings to their own ancestors, friends, the natural world, and each other. As the hallowed air melted my heart and stilled my mind, I found myself thinking this:

"I honor you, Father. I honor you for your love, for your heart, for your pain and struggle. I honor you for the many gifts you have given me. And I invite you, encourage you, ask you to take your place among the Ancestors. You have a place of honor there. There is nothing to fear there. You have many blessings to receive and to give. Let go, and take your place of honor among the Ancestors."

It was not until the following night, as I sat alone with my father in that sterile room, that I realized why I had felt irritated and unsettled when I returned home after the sweat. It was as if some fear of mine had been shaken loose in me. A power had been released that had galvanized lines of force both very real and yet beyond the ability of my mind to comprehend.

I gradually became aware that what I had feared was to actually let go of my relationship with my dad. There were so many unresolved issues, so many things I wanted to say to him, so many things that I wanted him to say to me. But in those intense moments within the sacred space of the sweat, I had, without realizing it, once again let go.

That letting go allowed a critical shift to take place. Since my dad had become comatose and I could no longer relate to him on a cognitive, rational level, I had been feeling helpless, for I desperately wanted to offer him solace. I suddenly realized that I was offering him solace, as he was offering solace to me, through my heart and my consciousness, by simply being there with him, holding his hand.

Sitting there late that night—holding his bony, tightly gripping hand, looking at his ghastly, sunken face—I suddenly knew why it wasn't sorrow and anguish that I felt, but compassion and appreciation. I knew that I would miss his body; his heart, his charm, his wit; yes, even his sometimes brutal edge. And I knew that in proper season I would grieve that loss with much pain and sadness.

But in that moment, I was washed with profound feelings of peace, assurance, and appreciation. For I knew, in my deepest heart of hearts, that my father was returning to the Light. And in so doing, he was illuminating my path.

Because God Made Me!

Rama Berch

The pain in my left shoulder blade always felt like an ice pick stuck in my bones. It had been a reliable gauge of my stress level for years. I'd learned to use it as a reminder that there were other things in life than the pressures of raising a family as a single mother and the amount of work necessary to provide a living for all of us. Then the children were gone, but my work style persisted: I must do—do more— do it all!

I'd taken the familiar ice pick with me to a yoga weekend, featuring personalized yoga therapy sessions as well as meditations and yoga classes. On the third day my yoga therapist said it was time to "go for it." She held me in a pose that concentrated on my shoulders, by pulling my arms back and supporting them. She held them there far longer than I could have done myself, asking how it felt. It felt great!

After a while, the ice pick seemed to be digging deeper. It hurt . . . but it felt like something was happening, so I decided to stay with it. I breathed long and deep as I broke into a cold sweat. Her voice gradually grew fainter as I submerged into the experience, until it was like a deep meditation.

Suddenly I was a bird. Sitting on a high tree branch with two other birds, I had folded my wings and was sitting quietly. I could see the ground below, the sky above, and the tops of the shorter trees nearby.

One of the other birds lifted his wings and flew away, looking for food. The thought arose in me, "I will not fly for food." And I knew what those words meant, that hunger and need would no longer motivate me into my old pattern of incessant activity. I continued to sit with the other bird nearby.

Then a flock of birds flew over, and my neighbor joined them. The thought arose, "I will not fly for company." I knew the deeper meaning: that I would no longer be driven by the need for companionship, through sex or simply social interaction.

So I sat alone. I was content in my aloneness, yet something was incomplete.

Below me, a child ran into the dirt clearing at the base of my tree. He began to call up to me, making human sounds I could not understand. Two older children joined him. I asked myself, "Do I fly?" and the answer came with ease: "No, they are no threat. They are only curious."

The children laughed and kept calling together, until some adults came. The adults began to confer, and I realized they wanted to capture or kill me. They bought equipment, including nets and ropes. Still I would not fly. They threw stones, but I was too high and the stones could not reach me. There was no reason for me to fly, for I was safe.

Finally someone arrived in a car and carried out rifles. To me they looked like long sticks, yet I knew these sticks could reach all the way up to kill me. But the untroubled feeling inside persisted, until it became words: "I will not fly for fear."

The adults talked, and finally aimed their guns. A few bullets whizzed past. I knew I could die, but I did not move. More important to me was knowing, "I will not fly for fear." Fear would no longer impel me in my life. But would I die?

I sat with that choice, willing to die rather than fly. After a seemingly endless moment, a voice spoke deep within me, different from before. It was a deep voice, God speaking within me, saying, "Fly. Because I made you."

At that moment, I leapt into the air. With great joy, I soared to the tune of the impulse inside: "I fly because God made me! I fly because God made me!"

I soared over the trees, toward the horizon. I streaked faster, across the tops of mountains, toward the sea. Powered by joy, I flew higher into the sky, headed home toward God.

I knew I would never again feel trapped in the frenetic pace of life. I knew that I would now choose to do it all.

Now I participate for the only reason worth living. Because God made me!

And my shoulder pain is gone.

My Eye

Carol Tisch

Every few years, during my entire childhood and adolescence, I had the same nightmare. In it, I could not see. I wasn't actually blind: the dream-images would flicker in and out, as though I couldn't keep my eyes open. I would struggle with all of my might to keep them open, but could never go more than a second or two before everything went black again. In the dream I always felt very powerless and fearful as I tried to go about my life and be productive in spite of this strange handicap.

One of the last times I had the dream was especially frightening. This time I was at a new school, desperately trying to find my way to classes through a sea of students and a maze of buildings and stairs, unable to see.

Much to my amazement, when I was eighteen years old the dream became a reality.

I was in the first month of my freshman year of college. It was the first time I'd been away from home, and I was busily going about the activities of a new, enthusiastic student. I had just joined a sorority, I was living in my very first apartment with several other students, and I was taking a heavy course load.

One Sunday morning I awoke and my left eye was in incredible pain. I had been wearing soft contact lenses for years, and at this time was using the kind you sleep with for two weeks at a time. I was very disciplined with them; I always took them out and cleaned them on schedule. I had just gone for a checkup with my optometrist prior to going off to school, and had been told that all was well. That morning, I immediately removed both lenses and tried to go back to sleep, but the pain was too excruciating. After a few hours, I became so concerned that I had one of my roommates take me to UCLA's Jules Stein Eye Center, a world-famous facility.

One of the doctors told me that my contact lens had somehow given me a corneal abrasion. He explained, though, that the eye is the fastest-healing part of the body. He would simply patch it and the eye would heal in twenty-four hours. Relieved, I returned home.

The next day, the same doctor removed my patch. He was good-naturedly chatting away when, looking around the room, I realized I could not see out of that eye. It was as though it had a film of Vaseline over it: I could see light and dark, but that was all. When I told the doctor what I was experiencing, he immediately became serious. He examined my eye, then suddenly stopped and said, "Uh . . . I'll be right back."

Within moments, five doctors entered the room. One by one they examined my eye with various instruments, none of them saying a word. After a few minutes one of them said, "Uh . . . we'll be right back," and they went off to have a conference in the hallway.

Why couldn't they speak in front of me? What was the matter with my eye? I was becoming very scared.

After what seemed an eternity, they returned and explained that the "abrasion" was actually an ulcer that had grown since the day before and was now infected. They prescribed some eye drops and instructed me to administer them every hour throughout the day and every two hours all night long. I was to return every day to be checked on my progress.

For the next month the eye problem became the center of my life. All day and night I would take my drops; every day I would return to the center to be examined. I knew from the way the doctors treated me that they were very concerned. Whenever I arrived the waiting room would be packed, yet I never waited more than a few minutes. The moment one of my team of doctors saw me, I would be taken into a room and examined.

Meanwhile, I tried to lead a normal life. I went to all of my classes and sorority functions, always carrying my drops with me. But I was frightened to discover that my vision was becoming just the same as it was in my nightmares. I couldn't see out of my left eye, and the right eye became so light-sensitive from having to compensate that *I could not keep it open.* So I was seeing everything in "flicker-vision." And here I was, in a new school, trying to find my way through a sea of students and a maze of buildings and stairs.

The doctors could not figure out what was causing the infection. They ran me through a series of tests. They even took scrapings of the top layer of the eye. None of the tests were conclusive. So they really didn't know how to treat me, and the ulcer was not improving.

After three weeks they finally told me what was going on; at least, they told me why they were so worried. It seemed that about thirty other people had experienced the same condition as a result of wearing extended-wear contact lenses. These people not only didn't recover their sight—they lost their eyes.

Another week passed, and still no improvement. My main doctor, Calvin, told me they would admit me into the hospital the next day if there was still no progress, so that they could monitor me twenty-four hours a day.

Well, I'd never stayed in a hospital before. This, and the minor technicality that I might lose my eyeball, prompted me to do something drastic. I decided to pray.

I went home, turned on some soothing George Winston piano music, and prayed like I have never prayed before. I saw white light entering the eye, and visualized the ulcer closing up. I did this all night long. I went into some sort of altered state, because I felt very peaceful and calm and my fear completely subsided.

The next day I entered the examination room anxious to hear Calvin's decision. One look at my eye, and he was incredulous.

"What have you done?" he exclaimed. "The ulcer is half gone!"

I told him about my night. He was very pleased. I was able to go home and stay in school. One week later, the ulcer was completely gone. It didn't even leave a scar.

And, having lived the nightmare, I never dreamt it again.

The Power of Healing Thoughts

Les Sinclair

For many years I have participated as a leader in a not-for-profit organization called The New Warrior Training. Our mission statement reads: "We are an order of men, called to reclaim the sacred masculine for our time, through initiation, training and action in the world."

On Thursday, August 12, 1994, before I took off for a San Diego-based training, I spoke to my eighty-year-old mother, Ida. Ailing in a hospital in Melbourne, Australia, she had been very ill for years. She'd fought hard to overcome her disease, but now I was alarmed by the frailty of her voice, in which I thought I detected a lack of desire to keep living. I told her that I would be away for the weekend and would call her on my return. As I got off the phone, I started to weep at the thought that this might be the last time I heard her voice.

One of many spiritual experiences forming part of a New Warrior Training is a healing sweat lodge, the oldest cleansing ritual known to mankind. We borrow this tradition from our Native American brothers. For us, these sweats are not based in religion, but they are spiritually connecting. During the sweat, acknowledgments and blessings are offered. The men honor Mother Earth, to whom our bare bodies are connected. We honor in gratitude her plants and animals that provide our sustenance. We offer prayers and acknowledgments to our wives, children, parents, and families.

This time, as I sat there in the dark, I silently offered a prayer for my mother. In my mind's eye I saw her troubled face, and wished her to be free of her suffering. I saw myself as a little boy with her in a park, somewhere in a Melbourne suburb. A black dog approached us and seemed about to bite me. Mum shooed the dog away and quieted my fears, putting her arms around me. I reflected on how, to this day, I had always felt her protective nurturing. Mum always thought of others first. Her heartfelt nature was built that way. In prayerful inner dialogue, I told her that I loved her, and that it was all right for her to choose what she really wanted.

Then I asked the men in the sweat lodge to send healing light to my mother. A spontaneous sound emerged from them as they huddled together, first as a low, soft *"Om,"* then louder, becoming a joyous *"Ah!"* The lodge vibrated with energy, and when the sound subsided, I felt exhilarated and peaceful.

That night, when I returned home, I called my brother Geoff in Australia to inquire about our mother. To my surprise and delight, he told me that she had made a remarkable recovery.

I quickly called the hospital and was connected to Mum. Her voice was stronger, and cheery. Without my telling her about the sweat lodge, she volunteered that she had felt an inexplicable feeling of energy overcome her. Prior to it, she told me, she had wanted to die—but now she was choosing to live.

I told her how forty or so men had prayed and sent her healing light for her speedy recovery. "Well," she nonchalantly replied, "it worked, didn't it? And please, thank all those nice men for me."

A year later, my mother died. However, I did not grieve her passing in the usual way people do. I simply chose to celebrate her gifts, and acknowledge the impact she made on my life. I chose to remember my mother by her thoughts and actions, and the legacy of love she left me.

In the final measure of her life, I judge her capacity to love me and others unconditionally to be her greatest gift. Because of her, I believe my thoughts and actions make a difference in this world. And I believe that the men in the sweat lodge made a difference that day.

If I Were Sitting on a Cloud

Eric Scott Pearl

If I were sitting on a cloud, scouring the planet for just the right person upon whom to bestow one of the rarest gifts in the universe, I don't know whether I would choose myself from among the multitudes of people, point my finger, and say, "Him! Give it to him." And maybe it didn't happen quite that way. But that's the way it feels.

I'd spent twelve years building one of the largest chiropractic practices in Los Angeles. Now I was visiting Venice, California, with my assistant—who suddenly started insisting that I get my cards read by a woman who'd set up shop on the beach.

"I don't want to get my cards read on the *beach*," I laughed. "If she were all that wonderful, people would be coming to her! She wouldn't be having to flag down unsuspecting beachgoers."

"I met her at a party and told her we'd be here," my assistant confessed. "I'd be very embarrassed if you didn't get a reading."

So, in exchange for my ten dollars I received a very nice yet unremarkable reading. At the end she said, "You need to have this special work done. It's called an Axiatonal Alignment. It reconnects your body's meridian lines to the grid lines on the planet that connect us to the stars and other planets."

"How much?"

"Three hundred and thirty-three dollars."

"No, thank you!"

You'd think that would be the end of it, but I couldn't get this "Axiatonal Alignment" out of my head. This was going to haunt me until I gave in. I cracked open my cookie jar.

There would be two sessions, two days apart. Day one, I thought, *I can't believe I'm giving this woman $333 so she can draw lines on my body with her fingers.* Lying there, though, thinking of all the better uses the money could've been put to, I suddenly heard my mind say, "Well, you've already paid. You may as well cut the negative chatter." So I lay quietly, ready and open, while she went to work. I experienced nothing. But I'd paid for both sessions, and I was coming back on Sunday for part two.

That night, about an hour after I'd gone to sleep, the lamp next to my bed turned itself on, and I awoke with the very real sensation that there were people in my home. I searched the house with my Doberman, a knife, and a can of pepper spray, and found no one.

Part two started out seeming as unremarkable as part one, but it soon became apparent that it was to be anything but. First, my legs didn't want to lie still. Soon the rest of my body felt the same, interspersed with almost unbearable chills. I didn't dare move, though. Why? Because I'd paid my $333 and I was going to get my money's worth out of this.

Soon it was over. It was a hot August day and we were in a non–air-conditioned apartment, but I felt near frozen. My teeth chattered as this kind woman rushed to wrap me in a blanket, where I remained for five minutes until my body temperature returned to normal.

I don't understand what happened, nor can I explain it, but I was no longer the person I'd been a few days before. I drifted into my car and thought my way home.

I always have my patients lie on the table with their eyes closed for a minute or so following their adjustments, to allow things to "set." The next day, seven patients asked if anyone had come into the room while they lay there. Three of them said it felt as if people were running around the table, and two sheepishly confided that it seemed as if people were *flying* around the table. Meanwhile, other patients and staff were saying things like, "You look so different! Your voice sounds so different! What happened to you over the weekend?"

Soon patients were reporting that they could feel where my hands were before I touched them, when they were still inches to feet away. It became a game to see how accurately they could locate them. Then it became more than a game, as people started receiving healings.

At first they seemed minor: aches, pains, and the like. After their chiropractic adjustment, I would tell patients to close their eyes and would pass my hands over them for a minute or two. When they got up, their pain gone, they asked me what I had done.

"Nothing . . . and don't tell anyone," became my standard reply. This was about as effective as Nancy Reagan's "Just Say No" approach to drugs. Soon people were coming in from all over for these "healings"—and I still had no idea what was going on.

I checked with the woman who had given me the Axiatonal Alignment. "It must have come from something that was already in you," she said. "I don't know of anyone who's ever responded like this. It's fascinating."

Early October found me "manifesting." I had held my hands over a woman's knee, which had been bothering her as a result of a childhood bone disease. When I removed my hands, her knee felt better. My hands were covered with blisters, tiny ones that lasted for three to four hours. This occurred many times.

Then it happened. My palm bled. I kid you not. Not in streams outpouring, as in old movies or the *National Enquirer*, but more as if I had stuck my palm with a pin. Yet it was blood just the same.

"It's an initiation!" more than one person insisted.

Into what?

November found me in the office of a world-renowned psychic. He spread his cards in a very businesslike fashion, his face carefully expressionless. Then he looked me straight in the eyes with a slightly quizzical expression and asked, "What is it that you do?"

"I'm a chiropractor."

"Oh, no, it's much more than that," he said. "Something comes out through your hands and people receive healings. . . . You will be on television," he continued, "and people will be coming from all over the country to see you." Then he told me I would be writing books.

"Let me tell you," I shot back with a knowing smile, "if there's one thing I'm sure of, it's that I won't be writing any books."

Books and I had never gotten along. By this point in my life I'd read maybe two books, one of which I was still coloring. But then, life was to bring many changes. Psychics, healers, and channelers started to come from all over the country, saying they'd been told in their meditations to work on me, refusing any compensation. My love affair with alcohol cooled to a casual friendship: no one was more surprised than I. Strangest of all, my addiction to television was replaced by—dare I say it—books. I couldn't read enough: Eastern philosophy, life after death, channeled information, even UFO experiences.

Meanwhile, I would lie down to sleep at night and my legs would vibrate. My hands felt as if they were constantly "on." The bones of my skull would also vibrate, and my ears would buzz. Later, tones would come to me, and on rare occasions what sounded like voices in choir.

"That's it," I told myself. "I've lost my sanity."

And my patients? They were seeing whites, golds and purples that they had never seen before, colors of an inexpressible, even unearthly beauty.

And yes, patients saw angels. At first I didn't pay much attention to the angel stories . . . until people began describing the same angels, the same messages, the same names. We're not talking common angel names like Michael or Ariel—nor are we talking Moses or Buddha, although a lot of people do say they see Jesus. We're talking names like Parsillia and George.

George appears to children and others who might be unnerved at seeing an angel. You see, George appears first as a small parrot.

The first person to see George was an eleven-year-old girl. Jaime and her mother flew in from New Jersey because she had scoliosis of the spine, quite noticeably disfiguring the body of this unusually bright and otherwise very attractive girl. When Jaime came out of her session, she told her mother and me, "I just saw this tiny little multicolored parrot. And he told me his name was George. And then he wasn't a parrot at all, he wasn't even a life form." *Life form:* now there's a phrase for an eleven-year-old. "Then he just became my friend."

This was followed by more George sightings. The other patients knew nothing of George: I kept his name and description in confidence, as I have with all the angels, so as not to influence people. Even in this writing, I've changed the names.

Parsillia comes with specific messages. First, she often lets you know that you will be healed. Then she tells you that you are to "spread the word."

The first person to see Parsillia was a woman from Oregon named Michele. Suffering from Chronic Fatigue Syndrome and fibromyalgia, she had no appetite and weighed all of eighty-seven pounds. She could scarcely get up from a chair by herself. To make her pain somewhat bearable, she would have to be carried from her bed and placed under a hot running shower, up to four times each night. Obviously, she couldn't work. And her six-year-old would often have to make dinner for his three-year-old brother: peanut butter sandwiches.

Michele, like most of my patients, had never seen an angel or heard voices before. It took her three days to get the angel's name. Parsillia told her that she would be healed— and that she was to spread the word via television.

Approximately one year later, Michele was a guest along with me on a talk show. She was all smiles—and quite a few tears. Her weight is now normal, her complexion healthy. She holds a full-time job and exercises regularly. And she cooks dinner for her family every evening. No more peanut butter sandwiches.

Another visitor is a man with white hair, a white mustache and a white coat. Other times, he appears in a robe with his head covered. Debbie, a Southern California mother of three, was the first to see this angel.

Debbie was diagnosed in March 1995 with terminal pancreatic cancer, and told she had maybe two months to live. In our first session, Debbie saw the man in his robe and head covering. He touched her wrist, sending a surge of energy through her body. He then bowed and walked away, leaving her in the presence of a very bright, welcoming light. Tears filled her eyes. She next found herself in a tunnel, traveling through the galaxy, feeling "stuff" leaving her body through her feet and head.

By Debbie's third session, her tumor was 80 percent gone. Eight months later, her doctors felt she was a candidate for surgery to remove the remaining 20 percent. Just prior to her surgery date, she returned for another session. A day and a half later, she went to the hospital. After some tests, however, they sent her home. Apparently, in the time since our session, her tumor had vanished completely. Nothing remained but scar tissue.

Patients also commonly see a circle of doctors wearing white coats. They can be seen conferring, yet they can't be heard. Another regular is a young Native American girl who places a leather band with shiny square ornaments on your forehead. Often, a Native American male also comes and stands in the room. Another visitor is a handsome angel, usually described as eight or ten feet tall, with huge, densely feathered white wings. I am told that he stands behind me with his arms around my waist, peering over my right shoulder, silently guiding my hands.

Jered was four when his mother first brought him in. He wore braces on knees that would no longer hold him up. Words no longer came from his mouth, only an endless flow of saliva. His eyes wandered, unable to focus. Their light had been reduced to a vacant expression that showed barely a glimmer of the beautiful being within.

As he lay on the table, motionless and almost without expression, Jered's mother told me he was losing the myelin coating of his brain, over which nerve impulses travel. He had been suffering fifty grand mal seizures a day until medication reduced them to an average of sixteen. For a year she had helplessly watched him deteriorate, until she found herself left not with the child she once knew but with what she could only describe as an "amoeba."

Whenever my hand approached the left side of his head, Jered would reach for it. "Look, he knows where your hand is. He's reaching. He never does that," his mother quickly pointed out. "That's where the myelin is missing." Jered became so active that by the end of the session his mother had to sit by him on the table, lightly holding his hands, placatingly singing to him.

That day, Jered's violent seizures stopped. Completely. His second session found him grasping at doorknobs and beginning to turn them. He was able to focus on objects. On his way out of the office, he pointed to a floral arrangement: "Flowers," he said, smiling. His mother started to cry.

That night, Jered was discovered reciting the letters of the alphabet with Vanna White while watching *Wheel of Fortune*. And before he went to sleep, this formerly speechless cherub looked up toward his mother and said, "Mommy, sing to me." Five weeks later Jered was back at school. On the playground. Catching balls.

Not everyone received a recognizable healing. Why couldn't I predict what someone's response would be? How was all this happening?

I had always been an in-charge type of person. Others might take a wait-and-see attitude; I preferred to control outcomes.

So imagine my surprise when it dawned on me that for these healings to really accelerate, I had to get out of the way and quit directing. I had to step back and let a higher power guide.

"Who's saying this?" I thought—but darned if it weren't true. Not only did the energy know where to go and what to do without the slightest instruction from me, but the more I got my attention out of the picture, the more powerful the response. Some of my best healings occurred when I was thinking about my grocery list.

Then, one day, I heard a voice.

"Receive, don't send."

"Who said that?" I asked. "You've got the wrong person here for that kind of advice. My ego is still recovering from 'Get out of the way and let a higher power guide.' How am

I going to get these healings through to these people if I don't 'send' them?"

"Receive, don't send."

"I heard you the first time. Now answer my question," I mentally retorted.

Silence.

I went in to see the next patient. Grateful that she couldn't read my uncertainty, I began, palms open, at her feet.

This time, somehow, I received from the patient through my hands. I received from the heavens through the top of my head. It was loving, it was humbling, it was confusing. It felt awkward. And then I saw the patient begin to respond—and it felt right.

At that point I truly embraced the concept I had been espousing, yet not fully understanding, all along: I am not the healer. Only God is the healer. And for some reason, I'm invited into the room.

The session was over. My patient got up from the table and said, "Thank you!"

"Don't thank me," I replied. "I didn't do it."

"Well, of course you did!"

Suddenly I thought that maybe that person sitting up there on that cloud didn't make such a mistake after all. Maybe I was selected for this gift because I *don't* wear robes and turbans, because I *don't* hang tapestries and burn incense, because I *don't* walk around barefoot eating bowls of macrobiotic dirt with chopsticks. Maybe it's because I'm accessible and speak in relatively plain terms.

"It's like this," I explained. "It's as if you've just had a wonderful chocolate malted ... and you're thanking the straw."

She laughed.

I think we both got it.

A Healing in Spirit

Stephan A. Schwartz

Bob was twenty-five, sallow, and very sick. Diagnosed HIV-positive, as he told us, only eighteen months before, it was apparent enough now that he was in the grip of full-blown AIDS. His handsome features were already being disfigured by the characteristic lesions of Kaposi's Sarcoma. I don't know how Bob found out about our study, but one Tuesday morning he'd presented himself at the clinic.

We were studying what is often called "energy healing." We'd invited fourteen men and women—seven experienced healers, from evangelical Christians practicing traditional laying-on of hands to channeling space people, and seven other volunteers, none of whom had ever tried anything of the sort before—to "treat" one of fourteen men and women who were suffering everything from migraines to cancer.

Although we hoped real healing would take place, as investigators we were looking elsewhere. Our research was simple in concept. Physics tells us that all matter is a form of energy, and that the passage of energy through matter leaves an at least theoretically measurable material trace. Thus, "healing energy" (whatever that was), if it existed, should leave its own trace—measurable, perhaps, in the simplest chemical compounds. During the healing sessions, therefore, our volunteers would wear small vials of triple-distilled water strapped to their hands. We would analyze the vials' contents before and after, along with the contents of "control" vials containing water from the same original samples, but unexposed to the healing energy. If the water in the various samples could be shown to differ somehow, then we would have found at least one clue as to just what healing energy—and "energy healing"—is.

Our focus, then, was on the water. Our twenty-eight volunteers, of course, had their own concerns. The fourteen people who were to receive healing were each randomly matched by computer to one of the fourteen healers. The luck of the draw put Bob with Ben, a forty-year-old film producer with a fundamentalist Christian background who had never tried to do healing before. Even in the initial interviews, Ben displayed an almost aggressive masculinity; he'd also made it fairly clear that he was profoundly homophobic.

When we saw the pairing, we realized we faced a dilemma. The healers were not being told the medical conditions of the person they were to heal—and in most cases there was no way they could know. But Bob, with the by then well-known markings of KS, was a different matter. We had to assume that Ben would immediately know his condition, and we knew that Ben was not only homophobic, but terrified of AIDS: he'd made a point of telling us so during a pretrial interview. Could we, in all fairness, not warn Ben that we were asking him to come literally face to face with one of his worst fears? Was it fair to assign Bob to a healer who not only found his lifestyle repugnant, but who was deathly afraid of the disease he carried?

While Bob and Ben filled out a long series of questionnaires, we wrestled with these issues. We finally decided that we should at least start by telling Ben: If we felt from his reaction that he could keep his fears in check, without signaling Bob, then we could still consider including these two in the experiment.

When Ben heard the news he blanched and asked to be left alone. He walked into one of the small rooms set aside for the healing sessions and closed the door—apparently forgetting that everything in the rooms was being video-taped, as did we. The tape would later show Ben pacing up and down as he struggled with his inner fears and demons. After about five minutes he came out and said, "We came here to heal. Let's go."

Ben didn't waver, even when he saw that Bob could just barely rise alone from the chair in which he'd been sitting, answering his questionnaires. "It's just my arthritis," Bob said. "Whenever I sit for more than ten minutes my body locks up." Ben smiled, and helped Bob into the room.

Bob leaned heavily on Ben as he struggled to get up onto and lie back on one of the massage tables we were using. "I'm sorry," was all he said.

For a moment both of them were silent. Then Ben began to move his hands slowly over Bob, about five inches above his body.

"How long have you had this?" Ben asked.

"I probably became HIV-positive a few weeks after I came out," Bob replied. "It was like some kind of punish-ment, I thought at first." The two men locked eyes, then glanced away.

"What are the major problems?" Ben asked, obviously struggling to keep his voice professional.

"Oh, God, I don't know. There are so many things. Right now, though, I guess it's the arthritis. I used to be a dancer before . . . before all this. And I'm cold. God, I'm cold all the time."

"Cold?"

"Yeah, I can't get warm. It's the AIDS," Bob said, locking eyes with Ben. "It screws up your circulation. I haven't been warm in, oh, maybe four months. Even when I take hot baths, it only lasts for a few minutes. I'm just cold, deep down inside, all the time."

For the next thirty minutes, Ben worked on Bob with a concentration that made conversation superfluous. Even via the video camera placed ten feet away, it was easy to see that the experience was an intense one for Bob. His eyes closed, and his body gradually relaxed. He was breathing through his open mouth as if in sleep, yet he was awake, speaking words so softly only Ben could hear them.

Ben worked carefully, slowly going over Bob's body again and again. At times he moved his hands as though he were pulling something invisible, yet thick and clinging, out of Bob's body: he would pull it out and throw "it" away with a flick of his hands.

Finally, he stopped. He stepped back from the table and looked down at Bob. Tears were running down his cheeks.

After a minute or two, Bob opened his eyes, looking slightly stunned. It took a moment more for him to collect himself. Then, as if without a care, and with easy grace, he rose from the table—and was halfway across the room before he suddenly stopped. He looked at Ben, and then looked down at his feet.

With a broad smile, he did a little dance step. Both men started to laugh. Ben stepped forward and hugged Bob.

"Thank you, Ben. Thank you so much."

"I don't think God punishes people by giving them AIDS," Ben said. "I might have thought that once, but now I think maybe His punishment is reserved for people whose hearts are closed to a brother's suffering."

As Bob came out of the room, he turned to the researcher monitoring the experiment and said, "I'm warm. For the first time in four months, I feel warm inside."

Was it all just subjective, a kind of placebo effect?

An hour later, when we examined them, we found that the contents of each of the vials from that healing session had, in fact, changed. It was still just water, of course, but the way the oxygen and hydrogen atoms linked together to form its molecules was different from in the control samples. But that's another story.

Bob stayed in touch with us. Over the next weeks, he reported that his arthritis had returned, although it was not quite as bad. To him, though, the most important effect of his healing session with Ben was that he continued to be warm. What he'd called "the chill of the grave" hadn't returned to torment him. He'd regained a feeling he'd thought was lost forever.

Three months later, Bob contracted pneumonia. A week afterward, he was dead.

Bob wasn't "healed," ultimately. But Bob's death forced me to reconsider everything I'd thought about healing.

We all expect the big finish, the lame child who throws away his crutches and walks. Sometimes, I realized, healing is just warmth, and a change of feeling.

5

HELP
FROM
ABOVE

Angels to the Rescue

Verlaine Crawford

The elevator quickly dropped the four floors and I stepped out into the small room in the center of the underground parking garage. There were two elevators and two doors. I headed toward the door closest to where my car was parked, passing a man dressed in a guard's uniform. As I glanced at him, I looked into his eyes, and a voice in my head said, "Run!"

"Run?" I repeated to myself. "Why should I run?"

Suddenly I felt an arm around my neck and saw a knife in front of me, pointed at my throat. He was holding me so tight I couldn't breathe. I managed to pry his arm slightly away from my neck so I could take a breath and said, "Calm down. You're hurting me." I was trying to remain calm myself. I couldn't believe what was happening.

He'd transferred the knife to my back and was pushing me toward the other door when the second elevator's bell rang and the door opened. Two men stepped out and stopped in surprise.

The guard stabbed me in the back and pushed me toward them. He ran out the door into the parking garage and got away.

The two men pulled me into the elevator. I felt my lung collapse. As I slumped to the floor, the pain was unbearable. I thought I was dying.

"If you will let me live," I asked God deep in my heart,

"please make me an instrument of your peace. I will serve you all the days of my life." I could feel the blood filling my chest cavity, and I felt faint.

Up on the main floor of this very impressive building on Wilshire Boulevard in Los Angeles, I sat on the guard desk, held by a stranger. He kept reassuring me that I would be fine, as police filed in front of me asking over and over again, "What happened?" Finally the ambulance arrived and I was taken to the hospital, where they punched a hole in my chest to insert a tube so my lung could reinflate. It took several weeks to recover, and I was in a state of fear and bewilderment.

When I returned to work, I went to visit the two men who had saved my life. They were lawyers working for a firm on the thirtieth floor of the building. They told me their side of the story.

That evening, they had gone to a coffee shop to have dinner before returning to their office to do some late-evening work. They got in the elevator to go back to their office when suddenly it felt as if they were being pushed out of the elevator going up, and moved across the hallway to get into the elevator going down. "Oh, I guess we could get our uniforms from the car," they said to each other as an excuse for this strange action: They were going to play baseball later that evening. When the elevator opened, I was standing in front of them with the guard holding me.

I asked them what made them leave one elevator and get into another. "We certainly had no intention of going down to the parking garage," one of them said. "It felt like we were being pulled and pushed. There was a feeling of powerful energy all around us."

"What do you mean?"

He got quiet and looked a little embarrassed. "It felt strange, warm, inviting . . . like the angels were calling us."

The other attorney looked at his partner and then looked around the room to be certain no one was listening. His face turned red as he slowly nodded his head, and said quietly, "Yes, I felt it, too. Maybe the angels wanted us to save your life."

The years have passed and my vow to be a messenger of peace has remained uppermost in my mind. I have been able to help create many worthwhile enterprises, and have been called to teach around the world. With love, humility and deep appreciation for these additional twenty-five years of life, I say thank you, angels, mighty messengers of God.

Do You Want to Live?

Judy Martin

"Martin, get on the set, you've got five minutes," Bill blared over the intercom, bringing on that familiar shot of adrenaline that makes your stomach spin.

Bill was a sharp, award-winning news director, and he hated when "talent" was late. As usual, I was still carefully lining my eyes only minutes before I would greet Long Island with a big smile and the evening update. That day, I was having trouble doing my eyes, since I was simultaneously sobbing on the phone while talking with my friend and TV mentor, Allie.

"Judy, are you listening? You're good," Allie said in an aggravated tone. "Dammit, I trained you!"

I'd had about three years of experience as a news reporter. I'd seen the gore, covered the political blunders ...

and I was starting to become numb, just like the pros. Somehow I felt empty, even with everything I had accomplished.

The day before, I'd received a call from another local station, wanting to see my resume tape. I was unhappy at my current job, it was time to move on—but I felt I wasn't good enough. I felt like giving up and trashing everything.

"Judy, where is your faith? Stop feeling sorry for yourself." Allie was not cutting me any slack. The son of a Lutheran minister, Allie always had this peace about him. He was always so patient. In fact, it bothered me as a rule, and today's abrupt departure from character was quite refreshing and amusing.

"Martin, please join us in the studio, now!" Bill was not happy. Even Allie could hear his scream over the phone.

"Allie, I love you. Thanks."

I hung up the phone, took a breath, and thought about what he'd said. Did I have any faith anymore? During my morning jogs on the boardwalk in Long Beach I would walk back and forth and pray to God, Saint Jude, whoever would listen, for peace in my work and life. I'd walk until my face was numb and I couldn't feel the cold wind blasting me anymore. Becoming numb was not too hard for me, or for my heart. Being a news reporter was making me sick. I didn't feel I was being productive. My parents had taught me to give back, and I longed to be a special assignment reporter dealing with health, children, women's issues, or some other beat that would help people get healing information.

I ran into the studio, my earpiece barely clinging to my head, lipstick in one hand, script in the other. Sitting in my chair, I squirmed to get comfortable on the phone book that was always placed there for me.

I had a perfect read of the first few stories, and then the lights suddenly felt hotter than usual. I became dizzy and started slipping around on the phone book. Looking down at my scripts, I noticed my hands had turned a deep red. They suddenly felt like they were on fire, and that fire was creeping up my arms. We went to commercial. "Just a few more stories," I thought.

In a flash, we came back. As the update neared its end, the rash on my hands and arms was now visible on my neck. My cameraman stepped away from the gigantic machine pointed at my face to see if it was his camera that was making me look funny. With a look of horror, he didn't say anything about my appearance, but instead offered a word of support. "Jude, it'll be over in just thirty seconds," he whispered. "We'll get through it."

When the show ended I ran off the set straight to the bathroom. In the mirror I saw the markings of a Pekinese dog. My eyes were so swollen they were mere slants on my face, which was beet red. Inch-square lumps had formed on my hands and arms. Lifting my blouse, I saw that my stomach had little lumps growing on it. My body was on fire.

Bill was banging on the door, asking, "Jude, are you okay?" I told him I was fine and was going home, then crumpled onto the bathroom floor and cried. The second half of the show had to go on; my part was done.

I figured this was some allergic reaction, but I hadn't eaten anything unusual. Bolting from the bathroom, I grabbed my bag from the newsroom and made a mad dash for my mother's house on the South Shore.

Driving on the Long Island Expressway at seven-thirty in the evening, my body was now not only on fire, it was itchy. Everywhere I scratched, I did damage; I dug into my thighs so hard I was bleeding. Looking in the rearview mirror every chance I got, I was alarmed to see that the little bumps on my neck were joining one another to form huge welts. Crying and praying out loud, I noticed my voice was hoarse and I was having difficulty swallowing.

This is it, I thought. I was on my way out.

The joints in my limbs were starting to freeze up from the swelling, my eyesight was poor, and my throat was closing. I went into this survival mode. It appeared that the car was driving itself, off the highway to the nearest hospital.

Suddenly, calmness came over me. Isn't this what I wanted? To leave the planet so I wouldn't have to deal with life? The pain of my present unhappiness in life somehow overshadowed the physical pain I was experiencing. Death seemed to be easier. I continued to pray as I was pulling into the hospital parking lot. For what, I didn't know. I just wanted the pain to go away.

A nurse took one look at me, and she and an attendant practically carried me into the ER and put me on a stretcher. I began to calm down a bit.

The hospital ceiling was so white. Bright, shiny metal hovered over me. There were about four doctors and nurses around me. They ripped my shirt open and put those sticky EKG devices on me. I heard a voice rumbling, "Judy, tell me what you took. Did you take any pills?"

Great, I thought. *They think I'm a drug addict.*

"Did you eat anything unusual?"

Nothing, I thought, but I couldn't speak. I had lost all feeling and all control.

Without warning, I suddenly felt I was floating near the ceiling. I didn't feel the prodding, the pain, the itching. I just stared at the ceiling. There was a sensation of numb ecstasy.

In an instant, however, I was brought back to awareness by an infusion of adrenaline and other drugs. All the uncomfortable feelings in my body were back—but the tension in my throat eased, and it appeared I was going to live.

After staying the night for observation, home at Mom's was like being in the womb. I was sleeping in my old room. Thoughts of childhood, of the comfort of being in my mother's care, rambled through my brain.

The swelling had gone down considerably. I slept for a few hours, then my mother woke me for medication and left me to go down to the kitchen.

Within minutes, it started again. This time the swelling came on at record speed, skipping the little lump stage in favor of welts the size of my body parts. My throat was closing rapidly. I tried, but couldn't call out to my mother.

I heard a voice—my voice—say, "Do you want to die?"

A tingling sensation filled every inch of my body, like

the pins and needles you get when your foot falls asleep. I somehow got out of bed, and felt like I floated downstairs.

In the kitchen, my mother was making eggs over easy. I thought, *She never does that. She likes them scrambled.* Now she was pouring garlic salt over the eggs. A snack, I supposed, for watching *General Hospital,* which I noticed was on the TV in the den. I wandered into the dining room, where my mother has pictures of several saints on the wall.

My body felt funny. I looked at my hand. It was transparent.

It occurred to me that I was dreaming that I was floating around the house. It's the only way I can describe it.

Suddenly I was jerked back into my bedroom. Once again, I was walking toward the door: I guess I just really didn't want to stay. But there were other plans for me.

At that moment, heading for the door, I felt a strong presence behind me. I turned and, to my surprise, I was lying there in bed. My physical body had been in bed all this time, while I was checking out my mother in the kitchen and taking a tour of the house.

It didn't alarm me. In fact, it felt very normal. I started to walk away again—but then I felt this jerking motion at my back and fell on my rear. My body was still in the bed, and next to the bed, standing brilliantly in a beautiful white dress . . . was me. I noticed I had brown hair, without the highlights I'd put in recently.

Who was this person who looked like me? After much thought, I realized it must be the higher self I had prayed to on the boardwalk, on the set, and in the emergency room.

She smiled at me and gestured for me to get back into bed.

Whisked back into my body, I gazed up at her as she tucked me in and covered me with a blanket of white light. Just looking at her made me feel protected and loved. She wagged her finger at me, as if to say, "No, no, no! It's not your time, you have work to do."

I looked at the clock on the wall. It was four in the afternoon, and I could hear the closing music of *General*

Hospital. I ran downstairs to tell my mother what had happened.

As I walked into the den, I said, "So, you had eggs for lunch. Over easy, with garlic salt."

She laughed quizzically. "How did you know?"

I knew now it wasn't my time to go. It was my time to take control, and have the courage to move on. I went back to the studio the next week and gave my notice, taking the chance that I would get enough freelance work to survive.

It all worked out. My freelance work at News 12 Long Island led to full-time work: I became the station's education and social issues editor.

Through faith in God and confidence in my higher self, I took a leap of faith, and ended up with a new mission, a new sense of purpose.

The Beginnings of Wisdom

Judith Orloff, M.D.

It was 3:00 A.M., the summer of 1968. A magical Southern California night. I was sixteen years old and had spent the weekend partying at a friend's house in Santa Monica, oblivious to my exhaustion. The soft, warm Santa Anas whipped through the eucalyptus trees, blowing tumbleweeds down deserted city streets. These winds were seductive, unsettling, conveying a slight edge of danger.

The scene was Second Street, two blocks from the beach, in a one-bedroom white clapboard bungalow where my

friends and I hung out. We were like animals huddled together for a kind of safety, apart from what we saw as a
menacing outside world. Brightly painted madras bed-
spreads hung from the ceiling, and candles in empty Red
Mountain wine bottles flickered on the floor. Barefoot and
stretched out on the couch, I was listening to Bob Dylan's
"Girl from North Country." I was restless; I wanted something to do.

A young blond man I'd met only an hour before invited
me to go for a ride up into the hills. He was a James Dean
type, cool and sexy, dressed in a brown leather jacket and
cowboy boots, a pack of Camels sticking out of the back
pocket of his faded jeans: the kind of guy I always fell for
but who never paid much attention to me. I wouldn't have
missed this opportunity for anything.

The two of us headed out, stepping over couples who
were making out on a few bare mattresses placed strategi-
cally on the living room carpet. We jumped into my green
Austin Mini Cooper, my companion at the wheel, and took
off for Tuna Canyon, one of the darkest, most desolate
spots in the Santa Monica range, a remote place the Chu-
mash Indians had consecrated, made sacred.

The road snaked up into the mountains to an elevation
of about 1,500 feet; we could see the entire Malibu coastline
laid out before us in a crescent of lights all the way from
Point Dume down to the southernmost tip of the Palos
Verdes Peninsula. The balmy night air blew through my
hair, filling my nostrils with the scent of pungent sage and
fresh earth. A few lone coyotes howled to one another in
the distance.

For a moment, the man I was with glanced over at me
and I felt something inside me stir. The softness of his voice,
the easy way he moved his body excited me, but I did my
best not to show it, determined to play the game of acting as
if I didn't care. The heat of his arm extended across my
body, his hand now on my leg. I reached my hand over to
meet his, slowly stroking each fingertip, one by one. I felt intoxicated: He was a stranger, completely unknown to me. It

was the ultimate risk. The closer our destination became, the more my excitement grew. I was anticipating what would happen when we reached the breathtaking view at the top.

The higher we climbed, the more treacherous the curves in the road became. But we were paying little attention, talking nonstop, high on a potent amphetamine we'd taken an hour before at the house. On the last curve before the top, he didn't respond quickly enough and the right front tire plowed into the soft gravel along the shoulder. The car lurched wildly as he wrestled with the steering wheel in a frantic effort to regain control. He slammed on the brakes. I heard the tires shriek and then we were skidding off the pavement and hurtling over the edge of the cliff, plunging down into the darkness below.

I recall only fragments of what happened next. I do know that time slowed down and I began to notice things. The night sky was swirling beneath my feet instead of above me. I could hear peculiar sounds as though amusement park bumper cars were crashing into each other. I made the emotionless observation that something was distinctly odd, but couldn't quite pinpoint what it was. The horror of my predicament—my imminent death—never really registered. Instead, something shifted; I found myself standing in a sort of tunnel, feeling safe and secure. It didn't occur to me to question where I was or how I got there. Although far in the distance I could hear the wind rushing past the open windows of the car, I was now suspended in this peaceful sanctuary while we fell through space toward the canyon floor hundreds of feet below.

With no impulse to move or to be anywhere other than where I found myself, I looked around the tunnel now surrounding me. It was an amazingly still, long, cylindrical space, its gray color gleaming as if illuminated from behind by a subtle, shimmering source. Though the tunnel did not seem solid, as in ordinary reality, its translucent walls appeared to extend endlessly in both directions, comprised of a swirling, vaporous material resembling billions of orbiting atoms moving at enormous speeds. Other than enclosing me, this surreal world was completely empty, but comfortable and soothing: There were no harsh edges, and the whole tunnel seemed to be vibrating gently. In fact, my body now also looked translucent and was vibrating, as if it had changed form to suit this new environment. I felt utterly at peace, contained, and self-contained, in a place that seemed to be without limits, going on forever.

Suddenly I remembered being a little girl, looking up into space while sitting on my rooftop, fascinated by the sky and the planets, sensing an invisible presence. For hours I'd stare at what I couldn't see but could feel more strongly than anything material. From my earliest memory, I always believed in God. Not so much the God of the Jewish religion in which I was raised, or any other religion for that matter, but a formless, ever-present being that twinkled through all things and lovingly watched over me. That same presence was now with me in the tunnel, more familiar and closer than it ever had been when I was a child. Enveloped by it, as if wrapped in a warm cashmere blanket on a cold winter's night, I was in perfect balance, impervious to harm, protected by an invisible but somehow tangible, sustaining life force.

Time had stopped, each moment stretching out into eternity. From what felt like a great distance away, I gazed through the shattered windshield, noticing soft moonlight streaming through the canyon. The car bounded off huge boulders, turning end over end through the air as we plummeted down the mountainside. And yet I never perceived that I was in the slightest danger; I experienced not a single moment of fear. With the coolness of a detached observer, I counted the times the car somersaulted: once, twice, three, four, all the way up to eight. Protected by the shelter of the tunnel, I remained in a void, suspended in free fall, not knowing if this was life or death.

As abruptly as I'd been pulled into it, I was jolted out of the tunnel and back into the present, just as the car crashed

down on solid ground. With a high, shuddering bounce
and a grating sound of steel against rock, we careened to a
grinding halt, the front wheels of the car projecting over a
narrow ledge. We were precariously balanced, actually tee-
tering on the precipice.

Thrown by the impact of our landing, my companion
and I had both ended up in the backseat. Fragments of broken glass were scattered all over the inside of the car, but
miraculously, neither of us was hurt. We quickly realized,
though, that we were still in danger: At any moment the car
might slide forward and tumble into a large ravine below.
We had to get out of there fast.

A live oak tree trying to crawl in through the window
appeared to be our only available support. Without looking
back I grabbed on to its branches and managed to pull myself out of the mangled car. My companion close behind,
we scrambled up the side of the cliff, pushing through
thickets of manzanita and wild mustard, barely penetrable
scrub brush and wild chaparral. Trying to avoid the loose,
unstable mounds of dirt and slippery leaves beneath our
feet, we used shrubs as ropes to pull ourselves up the sheer
hillside. Yet even as we inched our way to the top, I kept
asking myself, Why were our lives spared? We should have
been killed. Instead, we were walking away with hardly a
scratch. And already the image of the tunnel haunted me.

Very relieved to be on solid ground again, we were soon
able to hitchhike a ride down the winding canyon roads
back into the city. Faint rays of pink dawn light were beginning to illuminate the hills. I don't think either of us said a
single word the entire time, but I'm not certain. I have little
recall of the trip. Staring off into space, I replayed the accident over and over in my mind, unable to account for how
we could still be alive. Only a miracle could have saved us.

For many days, I blanked out the details of the actual fall
but retained a few disjointed images. I could distinctly remember the car rolling over the cliff and the giddy, weight-
less, out-of-control sensations during the drop. It was like

going over the first big dip on a gigantic roller coaster. I also recalled how every cell in my body had screamed in protest in the instant of the screeching, bone-jarring landing. As for the tunnel, I had no idea what to make of it. It was an enigma, a mystery I would continue to try to unravel for a long time to come.

The Birth of a Miracle

Marcelene Dyer

I was twenty-three years old and my first child was due any day now. Although my girlfriends and relatives couldn't wait to tell me horror stories about their children's births, I wasn't frightened. I didn't feel stronger or better than them. I just didn't give much thought to the actual job of giving birth. Having never experienced pain on any excruciating level before probably allowed my naiveté. Reading that the average length of labor for the first child was twenty-eight hours, I believed I could endure one day out of my life for this. Finally, I just knew I could do it. Simple. I was peaceful.

Each night, I prayed for the strength to handle whatever it took to give birth to this child. I prayed for the courage to look to the core of each contraction, honoring the process of my body opening for my child to push its way out and into my arms. I asked God and Jesus and Mother Mary to lend me strength. Thinking maybe God had helpers in the field of childbirth, I prayed to angels and goddesses for the strength and courage I sought.

On March 25th at 1:20 in the morning, I awoke to a popping sound. I felt this pop, actually. As I headed for the bathroom, I realized water was dripping down my leg. Excitedly I called to tell my mother that my water had broken. "I'm going to have my baby sometime today!"

When I arrived at the hospital I was immediately examined and admitted. The amniotic fluid surrounding my baby was indeed leaking.

As she left me in the empty labor room, the nurse told me, "Try to get some sleep before actual labor begins." Making myself comfortable, I looked at the huge clock on the wall: It was 2:00 A.M. I closed my eyes.

Suddenly, the longest, most intense pain arose from my belly. It hurt so much, more than anything I'd ever felt in my life. My entire body was engulfed with this pain. I grabbed onto the bedrails, my knuckles turning white as I held fast.

Then I felt the most gentle touch. A woman's soft hand began to brush back my long hair. I looked up at her. She was so pretty, with soft, reddish-brown hair and sweet, loving eyes.

"This is my first contraction," I said, "and I have a lot more of these to endure. I don't know what to do. Can you help me?"

"There is a place within your body to breathe and give birth to your child. Go there now and you will not suffer."

I took a deep breath and closed my eyes.

An instant later, I opened them and saw she was gone. Looking at the clock, I was shocked to see the time. It read 4:20. Two hours and twenty minutes had passed!

I knew my body was ready to push the baby out. I rang for the nurse. The same nurse who'd signed me in arrived, and asked if I'd had a good sleep. Not aware of having slept, I ignored her question and said, "I'm ready to have my baby."

Of course, she was amused, since I hadn't been through any labor yet. She laughed and said, "You probably just need to use the bathroom. There's pressure from the baby since your water broke."

"No," I said, "I'm sure I need to push." She gave me such a look of contempt that I very timidly asked if she could just check me and make sure.

Reluctantly, she did—and what a change of demeanor! Without a word, she left. She came back with another nurse, and they quickly wheeled me into the delivery room.

Soon the doctor came in, examined me, and stated I was fully dilated and could begin pushing on the next contraction. When I told him that I'd only had one contraction at two o'clock, and none since, he looked to the nurses. They raised their shoulders in bewilderment. Picking up my chart, he jokingly asked what painkillers they'd given me.

"None," they replied in unison. One of them said, "She was asleep the whole time."

So the doctor simply told me to begin pushing when I felt like it. Three or four pushes later, my baby was born.

I'm a mother! I have a newborn son. As he's laid on my belly, I reach for him. I kiss his head, his face, his ears, and smell that new baby smell. Heavenly. He's perfect. My silent prayers go out to God. "Thank you. Thank you."

It is now 4:41 A.M., and I have been blessed beyond words.

Later in the day, I met another floor nurse who questioned me about my labor. I felt odd talking about it. I told her about the one contraction, about the sweetest nurse who helped me, and how, although a hundred and forty minutes flew by, it seemed like only a moment and I was ready to give birth. She asked me to describe the nurse who helped me, then left.

Later, the same nurse came back, wheeling my son, Shane Michael, into my room in his isolette. Handing him to me, she said, "I've talked to the other nurses about your experience last night. We have eight labor and delivery nurses, some full-time, a few part-time. Not one of us fits your description of the nurse who stood by your bed. She doesn't work here, so I don't know what you experienced giving birth to your son. We're all talking about you. I just wanted you to know."

Twenty-three years have passed since that day. Am I any clearer about it? No. I don't know how to explain it. I just accept the gift of my prayers being heard and answered on a most profound level.

All my life, I'd only wanted to become a mother. This was my one true goal. It came true times seven, and as the birth mother of seven children, I can honestly say mothering is my greatest joy. As each child is unique, each birth is unique also. I am respectful of each experience—but the birth of my first child was awesome, mystical. Twenty-three years later, I am still growing into the experience.

I feel that God allowed me to feel the one contraction to know the depth of His gift. I asked for strength and courage. He gave me instead a joyous childbirth, and spared me the pain.

I am forever thankful, forever humbled. "Ask and ye shall receive. . . ." Remember to ask.

Greg Davis, Come Home

Pam Davis

We moved to our state capital in the late 1970s. This was a very exciting period in our lives, once I adjusted to the change. My husband had a prestigious job working for the governor, and we were able to enjoy the beautiful surroundings and the friendly, hospitable people. I was a homemaker, and had the opportunity to dabble in various spiritual classes, seminars and workshops. I was taking some classes in psychic awareness and Silva Mind Control, among other things. I would practice my newfound skills in mental telepathy by attempting to send people messages by thought alone, and by trying to guess who was calling before I picked up the phone.

In 1981, our last year there, our son Greg was graduating from high school. My husband had made a date with him to go shopping for a music system, as a graduation present.

Well, the night before the shopping expedition, Greg slept at a friend's house. The next day he called me to say that the group was going swimming in a lake at an Indian reservation, and asked if he could go with them. Apparently, both of us had forgotten about his date with his father: I told him to go and have a good time.

When I told my husband of Greg's plans he was upset, to say the least. He stormed out of the house, muttering, "If that's all it means to him, the hell with it."

I felt so bad for the whole situation and for the tension

between the two men in my life. I was cleaning up the kitchen, and while sweeping the floor I kept repeating in my mind, over and over, "Greg Davis, come home. Greg Davis, please come home."

About a half hour later, I was still in the kitchen when Greg came bounding into the house. I could hardly believe it. I asked him what he was doing home so soon, since he'd planned to be out most of the day. He said that while he was swimming in the lake, he saw me motioning for him to come home. He'd told his friends that he had to go home right away, that his mother needed him. I was beside myself with amazement and joy that this mental telepathy really worked!

My husband came home a short while later. When I told him that Greg was home, he said, "You probably called him." I told him that I had, but not on a telephone. They went and had a loving time together, picked out a great system, and all was well for a moment in time.

Thank You, Anna

Laura Goerlitz

Recently I met a young woman who has the gift of seeing and receiving information from angels. She told me that I had many angels with me, and that one of them was named Anna. She said that Anna was one of my "main" angels and that if I needed her guidance, to ask for it.

One night my eight-year-old son was having trouble

getting to sleep after an allergic reaction. His allergies affect his brain, and make him hyperactive and angry. I knew he must have eaten something he shouldn't. I needed to know what it was, so I could help counteract it with the right medicine, but he wouldn't tell me.

Finally, I gave up asking. Lying next to him to calm his restlessness and help him go to sleep, I remembered what my friend said about asking angels for help. I began to ask Anna if she could ask my son's angels to help him admit that he ate something.

But before I could finish my request, my son said in a sweet, calm voice, "Mommy, I want to tell you something."

"What?" I asked.

"I ate something." And then he told me what it was.

I was astonished at what had just happened. I raised my hand in the air and quietly said, "Thank you, Anna."

Just as I said it, my son said, "What's that?"

"What's what?"

"Over there."

It was completely dark, but as I turned over and looked where he was pointing, I saw a white light near the wall next to the closed door of the room. It was about as tall as an adult and as wide, except wider at the shoulders and upper arms.

I picked up the flashlight that my son kept next to his bed and walked in the direction of the light, but stayed across the room from it—even though it didn't frighten me. I noticed there was no light coming through the window, and that it was so dark I couldn't see anything else in the room.

As I stood directly across from it, I turned the flashlight on it. All I saw was the wall, as usual. Then I turned off the flashlight, and the light that had been there was gone.

I told my son it was probably a reflection from outside. He didn't think so—and neither did I—but I reassured him that it was so he wouldn't be frightened. He soon fell asleep.

I felt it was Anna, letting me know she was around when I needed her. Still, I wanted to make sure I wasn't deceiving myself, so several times over the following months I would lie in my boy's room, watching for the light. Neither the porch light, passing headlights, or moonlight created the same light as before.

Since then, I've let my son know that the light was an angel, and that the experience we had was a very special one. Now he knows that his angels are there to help and protect him.

Free at Last

Deborah Ford

It was day ten at the Palm Beach Institute for Drug Research's drug rehabilitation program, and I was hearing the familiar voice in my head saying, "You gotta get outta here!" I felt heartsick. This was the fourth treatment center I'd checked into, and I was facing yet again the demoralizing possibility that I would never make it into recovery. The vicious circle, I feared, would continue forever.

That day, in group, I was overwhelmed with feelings of despair and failure. I went into the bathroom to be alone.

I was certain I would never get through this. Overcome with hopelessness, I got down on my hands and knees and, for the first time in my life, prayed to God to help me make it through another day. I must have stayed in that position for ten minutes or more, I don't know. When I got up, for the first time in years I felt safe. I was confident I could finish the rest of the day, and went back to join the group.

The next few weeks were far from easy. Always there

was the nearly unbearable urge to leave, to run away from the pain. But whenever that feeling arose, I would go to the bathroom, drop to my knees, and pray.

I made it through the twenty-eight days of the treatment program. I was shocked and thrilled. This was the longest I had been without drugs in fifteen years.

My mother picked me up from the treatment center and dropped me off at my apartment. I was so excited, so happy to be home; I felt more alive than I had in years. I reached into my purse and pulled out my house key . . . along with a Percodan, my drug of choice for the past few years.

My heart sank. This was a test, and I wasn't going to make it.

Those pills had always had the power. My apartment had been searched to make sure I wouldn't be immediately faced with temptation. They'd even searched my purse at the treatment center to make sure it was clean—but here in my hand was this one little pill. I knew that if that pill got into my body, I would be right back where I'd started.

Standing there on the doorstep of my apartment I started crying hysterically. I knew exactly what would happen as soon as I went inside. I had done it so many times before . . .

I again found myself on my hands and knees. I said a prayer I had learned in the treatment center:

God, I offer myself to thee—to build with me and to do
    with me as Thou wilt.
Relieve me of the bondage of self, that I may better do
    Thy will.
Take away my difficulties, that victory over them may
    bear witness
to those I would help, of Thy Power, Thy Love, and Thy
    Way of life.
May I do Thy will always!*

---

* From *Alcoholics Anonymous*, p. 63. Reprinted with permission of Alcoholics Anonymous World Services, Inc., New York, New York.

The next thing I remember, I was lying on the floor of my bathroom, knowing that I had flushed the Percodan down the toilet. I felt as though I had been carried there by a power greater than myself or my addiction, and that I would never have to worry about facing it alone again. Whatever or whoever carried me from the doorstep to the bathroom would always be with me.

At the time of this writing, it has been eleven years since I have used drugs.

The Powerful Protection of HU

Linda C. Anderson

A public parking lot is adjacent to my garage. One afternoon as I drove up and pressed the button for the garage door opener, it didn't work.

This puzzled me. The opener had always worked.

When I got out to open the garage door myself, a man who had been sitting in a car in the parking lot jumped out and rushed toward me.

I heard an inner voice I recognized as the Mahanta, my spiritual guide, give clear commands. "Get back in the car. Lock the door."

I immediately did as I was told.

The man swerved to run in another direction. He seemed to be pretending that he wasn't really pursuing me.

I again pressed the button to open the garage door. This time the door slid up easily.

I parked the car. Got out. Checked behind me. Then

pressed the button to close the garage door. I hurried out the side door of the garage and rushed across the yard to my house.

As I tried to unlock the door, I saw the man run into the yard. I froze. No one else was around. Evil seemed to ooze from him. I knew he intended to hurt me.

I began to sing "HU" very quietly. This is an ancient name for God, pronounced like the word *hue*, that has the power to uplift a person spiritually for direct experience with the Holy Spirit. I also called upon the Mahanta for help.

My pursuer looked directly at me. But a field of clear light had surrounded me, and he couldn't see me at all! I was invisible!

The puzzled man kept looking my way. He had been watching and knew I had to be there. He actually turned in circles, amazed at not being able to see me where he knew I must be. Finally he ran around the house to find me.

As he searched for me, I moved and hid on the side of the garage. I watched as he returned to his car, jumped in, and sped away.

Stunned and shaken by the experience, I rushed into the house.

Within one minute, my husband arrived home from work early. I ran to tell him about the man chasing me.

My husband said that he had been working when suddenly the Mahanta urged him, with a strong inner nudge, to go home right away. He dropped everything he was doing and ran out to his car, sensing that I was in some kind of danger. If the man had succeeded in attacking me, my husband would have been home in time to help.

We hugged each other and thanked God for this powerful gift of HU and the loving protection of the Mahanta.

When I filed a police report on the incident, I told about everything but becoming invisible. I didn't think the officer would believe that part. But it happened. And that stalker is probably still wondering how his intended prey disappeared.

The Voice from the Grave

Elena M. Esparza

My name is Nena Esparza. I've been a widow for the last ten years. I live alone, in the same house that I've resided in for the last thirty years, the same house where my husband and I raised our five sons. I have worked for many years as a chef in the school cafeteria in our town. Though the work is hard, I am a good cook and I enjoy what I do. I have a large, close-knit family. My sister lives next door, and there are my sons and their families and my brother who visit often. There is always coffee on the stove and friends at my table.

The event I would like to recount to you took place just after my husband Ernie died, in 1986.

I arrived home from work one evening. The day was satisfying, but I was tired. As usual, I unlocked the kitchen door and walked inside. The house was quiet and empty. All I wanted to do was soak in a hot tub and relax on the couch, maybe read a bit.

At the time, my boys were converting the second bedroom, an extremely large room, into an apartment. Although I hadn't thought of quitting my job, my sons were always thinking of ways to make my retirement, when it came, a little easier. The rent from the apartment would be a sweet cushion for my pension.

However, now the house was under construction. One wall in the living room, the one that connected to the soon-to-be apartment, was still only framed. You know, that's what builders call a wall that has only two-by-fours and plastic.

As I walked through the house to make sure everything was locked before taking my bath, I noticed that my cousin Justina had been there earlier in the day. As we had discussed, she had left two queen-sized mattresses, and they were now leaning against one wall in the apartment. I knew that she would be by on the weekend to take them to her home in Tijuana, Mexico.

After making sure that the windows and doors were secure, I proceeded to linger in the bath for a while. Then I put on a warm nightgown. I wanted to sit on the couch in the living room to relax before starting on dinner.

As I entered the living room, I heard someone call my name—not just once, but repeatedly, as if looking for me. The voice seemed to be coming from the apartment.

I walked into the apartment, fully expecting to see someone there, even though I had just locked the house up tight. I felt that someone must be in the house, as the voice sounded so near. I searched the room and found no one. I continued to search the entire house, and found no one. Feeling not a little foolish, I retreated to the couch where, naturally, I fell asleep.

The voice startled me awake. It sounded much more urgent this time, even desperate. My mind kept telling me that the voice was my husband, Ernie, although the voice sounded nothing like Ernie.

I arose to look through the house again. Upon entering the apartment room, I saw smoke. I immediately understood the voice's urgency. The mattresses Justina had delivered in the morning were propped up against a heater. They had been smoldering, and were obviously ready to burst into flames. I unlocked and opened the sliding glass door and, with strength that I really didn't know I possessed, I dragged the mattresses outside and drowned the fire with water from the hose.

My home is an older, wood-framed house. Had the

mattresses caught fire as I slept, it would have burned to the ground. I still don't know whose voice saved me from that terrible fate, but I like to think it was Ernie, safeguarding me from above.

Lion of God

Brynn Amber Rials

It was a cold December night in 1993, and I was seven and a half months pregnant with my first baby. My husband and I had just left a dinner party and were heading back to our mountain home. As I drove, my husband asleep in the back seat, I was reviewing my life and praying to God to show me the path he wished me to take.

I was just asking him to give me some sort of experience to bring me closer to him when we hit a patch of ice on a snow-covered bridge. Reacting without thought, I hit the brake when we started to spin out, causing the car to flip into the air and roll over. Since he'd been lying down without his seatbelt, my husband was thrown around the interior of the car, while I was held secure by mine.

Once the car came to a stop, I dimly heard my husband moving around, asking if I was okay. I was afraid to move, but I told him I thought so. He crawled out through the shattered hatchback of our all-terrain vehicle and started yelling for help, but no one could hear him.

Crawling back inside, he made his way to me. He asked me to try to pull my head up, and only then did I realize that my head was embedded in the snow outside the shattered window. Reaching up to see what was covering my face, I realized that the sun visor had swung forward to shield me.

We had always carried guardian angel pins in our cars for safety. In this car, the angel was pinned on the visor, and it was now pressed directly against my temple. Moving the visor and lifting my head, I saw that my swollen belly had been completely cradled and protected.

My husband unfastened my seatbelt and carefully pulled me through the car and out the hatch. Once outside, we could see that the car was totaled, and lying on such a steep incline that it seemed impossible that it hadn't continued to roll into the stream bed below.

It was then we realized that something divine had intervened and brought the car to a halt. My husband told me he'd felt the spirit of his deceased mother, while I'd felt the presence of an angel.

We ran into the road and flagged down some help. We were checked by paramedics, who found us in perfect condition. Neither of us had a single mark on us. They told us we could go home.

When we got there, I prayed to God to show me the face of the angel who had saved us. To my surprise and confusion, a vision of the huge, beautiful face of a lion rose before my mind's eye.

This didn't make any sense to me at all. I'd never heard of a lion-faced angel. But I was grateful just the same.

A few hours later, my doctor told me to go to the hospital to have the baby checked. While I was there, I told the nurses about our incredible experience, and how sure I was that we'd been saved by an angelic presence—although I didn't tell them the part about the lion, since I still wasn't sure what it meant.

They were all amazed, and one of them was so taken by the story that she began to cry. She started telling me about all the different angels described in the Bible, sent down to assist us in times of need. About ones that would come down on big rolling wheels, while others would appear as light, or sound. About four figures found in both the Old and New Testaments: A winged man or angel, a winged calf, an eagle . . . and a winged lion.

I was stunned. In that moment it was all clear: An absolute miracle of God had occurred, and our lives were changed forever.

An Angel's Hand

Victoria Bullis

I drive north to Santa Rosa every week to do a radio show. It's about an hour's drive each way, and the freeway gets pretty monotonous. One Sunday evening last spring, I decided to take a longer but more scenic route home, through blossoming trees and vineyards.

Dusk fell earlier than I had anticipated. Since the road wasn't well lit, I was paying close attention to the traffic ahead and driving under the speed limit. Even so, I was shocked to suddenly see a vintage Cadillac parked perpendicular across the two-lane highway, its nose slanted toward a ditch on my side of the road, only a very few feet ahead of me.

Immediately, everything became extremely surreal. I felt a bizarre sense of great peace while I slammed on my brakes. I remember hoping, very calmly, that I would make it through this without any major injuries.

My big old Mercedes usually takes a lot longer to stop than cars with less power. This time it stopped virtually instantaneously, with inches to spare. Several cars behind me were going off in both directions, either into the ditch or skidding to the other side of the road. By all accounts the vehicle just behind me was traveling so closely that even at our slow speed, it should have collided with mine. Instead, it easily missed, and ended up in the drainage ditch. There was no injury to anyone, no damage at all.

Just at the moment I knew we were about to collide, I saw a larger than life-size ethereal "hand" rise up between my car and the Cadillac. My car screeched to a halt.

Then, suddenly, an angel also slid up from somewhere between the two cars. She smiled at me and nodded, seeming to say that all was well. In a daze, I watched her come around to the driver's window.

As she floated toward me, I heard her say, as clearly as though she'd been speaking in a human voice, that I was going to be all right and to go on home.

She was beautiful. She had large feathered wings and was wearing a shimmering opalescent gown that trailed down to the pavement and disappeared into it.

I watched the driver of the Cadillac, who had been standing next to his car, casually get back into it, start it up, and drive away as though nothing at all unusual had just happened. Why he had been parked in that position, across the road, I'll never know.

I arrived home in a deep trance; I was devoid of any emotions whatsoever. Even though it was still early evening, I calmly undressed and went straight to bed. I fell asleep immediately.

I woke the next day feeling normal and rested. I wasn't at all shaken or amazed at what had taken place, even after I began to think about how very close I had come to a possibly fatal accident, and how I was saved. Oddly enough, to this day it has never really felt as though anything unusual *did* happen.

Several weeks later, I awakened one morning knowing

that I had just been dreaming about a similar incident that took place in Hong Kong in 1978. I'd just gotten off a double-decker bus, and was really tired. As buses usually passed by there only every twenty or thirty minutes, I wasn't thinking about the possibility of another one being right behind the first. Somehow, I'd managed to jump out of the way just in time.

Now, in the dream, I'd lived through it all again—but this time I saw another giant ethereal "hand" literally shoving me back from where I had been about to cross the road at a bend. I was propelled about a foot up in the air and seven or eight feet backward, yet I hadn't stumbled or fallen; I'd landed upright, with my shopping bags still in my hands.

That time, too, I'd remained in a state of total calm. I never even had the feeling that anything unusual had happened.

I've always believed that miraculous events occur, but only occasionally, and for a specific purpose. I'm not sure just why I was spared from disaster twice like this. I am certain, however, that there was a reason for it, that there is something I'm still meant to accomplish here.

And I somehow feel that I'll know it for what it is when it happens.

Crash

Robyn Burton-Tuva

It was March 1985, a hot, tropical day on the North Shore of Oahu. I had been in Waikiki with my girlfriend Cathy, playing on the beaches and in the ocean. Now it was becoming evening, and Cathy wanted to stay in and retire early. My friend Darrell asked me if I wanted to take a drive over to Brigham Young University, where I'd gone to college, and visit some friends. I eagerly accepted.

We stopped and got a bit of dinner on the way. When we came out it had started to drizzle, so we put the top up on Darrell's convertible.

We were driving on Kam Highway, a small two-lane road, laughing and reminiscing about our college days, when we suddenly stopped and stared at the car coming toward us. Surely they would notice they were in the wrong lane? Surely they would get back on their side? I'm not sure how far away they were when I saw them, but everything slowed way down. The last thing I remember thinking was, with the Pacific on our right and a mountain on our left, where were we supposed to go? The last thing I remember is the sound of the crash.

I came to with my face down between the seats. Darrell was calling my name. I untangled myself and tried to open my door, but it wouldn't. Darrell started to drag me across the front seat, and I grabbed my purse on the way out.

I stood up and looked at Darrell's car. It looked like an

accordion. Completely smashed, his Chrysler Le Baron looked like a toy car.

As I struggled to walk around our car, I saw Darrell trying to help the people in the other one. It was a VW Bug.

There were beads of water on the back of the car from the rain, and I brushed my hands across them. I wanted to wash off whatever was on my face. I felt something dripping on my face—I couldn't understand why. I reached into my purse and got my compact mirror to see what the problem was.

My lower lip was stuck on my lower teeth, and my upper teeth were broken right in half. I think the rest of them are in that dashboard to this day. Now I knew why my white outfit was red, which I thought I'd noticed before. I really couldn't grasp what was going on.

So I detached my lip from my teeth and walked over to help Darrell. I saw two Polynesian boys in the car, about nineteen. The passenger was unconscious and looked really bad. The driver was screaming. I could see thigh bone, broken in half, sticking through his skin and up through the steering wheel.

I also saw lots and lots and lots of beer cans scattered all around the Bug. The rage hit me harder than the car crash, and I started yelling, "A drunk driver hit me! Head on!"

Then I felt that my back wasn't supporting my body anymore, and I sat down on a tire that had flown off one of the cars. Soon I realized that that wasn't going to hold me up. I needed to lie down.

My body is failing me, I thought. *The grass is all wet. It's raining. I'm on the side of the road. Is anyone going to help us?*

Some tour buses came out of the Polynesian Cultural Center. Apparently, they radioed for help.

I closed my eyes and listened to Darrell trying to calm the driver down. Then I heard footsteps coming through the grass, and a man's voice ask me, "Where are you going?" I opened my eyes.

I thought, *Oh, thank goodness, it's a fireman. It must be a fireman. He's wearing his yellow fireman's suit.*

I tried to talk, but my mouth would hardly move. I mouthed, "B—Y—U."

He introduced himself as Stanley, and with a knowing smile asked me if I wanted a heavenly blessing. I nodded yes. Then I heard sirens approaching and looked toward them. It was odd, I thought, that this fireman was here already. I turned to look at him, and he was gone. "No!" I wanted him back.

The paramedic checked me over. Then he put me on a wooden board and went over to the others. Once again I heard the footsteps approaching.

All of a sudden the heavens started to open. I felt beyond calm, and a sense of complete love, perfect and overwhelming. I felt no pain, only the pure love of God. I knew I'd died and was going to heaven.

I felt Stanley put his hands on my head. He told me that my body would be completely healed, and that my heavenly Father loved me and I had much work to do on Earth.

The heavens closed. The warmth was replaced by the tropical drizzle.

Stanley said, "I once lived around here."

I closed my eyes. Stanley was gone.

At the hospital, the doctors in ER made sure I wasn't in danger, then turned their attention to the boy who'd been the passenger in the VW. I found out later that his name was Jessie.

I could see his face between the doctors and nurses as they frantically worked on him. He turned his head and looked at me, and smiled. I smiled back.

Then he flatlined. Jessie died there before my eyes.

The doctors sent me for x-rays. The first set came back unclear. When the second set came back, they were confused. The paramedic's report said I had a broken jaw, broken fingers, possible broken leg . . . and they weren't seeing anything of the sort. They even called the paramedic on the radio to make sure he'd given them the right report.

One of the doctors told me I was pretty banged up, but I

was in "remarkably good shape." He said I must have an angel on my shoulder.

I told him, "Tonight I sure did."

Sometime after they put me in a room, Darrell came in. He wasn't severely injured, just some broken ribs and bruises. I asked him to dial my mother in San Diego.

I told her I'd been in an accident, and about the boy dying. Then the Demerol kicked in. When I woke up, she was sitting next to my bed.

When I was able to make the flight home, I asked Mom to wheel me to the room of the other car's driver. His name was Walter.

I told him how angry I was the night of the accident. But I said that I was able to forgive him now, and that I was sorry about his friend.

I still have plenty of scars over my face and body as reminders. But I took something else away, too. I learned a big lesson in forgiveness and compassion.

6

VISION

Family Reunion

Thomas Pecora

Everything I am about to tell you is absolutely true. Because it is a highly personal account concerning a Native American sacred ceremony, I feel that it must be added that no sacred medicines or any other outside physical agencies were employed that might alter consciousness in any way. At the time of the experience, I was in the clearest state of mind, lucid and peaceful, devoid of apprehension or expectation.

My first contact with Duke Joseph Big Feather was over the phone. A mutual friend named Danny mentioned that he knew someone he felt I might have a connection with, and handed me the phone number. As an intuitive astrologer, I thought it might be intriguing to cast and interpret the birth chart of a Native American spiritual leader such as Big Feather. So one evening, pretty much on what I thought was a whim, I made the call.

The connection was immediate, as Big Feather "felt" extremely familiar. He also wasted no time letting me know what he thought my current life issues were. This I am not used to: I am accustomed to being the reader. The fact that he was going right to the heart of various personal and psychological matters, and with such ease and accuracy, took me by surprise and forced me to stop and think. At the end of our conversation he asked if I would calculate his chart, along with some charts for specific points in the future, and stop over in four days. Of course, I said yes.

Four days later I sat across the table from Big Feather, numerous charts spread out before us. I was very much in a type of "stream of consciousness," accessing and interpreting energy as I went, and not retaining most of it once it was spoken. This is my way. When it was finished and the energies began to dissipate, I looked up and noticed that Big Feather had his eyes trained on me. Unblinking, he nodded twice and merely said, "Aho." As I reconnected to myself, I realized that I was the one who had some questions now.

I learned that Duke Joseph Big Feather is the spiritual leader of an intertribal group called the Two Feathers Medicine Clan. They formed in the early 1800s, although their original work and traditions are centuries older. They were brought together by some very well-known Native Americans of their time, including medicine people and spiritual elders, to be the caretakers of ancient and sacred artifacts, ceremonies, traditions, medicines, burial grounds, and so forth that needed immediate protection for future generations and earth cycles.

I have come to understand that my own spiritual traditions, including my inner family and guides, are primarily Tibetan. Thus I found the parallels and my immediate feeling of familiarity to make perfect sense. In many ways, the Native Americans and the Tibetans have shared the same hardships and challenges.

At the close of our meeting, Big Feather asked me once more if I would return four days hence. Once again I said yes.

It was the evening of January 26, 1996. One of those incredible Chicago blizzards was whipping up, and the wind was literally howling. Between the snow and the high winds on the expressway, my car was being tossed around so much I had to pay very close attention just to stay on the road. I kept asking myself what was I doing.

As I got out of the car upon arriving, I was immediately hit by a gust of wind that almost knocked me over. It was pitch dark, except for some large, glowing embers flying out of the house's chimney. A fireplace was obviously roaring somewhere inside, and the sight of the swirling, violently blowing embers against the pitch-black winter sky made me once again feel like something "real" was about to occur. This was very high earth energy of a kind that I must admit I have not experienced since.

The moment I stepped inside the house, I realized something serious was happening. The atmosphere was completely different from my previous visit. First of all, there were other Native Americans there. They were just sitting, watching me with a sort of nonchalant, disinterested interest; not curiosity, but something else. All of them seemed completely nonjudgmental, and all bore the slightest hint of what looked like a grin. I was not at all anxious, just curious—unlike them. I must admit, however, that I wasn't too wild about those grins.

Duke Joseph Big Feather introduced me to the group only with, "This is the one I was telling you about." This rattled me a bit, so I just grinned back. Then he made the introductions. Joining us that evening were Cindy Crow Woman (president and Clan Mother), Jomary Wildflower (member), She Dog (a female member about seven years old, being trained in the ways of Medicine), and Roger (the drummer for this ceremony and an extended family member).

I did not know that I was there to take part in a high spiritual ceremony. Nor did I know I was to be the subject of this ceremony. I expected it a little, but I thought it best to just go with the flow. If I wasn't supposed to be there, I wouldn't have been there.

After some brief comments and explanations, Big Feather got up and said, "All right, let's get started."

The next thing I knew, we were going into an adjacent room, twice the size. It had a distinct atmosphere of being a sacred space, a space where the Work is done.

It was very difficult to see at first, as there was only one dim red light in the corner. The first thing I noticed, though, with a slight, instinctual sense of alarm, was that a special place had been set aside on the floor for me. There were a blanket to lay on, a decorated buffalo skull on the floor just above the pillow where my head was to go, and a great number of other items: sacred objects, I assumed.

I lay down. They placed on me, and under both my arms, different items belonging to the Spirits when they were physically here on Earth, as well as other very old articles of one significance or another. When they had finished, I was covered chin to toes with a heavy deer skin, and a large, heavy necklace was placed over the deer skin and around my shoulders and chest. I was then told that they would be playing some recordings of traditional and sacred spirit songs, while Roger played along on the drum, and all I had to do was go to sleep. I felt as though among the many things I could have done at that time, sleep was probably not one of them.

The songs were played very loudly, coming from speakers placed in the four corners of the ceiling. As the music and the drumming got louder, I realized that the women were quickly fanning my entire body, head to toe, with some sort of feathers. What felt like an incredible wind began to pick up all around me, no doubt caused by the frantic fanning of the feathers.

And then it begins.

The inner visions start. These are not visualizations or the wanderings of the imagination. These are detailed, sharper-than-life visions. I can move within them, examining them at will from any angle. They also come complete with their own sort of information and emotion. Very clear sight, sound, information and emotion. Not separate, but as *one*.

I am shown many things. First, I am shown the North American Plains Indians before the arrival of the Europeans. There are tepees as far as the eye can see. Smoke rises into a cloudless blue sky. Children are playing, women are laughing, men are talking to one another in various parts of the city, and a true city it is.

The primary thought pattern here is one of harmony. Harmony with universal law, with each other, and especially with Mother Earth. There literally is no separation between the people and their environment. Although I am trying my best to convey it all here, there are no adequate words to truly describe the beauty.

Then something very odd happens. Coming in from my right are a group of spiritual elders whom I instantly identify as being Tibetan. They are wearing their traditional maroon robes, and there is an immediate recognition between us. Just as quickly as that recognition comes, I see on my left a similar group of Native American spiritual elders. They, too, are clothed in attire appropriate for their traditions.

The two groups greet one another and begin to very rapidly exchange information. It would appear that they are familiar with one another.

As I watch, I begin to have the absolutely physical sensation of an older woman's fingers slowly touching my right shoulder. It is as if they want to know more about me, but without frightening me in any way. The touch is gentle, as light as a spider crawling on my shoulder, and infinitely wise, carrying the vibration of this elder medicine woman.

Because Crow Woman was on my right, I assume it is her, and part of the ceremony. Then I remember that I am covered by a heavy deer skin, while the fingers feel as though they are literally on my exposed skin. Slowly, I open my right eye just a sliver and look over. There is nothing there. Nothing at all, except the feeling of the old woman's fingers.

Then the fingers press, first down, then up. Again, gently, like someone pushing a soft cylindrical object on me. First on my chest, then on my stomach; down, then up, down, then up. This continues for about ten minutes. I open my eyes again to see who is pushing on my solar plexus and my heart center, but as before, no one is there.

Toward the end of the ceremony, I kept hearing the phrase repeating, louder and louder, "We are many, we are strong"—and the Spirits departed.

It was as if a very ancient agreement had been awakened at the appointed time. That is how it felt.

To this day I do not have conscious knowledge of all the details, but the Work would appear to be right on schedule. Very recently, I was asked by an important Native American spiritual elder for the phone number of the Dalai Lama's Tibetan contact person at the United Nations in New York City. This person is the only individual authorized to coordinate His Holiness's United States schedule. It would appear that the Native Americans and the Tibetans are joining together to reconnect and assist one another in their Work.

As above, so below.

I can only say that I was truly humbled and honored to be a witness to this Spiritual Family Reunion.

Tashi Deleck.
Mitakuye Oyasin.

A Spiritual Baptism

Dina Tevas Ingram

There was a sound as though a gale-force wind was rushing toward me. My entire being was dwarfed by its magnitude. Then, total silence. I heard a deep, reverent voice somewhere in the distance say, "the Master of all understanding." As I felt the words wash over me and echo through me, I realized that Reverend Della Reese had just introduced me to the Presence of God.

In September of 1996, I had come to Della Reese's Understanding Principles Church to interview her for a book I was writing called *Answered Prayers*. I was impressed by both the exuberance of the choir and the warmth of her congregation. It was the message of her sermon, however, that struck a chord in my soul, and inspired me to spend Sunday after Sunday in her church.

This *Touched by an Angel* star and jazz legend spoke of God as a living presence, accessible to all who open their hearts to Him. She spoke about God with the authority and love of someone speaking about her dearest and most intimate friend and companion, an omnipotent and omniscient partner with whom she speaks and from whom she receives guidance every moment of every day.

With passion and conviction, Reverend Reese said that through God, each of us could have all of our heart's desires, be all that we wanted to be, and achieve any goal we set for ourselves. "The Holy Spirit will bring you ideas straight from God," she said. "It will speak to you and turn around and speak for you, seeking out the very best of all the things you want and need to complete your life. It will cleanse you, guide you, comfort and take care of you, and it will fill you with a peace that surpasses all understanding. The deep things of God it will show you, and you will know and experience God not as an intellectual ideal, but spiritually, in your heart and soul, and be forever changed."

She recounted how "the Father" had healed her physically when doctors said there was no hope, restored her financially when she was left destitute by a former manager, gave her a hit television show at the age of sixty-two, and even guided her to her soulmate and present husband. She spoke about being baptized in the Spirit, and about experiencing God's presence on the deepest spiritual level— something I had always yearned for but thought beyond my reach, strictly reserved for mystics, saints, and those in acute crisis. When she announced that she would hold a spiritual baptism for all who were ready to accept the whole Spirit of God, my husband and I eagerly planned to attend.

On the day of the service, Reverend Reese's ministers first met with all those being baptized in a room adjacent to the church hall. We held hands and prayed that all would be done according to His will, and were led in meditation by one of the assistant ministers, who simply asked us to open our hearts to God. In dulcet tones she gave thanks that God was with us, and asked us to be willing to accept anything that might happen.

As the service began, an almost electrical feeling of expectancy surged from the deepest part of my being. Like a wave, it spread throughout my body to the very ends of my fingertips. I realized it was my turn to stand and move toward the aisle, where Reverend Reese was laying on hands and baptizing the initiates. I took a deep breath to regain my composure.

As Reverend Reese pressed her hands on my chest and back and prayed for the Spirit of God to fill and bless me, I closed my eyes and tried concentrating on her words, but her voice seemed to trail farther and farther away. Nothing I had read, heard, or been told had prepared me for what was about to happen. Nothing on Earth could have.

At that moment, I heard the roar of a massive force of wind rushing toward me. Then, total silence—save the voice of Reverend Reese. I knew I was in the presence of God. The awesome power of that sound and the vastness of God's presence were only matched by the tenderness with which they completely surrounded and engulfed me— enfolding me, filling me, and moving through me. I felt as though it was holding and caressing my very heart.

As it did, the heaviness of a thousand hurts, disappointments, and fears was lifted from me. Images, scenes, and faces of people I once associated with those feelings flashed through my mind, and I realized I no longer felt any pain.

Tears of release, relief, and exultation poured down my

face. I felt as though my soul was being cradled and lifted with love and by Love itself. Every cell in my body was being lifted up, and I felt my soul expanding, filling, and then encompassing my entire body. My being was at once within me and outside of me. All physical sense of my body and surroundings fell away.

I was one with God, and God was within me and all around me. Everything outside of me was within me and was me. Everything within me was outside of me and was me. There was no separation. There were no boundaries. There was no sense of individuality. Only oneness. I was part of a vast ocean of consciousness. Everything was God and nothing but God existed. In that moment, I remembered who I was, and Whose I was, and I knew I was home. My entire being vibrated with the joy of that knowledge, as though I was Joy itself. There was no beginning and no end. There was no past or future: All time was now and eternal.

And I knew this was eternity. There was no death, only Life. I knew Life is God, and God is Love, and I was inside of that Love that is God. I knew that everything material— all sadness, sickness, poverty, wealth, success, and fame— was an illusion. I realized that what I was experiencing was the one and only reality there is.

As gently and as completely as it had engulfed me, God's Presence left me. I found myself on the floor of the church, drenched in tears of joy and cradled in the lap of one of the ministers' many helpers who had volunteered to tend to the initiates. As he wiped the tears and sweat from my face and helped me to my seat, I looked into his face and saw Love. And I realized that that is what and who each and every one of us truly is.

Messages and Mountains

Jan Tuttleman

Dedicated to my late husband, Michael Kriegler

I had planned a quiet New Year's weekend getaway with my sister in Palm Springs. I felt the need for some quiet time away from home to reflect on the past year. My husband Michael had died that July, of a sudden heart attack, at age forty-one.

Michael was a remarkable man: brilliant, passionate, energetic, always questioning. He loved ideas, technology, films, his friends and, most of all, me and his girls. At twenty-two, he was diagnosed with Hodgkin's Disease, which he fought off and on for the next ten years. His zest for life stemmed from a feeling that he never knew how long he had to live. At forty-one, he had reached a level of personal and professional achievement that few of us will obtain in a long lifetime. Perhaps one answer to why he died so young lies in a quote from one of his favorite films, *Blade Runner*: "The flame that burns twice as bright burns half as long."

Nine months before Michael died—through the analysis of three separate, recurring dreams that all came together in one dream—I realized that I had been searching for a sense of spirituality and connection to God. Since then, I have

been studying yoga meditation and postures, dream analysis and astrology, and have connected more with Judaism.
Another world has opened up to me: my desires manifest
themselves and events are no longer coincidences, as I am
now able to find a deeper meaning in their connections. I
believe that Michael's death had a deeper meaning for my
life and his. At the time of his death, I was able to draw on
my spirituality for strength, for me and for our young
daughters, Emma and Sophie. It was as if my spiritual
awakening was preparing me for Michael's death.

My sister had to cancel her trip, but I felt that I could use
a few days away myself and kept my hotel reservation.
Shortly before, a friend had told me about Siddha Yoga
Meditation. I had shared with him the experiences of my
spiritual awakening, and the further unfolding of my spirituality since the death of my husband. He thought I might
benefit from being in the presence of a Siddha Guru.

A Siddha Guru has the power to give others the inner
experience of God. During a retreat, the most significant
event in Siddha Yoga, the Guru transmits to the attendees
the grace known as *shaktipat*: the awakening of one's dormant spiritual energy. After one receives *shaktipat*, the
awakened energy empowers one's daily practice, giving
access to the clarity, inspiration, and insights that lie within.
The same weekend that I would be in Palm Springs, the
Siddha Guru Swami Chidvilasananda, known as Gurumayi, would be there leading a two-day program. I decided
to attend.

Coming to the retreat early on Saturday morning, I was
astonished to discover that there would be over two thousand people attending. There wasn't enough room in the
main hall for everyone, so some of the people, including
me, sat in another room filled with video monitors.

For the first few hours, different people spoke, explaining the process of Siddha Yoga Meditation. Gurumayi then
entered the hall and gracefully took a seat on the platform.

She was truly beautiful, and her presence filled even the overflow room.

She started by leading the group in chanting "*Om Nama Shivaya*," a chant that pays homage to the God within ourselves. The sound of her voice was so pure. My eyes were closed, but I briefly opened them and looked at the video monitor. At that instant, it seemed that Gurumayi was looking directly at me, and I felt a strong spiritual closeness to her blossom inside me.

After the chanting, Gurumayi started a discourse, one of many she would give during the two days. I was stunned that the first thing she talked about was the love you can give to a dying man. Through being with someone as he or she is dying, you can give total, unselfish love to help the soul move peacefully to a higher level with God.

As I listened to her speak about an experience still so close to me, tears poured down my cheeks. Michael had been afraid of dying alone ever since he was first diagnosed with cancer. But Michael was in my arms when his heart stopped, and our small daughters were there in the room with us. At that moment, I felt such complete love for him. Gurumayi's message confirmed what I had already felt, that by holding Michael while he was dying, I gave him permission to pass on with grace and into peace with God.

Gurumayi also said that being with a dying person elevates you closer to God. The strength I felt after Michael's death could only have come from God. Hearing these messages from Gurumayi made me believe that there was a reason for me to be attending this program, that there was something in store for me.

Gurumayi then led a group meditation that lasted for over an hour. During this meditation, I began to experience a buzzing sensation in my head and shoulders. Energy pulsed through me, and I felt as though I was sitting up on the platform right next to Gurumayi. It was only she and me: I couldn't see anyone else, and briefly wondered where the other two thousand people in the room had gone. The closeness I felt to her was remarkable. She placed her hand on mine, and we sat there together. A feeling of greatness stirred within me, as if there was a power that was starting to be awakened. I was overwhelmed.

The next morning, as we chanted, I felt my heart opening with absolute trust. I felt myself surrender to Gurumayi, and heard the message, "God is love . . . from above," come into my head. Following the chanting, Gurumayi talked about fear and pride as elements keeping us from closeness to God. My surrender to Gurumayi allowed me to let go of my skepticism and absorb the experiences that were about to unfold.

Gurumayi started to lead us into meditation. My first sensation was that of leaving my body. I found myself first near Gurumayi's chair, seated next to her, then floating upwards around her head.

Then I was in my own chair again. I felt as if someone was behind me, allowing me to lean my body back and relax into theirs. My head tilted back slightly, my jaw relaxed and my mouth opened. Gurumayi said to me in my meditation: "Drink the sweet nectar of life." I closed my mouth and tasted a soft, sensual, loving sweetness within. The feeling was very pleasurable, and I felt a warmth and sense of joy fill my body.

I next found myself standing on a mountain, wrapped in the same prayer shawl I wore during the meditation. It was a desert mountain, brown, barren and rocky, with a snow-capped peak. The wind was blowing, but my shawl kept me warm.

I felt the presence of Gurumayi as she said to me, "You need to be given the mountain and the earth for your strength and support. Use it, you need it. You need to be given the wind, whether it be warm or cold, for your courage and energy. You do not need to be given God's love, for you already have God's love in your heart. It is there. Drink the sweet nectar of life."

A feeling of overwhelming happiness, joy, love and peace filled my soul, a feeling of completeness that I'd never known before. I truly felt God's love in my heart.

When I came out of the experience, everyone in the room was still meditating. I realized that I was in a very special, spiritual place, with an enormous amount of spiritual energy surrounding me. I decided to make use of it while I was there: If there was ever a time for me to reach my husband Michael, it was now.

I called out to the heavens, called for Michael. I felt that a space had physically opened, a window to the heavens. I asked for my love to be sent to Michael. I was combing the heavens with my love for him, searching for his soul.

I found myself back on the same mountain, and heard a voice say, "I can't be who I used to be. I can't come to you as a person."

As I looked up to the top of the mountain, a tiger appeared. He was a very large and powerful Bengal tiger. He came and lay down at my feet; I sat down and stroked him. I didn't ask anything of him. I told him how much the girls and I love him, how much he is still in our hearts and minds. His fur was thick and soft, and the sound of his purring was one of deep contentment. We just sat there together peacefully.

He then leapt up, as tigers do—or as Michael would have done—and we ran together playfully for a few moments. Then a voice in the distance said, "I have to go now," and the tiger headed up the mountain. I heard myself say goodbye.

At that moment, I profoundly realized that I had been with Michael, and that I had also just said goodbye to him—something I'd never been able to do, since he died so suddenly. Tears welled in my eyes and streamed down my face: It felt as if they were cleansing my soul. I watched the tiger go over the ridge of the mountain and disappear.

I wrapped myself closely in the shawl and headed down the mountain, and now a luscious garden appeared before me. It was spring: the roses were in bloom, wild flowers were abundant, and the trees were full of delicate white blossoms. The sun was shining and the air was warm. I walked through the garden, smelling the scents, taking in the whole experience. I no longer felt sad. A feeling of peacefulness came over me.

I came upon a green lawn under the trees next to a rose garden: I recognized it as my garden at home. Placing my shawl on the warm grass under a tree, I laid down upon it. A man came to me: It was a man I'd noticed earlier in the day, at the retreat, to whom I'd felt attracted during our brief conversation. He lay down next to me and started to kiss me. The sensation was as if I *was* "drinking the sweet nectar of life": the kiss was absolutely wonderful and delicious, recreating the feeling I'd had in my mouth when I first heard Gurumayi say those words to me. We started to make love under the trees.

Soon after, I heard the sound of the bells signifying that the meditation was over. I came out of the meditation with an overwhelming feeling of having been blessed.

I arrived home on New Year's Eve. I was lying in bed with my four-year-old daughter, Emma, and began chanting to her to help her fall asleep (something I frequently do). My voice sounded so pure, so beautiful, in a way I never remembered it sounding before. It was as if the sounds were coming from a different place within me, and were going somewhere much higher than they'd ever gone to before.

Before falling asleep, Emma looked up at me and said, "Mommy, it feels like the music is singing in my heart."

"Yes, Emma," I replied. "That's what it's supposed to do."

Meeting Tabuk

Ellen Lieberman Weil

It is said that when the student is ready for mystical teachings, the teacher appears.

I was twenty-six years old, working in New York City in real estate management with Toni Mack, an outspoken, vivacious woman in her late forties. She was tall and buxom, with thick red hair and long red fingernails. She was also a practicing mystic, but I did not know it. Watching me bounce around in my confusion and fears, reacting to life, she occasionally offered subtle spiritual guidance, but I didn't respond or recognize the inner depths of who she was.

One day, after five months of working together, we were alone in our office and I felt moved to ask her a spiritual question. Her answer touched a profound truth that had been dormant inside of me, and ignited a passion to understand the Universal Laws and myself in relation to them. At that moment my teacher appeared.

Seven years prior to our meeting, Toni was diagnosed with terminal cancer. After a radical mastectomy and chemotherapy she was given two to five months to live. She began to seek out accomplished teachers, and quickly delved into profound spiritual and mystical realms. Through a series of deep meditations and healing circles, her cancer was healed: to the doctors' amazement, they could not find a trace of it in her body.

Toni continued to seek knowledge and wisdom from the
Mystery Schools. She did so in a discreet manner, and only
a few individuals were aware of her practices.

I truly believe that Toni and I made an agreement prior
to this lifetime: that she would awaken first, and then be
the vessel to awaken me. She became a teacher, guide, and
mentor. She taught me about God, love, the universe. Most
importantly, she taught me to observe and understand myself, and to transform myself into someone more alive,
aware, loving, and empowered. As the years progressed,
she also became my best friend, mother, daughter, and occasionally, student.

After a year of almost daily teachings, she said, "You can
go no further unless you go inside."

"What do you mean?"

"So far you have been learning about the universe
through understanding universal laws and seeing how
they get played out in the external world. Now you must
temporarily shut out this external world, close your eyes,
breathe deeply, and explore other dimensions."

We turned off the phones in our office, and she proceeded to guide me into meditation. She showed me how
to invoke protection, then travel into other realms of reality
in search of spiritual masters and teachers. When I had
completed work with the first teacher, she told me, I would
be escorted by that teacher to a higher realm, where I
would meet the next.

My second teacher in these realms was named Tabuk.
We met in a country setting, on a beautiful green hillside
next to a large old tree. He was a small man with gray hair
and a white beard, and he exuded a calm, joyful presence.
His sparkling eyes were those of a sage, clear and deep.

As we stood by the tree talking, I began to tell him about
a situation at work that had been causing me much emotional pain. "My boss has turned against me. He's become
severely critical and disrespectful. He's constantly looking
for me to make a mistake, so he can pounce on me and then

badmouth me to his superiors. What do I do? How do I handle him? I try to anticipate his next move so that I can protect myself, but it's exhausting."

Instead of receiving a reply, I felt myself being lifted off the ground and placed inside of Tabuk's body. It was a phenomenal sensation! I was actually inside of him, looking out of his eyes; aware of myself, yet able to feel and experience everything he did. I felt his calm presence and strength. Looking out through his eyes, I felt the wisdom with which he viewed his surroundings. Most of all, I felt the profound love that filled his being and pulsated with his every breath. Then he spoke.

"Feel me. I am strong and fierce, yet I am soft and gentle. I have much power, yet I am peaceful and loving. I can defend myself, yet I remain kind and giving. Feel who I am. I have much joy and passion, yet I am not dramatic. I do not indulge in negative emotions."

As he spoke, I felt the truth and wisdom of his words resonate throughout my entire body. I was learning and internalizing his teaching on a vibrational level. It felt as though my cells were taking an imprint of his energies.

"Don't try to outsmart your boss. Take your focus and your energies away from what he is doing to you. Instead, focus on acknowledging who you are. Become aware of your being, of the 'I AM presence' that you are. As you turn your attention to building your self-esteem, your love of yourself and capacity to love others, he will not be able to affect or harm you.

"Observe how he is operating in the world—dishonestly, out of fear and greed. There is much weakness in the character of an individual who functions this way. Have compassion for him.

"Stand up for yourself, yes. But do it with a sense of love and compassion. It's about feeling your heart chakra, and letting your strength and power come from your heart, from love—and not from your fears. Your fears cause you to be scattered, impulsive, intense and overly dramatic. The power of love in your heart allows you to breathe deeply and slowly—to pause, and then respond, not react.

"No one has power over you unless you give them your power. Take your power back. Stop thinking and fearing and focusing energy on how he can hurt you. This is how you give your power away. Instead, bless him. Bless the outcome of the situation. Finally, after you take right action and bless the results, place it in God's hands. . . . And remember your sense of humor. You take things too seriously. Take the life-and-death attitude out of it. Remove yourself from indulging in the dramas, and start enjoying the process of life, of growth.

"Bless the good that will come from having to interact with him in your life. You will learn and grow here. The universe placed him in your life right now for a reason. This situation, which you think is disempowering you, is in truth just what you need to work with in order to become more empowered. If he wasn't here, you would have attracted another situation and another person to treat you the same way, in order to activate this very same lesson and healing. So use this experience in this way. And stop resisting who he is, stop trying to change him. Change yourself instead."

Tabuk then lifted me out of his body and placed me in front of him again. I was filled with joyful tears and intense love for him.

We stood looking into each other's eyes, smiling. He took my hands in his and said, "It's such a magnificent journey. Enjoy it!"

I felt overwhelming gratitude as I thanked him and said goodbye—knowing, without him having to tell me, that he would always be accessible to me as a teacher and a guide.

Thank you, Toni, for opening up the magic of the universe to me, and showing me the beauty and power of love. Thank you, Tabuk, and all the wondrous teachers on my path.

Finding P.E.I.S.

Tom Youngholm

I had accomplished all the things that society said would make me fulfilled: graduated from college, gotten married, had a good job, was well respected. I had filled my life with joy, but also with some hard realities: a broken marriage, unfulfilling relationships, almost getting killed by a bomb, having a gun stuck in my face, having my uninsured houseboat-restaurant sink to the bottom of the Gulf of Mexico, and now working as a waiter as I approached forty. I felt as though I'd tried it all, but there was still something missing. I just didn't know what it was. Little did I know that within the next hour, the missing pieces would appear, and my life and my perception of the world around me would be totally changed.

I was working at a restaurant in San Diego. Arriving home after one stressful shift, I sat down in my favorite chair and began to meditate.

I'd taken up meditation simply to relax. Even though my friends back in Chicago thought I had "gone Californian," for me, yoga and meditation were purely stress management techniques. I certainly wasn't looking for any spiritual connection. I had given up any thoughts or feelings about spirituality since I had given up my religion some twenty years earlier. God, angels, and anything other than physical reality were way beyond my interests.

I continued my meditation. All I could hear was the distant sound of my breath, as if it were emanating from a nearby well. The sense of my physicality was beginning to break down: I couldn't tell where my body ended and the chair began. I began to feel as if I were falling, and also getting smaller and smaller. This was very different from any other meditation I had ever experienced.

I had no idea how long I had been in this state when, all of a sudden, I felt a hand on my right shoulder. What really surprised me wasn't the fact that no one else was home—who could that hand be attached to?—but that I wasn't surprised. The hand felt warm, friendly and, most of all, loving. It seemed to be more in my shoulder than on it. I didn't have any thoughts at the time? I was just there, just feeling.

Whoever it was began to rock me gently from side to side. The rhythm was leading me to a place; not a physical place, but a place of consciousness, a place of "knowing." I felt as if I were a sponge absorbing concepts, emotions, and information, without being aware of what they were.

When my ego finally did rear its head, it asked, "Am I making all this up?"

A voice seemed to shout all at once from behind me, from inside my head, and from my lungs: "No!"

I jolted out of my chair. From that moment on, my life changed. I knew that I had been contacted by an angel or guide.

For the next three weeks I meditated every day, eventually becoming familiar with four different angels. Over the years to follow, I would sense their presence in many ways. Sometimes I would feel them through a tingling sensation on my scalp or nose. When they communicated with me, I might see words, as if on a ticker tape inside my head, or at times actually hear voices. Sometimes I would receive an insight directly, without the medium of language. The guides/angels might show themselves to me as flashes of blue or white, or as tiny sparkly lights. Most of all, though, I would feel their presence as love, love that moved through every cell of my body.

They helped me discover what I was missing in my life: balance. They told me I lacked balance of what they called P.E.I.S. (pronounced "peace"): Physical, Emotional, Intellectual, and Spiritual. I had always seen myself as basically a physical being—but now I know that I am a spiritual being having a physical experience.

My guides eventually told me what I was going to be when I grew up: a teacher. Six months later I was hired as a business consultant, and several months after that I began to teach the information that I had received from the guides.

Many times they told me to write, but I hated writing. They assured me that writing was just another way of teaching, and that everything would work out wonderfully. I couldn't explain it, but I, too, felt that confidence and knowingness within myself. After seven years of prodding by them, and against all odds, I took one year out of my life and borrowed money against my home and retirement savings. Fifty thousand dollars into debt, I self-published a book, *The Celestial Bar*, about my experiences and the information shared with me by my guides / angels. Within three months of self-publication, the book was picked up by one of the biggest publishers in New York, and I was given a handsome advance that more than covered all of my expenses. The book has now been translated into twenty-two languages.

Now I believe that every day brings the possibility of life-changing moments, mystical experiences, and miracles. Just my belief can make it so.

Kundalini Awakening

Marc Boney

This happened in the winter of 1975, when I was twenty-four. Like many momentous events in life, it was foretold in a numinous dream several nights before.

I was in my bed when all of a sudden I found myself astride a huge white stallion. As the horse started to buck and toss as if to throw me, I began to panic. At first I tried to cling to its mane, but I realized quickly that this was futile.

Somehow it came to me that if I relaxed my body and calmed myself, this would also quiet the animal. To my amazement, the stallion responded immediately. By exerting a slight pressure with my knees, I seemed to be able to communicate with it. My panic turned to exhilaration.

Upon awakening, I marveled at the vividness of the dream. What did it mean?

I was a seminarian at the time, preparing to be a "priest"—but not the Catholic kind who had educated me in high school, who had asked me to look into my heart to see if God was calling. As it turned out, He was, but not in the way they, or I, would ever have imagined. This was Kriya Yoga Seminary, training instructors in the practices of Kriya Yoga, brought to this country by Paramahansa Yogananda. Goswami Kriyananda of Chicago was our spiritual preceptor.

A good portion of my day was spent in individual *sadhana*, spiritual practices. Each morning, I would rise and sit in meditation, experimenting with the techniques I was being taught. I was also devouring literature on the spiritual traditions of the East, including a curious tome entitled *The Serpent Power*, by an Englishman who had lived in India for many years.

It described in great detail a divine force that was said to reside, coiled like a serpent, in the lowest *chakra*, or psychic center, at the base of the spine. Yogis, through their spiritual discipline, sought to awaken this force and have it travel up the center channel of the subtle body to the highest center of consciousness at the crown of the head, described as a "thousand-petaled lotus." This was said to result in direct experience of the Divine, and indescribable bliss.

Until that morning my experiences in meditation had been good, but not remarkable. I had been practicing Transcendental Meditation as taught by Maharishi Mahesh Yogi. I had achieved with this practice states of deep physical relaxation and mental stillness, and often feelings of great inner peace and well-being. Still . . .

That morning, after doing TM for about half an hour, I practiced one of the *"kriya* breaths" that we were being taught in the seminary. This involved the combination of *pranayama*, or breath control, with a mantra. After doing this for some time, my mind became very quiet, and I felt my attention drawn further and further inward. I had the impulse to chant the Gayatri Mantra, otherwise known as the *maha*, or "great" mantra, from the Vedic tradition that I was learning.

As I did, it happened.

I felt an indescribable sensation of liquid heat break open at the very base of my spine. Simultaneously, my entire being seemed to go into a state of expansion and suspended animation. External sensory awareness receded, and along with the intense sensation in my lower spine, an equally intense, brilliant white light appeared on the inner screen of my mind at the point between the eyebrows.

I seemed to have stopped breathing. For a long, long moment, instead of the inhale and exhale of the breath, an almost electrical current rose and fell in my spine. With each oscillation, the liquid heat also rose and fell—but only to the level of my solar plexus, where it seemed to encounter a block.

While almost unbearably pleasurable, the experience also began to frighten me. Somehow I felt that if the energy were to break through the block, there would be no turning back. Some primitive instinct of self-preservation took hold of me, and this fear began to dominate.

The energy in my spine receded, and I rapidly came out of the experience. I felt my breath return to normal.

But I was euphoric. *It's true! It's true! God in heaven, it's all true!* I can remember thinking. I wept with joy, awestruck, and laughed through my tears.

That was many years ago. I continue to do my daily *sadhana*, and have felt again at times that I was on the verge of such an experience. Alas, though I long for that intense spiritual bliss, it has not happened.

But I am not discouraged. I feel blessed to have had even a small taste. For my course is set now, my faith unshakable. Though like everyone else, I am pulled this way and that by my karma, by my unfulfilled desires, by the endless attractions of this world, I know in the inner recesses of my heart that nothing external ever will satisfy. I have been fortunate to experience firsthand the truth expressed by Lord Krishna in the *Bhagavad Gita*, when he tells Arjuna:

> That which is night for all beings,
>   therein the self-controlled is awake.
> That wherein beings are awake is night
>   for the sage who sees.
>   (Chapter 2, verse 69)

For a brief moment, I was truly awake. And though I am very far from being "the sage who sees," I have no doubt that it is possible.

Nor should anyone else. Those who have been enlight-
ened, in their compassion, have shown us the way out of
our suffering.

Birthday Meditation

Shirley MacLaine

Jack Romanos, publisher at Bantam, and Stuart Apple-
baum, chief of publicity, who had accompanied me on my
book tour the summer before, walked toward us. "Everyone is ready," said Jack. "Let's go on in for your birthday
presentation."

I walked into the main conference room, where several
dozen intelligent, literary-type people stood with cham-
pagne glasses in hand waiting to see what I was like.

Jack stood on a chair and talked about how apprehensive some people at Bantam had been before *Out on a Limb*
came out, then said that if the response was any indication
of what people wanted to read these days, it was a case of
how the public was ahead of the publisher. Lou Wolfe, Bantam's President, then presented me with a dozen roses and
two beautiful leather-bound books, one of the hardback
and the other of the paperback edition of my book, housed
in a magnificent keepsake box. The crowd from Bantam applauded, then asked to hear from me. I looked at my watch.
It was 3:55 P.M. In two minutes it would be my birth time. A
spiritual guide had told me that the energy one inherits on
one's birthday is very powerful, because the sun and its
complementary planets are emitting the same aligned en-

ergy that they did the moment you were born. You "own" that energy. It is yours to use in projecting whatever you want of it for the following years. In 1983 I had gone to a mountaintop in Colorado and "projected" positively what I wanted; the success of *Terms of Endearment*, the Oscar, *Limb*, and my Broadway show. I had tried not to allow any doubt or fear to enter my mind. I needed to "know" that what I had projected would come to pass. Everything that I had projected happened. Now, as I stood before the Bantam crowd, I remembered my projections the year before. There was no mountain this time and I couldn't be alone, so I stood on a chair and thanked everyone. I explained what I had done on my birthday the year before at exactly 3:57, and I asked everyone if they would please take one minute and, in a collective mood, send me some positive thoughts about the book I was going to begin writing as soon as I left the building. No one bowed their heads, but nearly everyone closed their eyes. Some probably thought I was a lunatic, but they indulged me anyway, and I have had enough to do with audiences to know that this one genuinely wished me well.

I sopped up the positive goodwill I could feel in the room and for one minute we were silent with each other. It was a kind of collective projection.

When the minute was over and I was officially one year older, I applauded them for going along with me, thanked them, and went out to get some looseleaf notebooks and new smooth ball-point pens.

Meeting My Mother

Michael Ackerman, D.C.

Since about the age of fifteen, I had been engaged in spiritual practices and reading about the lives of Eastern saints and spiritual masters. I was initiated into the meditation practices and Kriya Yoga of Self-Realization Fellowship, and I frequently practiced *mantra japa* and studied the application of various spiritual affirmations, all with the purpose of seeking the "light" and regaining the awareness of God constantly in my life.

I equated God with this "light." He was present for me in consciousness as a crystalline quality of transcendent stillness, untouched by any manner of material or mental *forms* ... the space in meditation where the breath wanted to stop, and the all-fulfilled mind became powerfully focused to a singular ecstatic point. To experience anything other than this state of consciousness, as was my opinion for most of the years of my spiritual practices, meant that I was seeing something somewhat less *pure* and not the ultimate experience.

I practiced bringing the meditative state into the world using a mantra I gained internally by intuition: "Krishna" on the inward breath, "Om" on the outward breath. After years of repeating it, within just a few repetitions of the mantra, the world would start transforming into a Christmasy, luminous experience—where all the objects within my vision would take on an aura of the divine. Krishna became not only a person for me, but the actual experience of the transcendent father principle behind all creation.

This was, however, a best-case scenario. Most of the time, despite my spiritual efforts, I confronted darkness and negativity around almost every corner. I begged and cried for God. For years I was so sensitive to the energy in my environment that I avoided most people and places and became very reclusive—and admittedly, almost always depressed. I could not sit in a chair where someone had been sitting in a negative mood, nor would I even shake hands with anyone for fear that I would absorb hard-to-release negative energy. I was a very pitiable and poor example of what a so-called "spiritually aware" person was supposed to look like. The dichotomy in my life between light and dark, between God and not-God, was palpably present for me all through the day. Striving to hold the vision of the light consistently, seeing all things as divine, I only met with temporary success, for inevitably another instance would come when my judgmental mind or someone else's negativity would result in a fall from this state of grace.

For seventeen years, this battle raged on with only gradual progress, until a major turning point in my life came. It was 1992, and a great saint was visiting the San Francisco Bay area. Her name was Mata Amritananda Mayi, or, for short, as we know her in the West, *"Amma"* or *"Ammachi"* (The Holy Mother). She was believed by many to be one of the world's most pure spiritual luminaries of our time, a self-realized master who was egoless and lived her life as an example to us of unconditional divine love.

I had received her blessings at a few of her programs during her previous 1990 and 1991 World Tour visits to the Bay Area, and I had been most impressed. All programs were free to the public, and she embraced and received everyone with what appeared to be inexhaustible divine motherly love and spiritual energy.

I decided I had had enough confusion (Yogananda's term was "spiritual indigestion") from the many paths I had studied and was trying to integrate. So this time I

approached the Holy Mother and I asked her, with full
faith that her reply would come only as divine truth, "Who
is my guru?"

After engaging me with her sparkling eyes, and mischievously asking me questions about myself I knew she already knew the answers to, she replied with a smile, "I will
take care of you."

So began what was to become one of the greatest trans-
formational periods of my life. I had finally found my guru
after almost twenty years of consciously searching for a
spiritual master. I had tried and mysteriously failed on
three occasions in the past to travel to India, so with bated
breath I asked her, "Would Amma like me to work as a doctor at her ashram in India?"

She said, "Oh, I don't think you will like it there. But if
you wish, you can come for a two-month period of time.
After this you will know firsthand what our life is like
there, and if you like it, you can stay."

I was awestruck and teary-eyed. My long-awaited
dream of being accepted by a spiritual master and someday
moving to India was now within reach. It was only a matter
of *my* ultimate decision to chose what my future would be.
To make a long story short, after attending as many programs on Ammachi's U.S. tour as my work schedule would
permit, I made arrangements for another doctor to take
over my practice, and in mid-September I left for a two-
and-a-half-month stay in India.

In the weeks before departing for India, I had several
people tell me that they foresaw my having a unique experience there, one that would profoundly impact the course
of my life. Well, the entire visit turned out to be one miraculously powerful experience after another. Hardly a day
went by when I did not find myself repeatedly moved to
tears by the divine grace that was so markedly present in
the opportunity to perform service work, and by the grace
that powerfully guided our learning to surrender to God in
the face of the constant incredible synchronicities and miracles that occurred in the presence of the spiritual master.

I am moved, especially, to describe one particularly powerful experience. I suspect strongly that it was *the one* foreseen by several of my intuitive friends, which was to significantly alter the course of my spiritual understanding.

Great teachers such as Amma place little importance on the mystical experiences of devotees, however, emphasizing much more the greater miracle of the steady transformation of our ego-centered minds into ones that become more centered in selfless love. With this considered, I still have decided to share this experience, because it was integral to this process of transformation in me toward realizing a more all-embracing love in my life.

It was approximately one month after my arrival in India, and I was struggling to try to more consistently repeat a mantra given to me by Amma (per my request, one year earlier) while engaged in all of my work at the ashram. It was a mantra invoking the Divine Mother, and I had had a hard time with the uncomfortable burning energy it brought up in me. So I sought Amma's counsel, in hope that she would compassionately see my predicament and allow me to change back to my previous "Krishna-Om" mantra, which, after all the years of practicing it, could lift me into divine bliss almost effortlessly.

Amma's reply was loving, but very disappointing: She suggested I continue with the mantra she'd given me, and that I not use my old mantra at all.

I left very heavy-hearted. Why was I not supposed to repeat a mantra that so easily lifted me up into God? Why was this Divine Mother mantra so burning and heavy for me? What was the difference if I invoked Krishna or Divine Mother, since both were names of God?

This heaviness of heart lead to a great depression, which continued through the day and into our evening program of group devotional singing. Amma usually joined these programs each night at the ashram, and inspired everyone with the magnitude of her heart-rending calls to God, which she fervently cried out while singing with us. During a Krishna *bhajan* (devotional song), she would repeatedly cry out for him, calling him by one of his many endearing names: "Krishna!" "Shyama!" "Chitta-chora!" It lifted me up when I heard these names, because of the many years of chanting my mantra and the divine vision it almost immediately conferred upon me. However, when it came to singing a *bhajan* for the Divine Mother, and Amma crying out one of Her many names, "Ma ... Ma ... Ma ... !," "Kali ... Kali ... Kali!," "Radhe!," I hadn't been able to feel any semblance of God. The vibration of the names, to me, just didn't *feel* like God.

That night, I was in a troubled mood. I couldn't understand why, if the name *Krishna* moved me so much, I couldn't continue with his mantra. During the next song to the Divine Mother, I concentrated inwardly on trying to feel, "who is *Ma*?" as Amma called out her name. "Amma, if you are taking Krishna away from me, show me who this *Ma* is!"

At that moment I felt a kind of hollow "pop" at the base of my spine, and I was immediately flooded with an incredible ocean of ecstatic vibratory energy, rising up through my spine and thrilling every atom of my being with the cosmic sound *OM*. To my inner vision, the temple, all people, and all things around me were pervaded and empowered by this tremendous sea of conscious, deeply personal loving energy. I knew as if for the first time in all eternity that I had finally found my Mother—the Mother I had always been searching for!

For three days, I wandered in a semi-altered state of consciousness. Everywhere I looked, I could tune into the sacred sound *OM* coming from animate and inanimate objects around the ashram. My perspective on God shifted from nearly twenty years of seeing him *only* as the transcendent stillness and *light* of the formless absolute—the Divine Father principle—to also the vibrant rich loving energy of all forms (sometimes even appearing *dark*, to my perception)—the Divine Mother principle. Whereas when I had felt "negative" energy before, it was often incompatible with my staying centered in the light and Divine Father consciousness, now I was able to offer this energy up to the Divine Mother, who would easily embrace and absorb it without breaking my communion with my new deeper vision of God.

Over the years my Divine Mother mantra worked to purify me more and more, opening up a whole new aspect of God that I had previously never truly seen. Meeting Ammachi and being given the gift of this experience was the dawning of a new period of growth and transformation: After all the years of spiritual practices dedicated to reaching the *light*, now I began my equally challenging journey of lovingly embracing the *darkness* that still remained within.

A Pilgrimage

Marcia Wieder

A few years ago, while living in Washington, D.C., I was home one evening finishing a wonderful book called *The Mists of Avalon*. Something inside me told me to go to the roof of my building. It was a warm summer night, so I thought, *Why not?*

With the full moon above me, I found myself slowly dancing around and softly singing, "I'm free to be, I'm free to be." My rational mind thought this was absurd, but the rest of me liked it. This lasted about twenty minutes.

I went home and felt like taking a bath. I lit a few candles, got into the tub to relax—and started to sense this funny voice in my head saying the word "Shasta." I wondered why I would be thinking about a soft drink.

After my bath, I went to the dictionary and looked up "Shasta." I saw a description of Mt. Shasta, in Northern

California. I decided to call my psychic friend and minister, Barbara Hamilton, who is versed in this sort of thing. She became very excited and told me that she'd had a very mystical experience on the mountain, and I should consider going there. *Yeah, sure,* I thought.

The next day I received a free ticket to California. Okay, I can take a hint, and I do practice recognizing signs. I enlisted my best girlfriend from Los Angeles in making this trek. She told her darling husband that she was off on an adventure with me for two weeks.

Before I knew it, while rendezvousing in San Francisco, I told her that the purpose of this trip was to reclaim my magical powers. I'm not sure that I knew what I was saying or that I believed it, but there we were and off we went.

We took four days to drive up the coast, even though we could have gotten there in about seven hours. We meditated, laughed, journaled, and hot-tubbed the whole way. We even dabbled with tarot cards, although neither one of us really knew much about them. I was a credible Washington businesswoman. I didn't do such things. However, here I was.

When we got to the mountain, it was so big that it was overwhelming. It would actually take us two more days to get the nerve to go up. Finally, on the Fourth of July, we did it.

Seated quietly on that mountain, I had this amazing memory. Whether the incident actually happened or not doesn't matter. But what I made it mean did matter.

I remembered blowing up on the mountain. It was like I put a little too much spice into the soup, and the whole mountain blew, including me. I had this image of being a wizard or something like that and standing over a cauldron.

I interpreted the experience to mean that I'd screwed up, that I couldn't be trusted and that my power was too much for me. I also made it mean that God and the universe and life in general could not be counted on.

At that moment, I felt extreme sadness. How many years

of my life, I wondered, had I carried around this judgment? How long had I been repressing my power, my self-expression, and my magic? I yelled out, as loud as I could, "No more! I reclaim my power here and now!" My friend said I yelled so loud it hurt her ears.

And I thought I heard back a soft whisper that said, "She who remembers is free."

She who remembers is free. By remembering who we are, powerful and magical people, we will be forever free. What a gift to receive on Independence Day.

Did it happen? Was it all symbolic, or perhaps a dream? It didn't matter, but the deep teaching from that day sure did.

Was it real? Well, when we came down from the mountain I noticed that I could now read the tarot cards without the interpretation book. I recognized the archetypes and symbols and remembered information that I had not learned in this lifetime. Shocked at first, I realized I had new found clarity and felt somewhat magical.

So I treated it as though it was real. I declared the day a major initiation in my life, and will forever hold and honor it that way. By the time we got back to San Francisco, I had decided to move to California. I was ready to live a very different kind of life.

My Choice

Rachel Naples

I was living below my potential and I knew it. What I didn't know was how to get out of the rut I'd found myself wallowing in. I was sure my brain was missing a synapse or something equally important.

I awakened one night in the middle of what I thought was a dream . . . but it was still happening as I lay in bed. I was engaged in conversation with a higher aspect of myself, and I was being given the opportunity to have breast cancer.

One thing was clear: It was up to me. Apparently there were a few things cancer had to teach me, but I could also choose to learn those lessons another way. There were several reasons I was attracting this disease to me, but perhaps the most important was that I had very low self-esteem at the time, although I wasn't aware of it.

I asked what the quality of life would be like after radiation. Now, this really disturbed my conscious mind, because I realized I was actually considering getting sick. That was *not* where I wanted to go, and I took a stand, rallying the other parts of my personality, imploring them to listen to me.

Then I found myself on a gurney in a beautiful healing room. There was a man there who I learned was a doctor from Canada, and he was sticking energy needles in my breasts—which, by the way, he did on many occasions after this. The group of beings who were with me, much like my physical friends, told me that this doctor was the one of the best for this type of healing. I remember saying, "He'd better be the best. This is my body we're talking about!" Although I was serious, we all had a few laughs.

This doctor gave me a mantra to "take back" with me. Then I must have fallen unconscious for a few moments, because I found myself, like Dorothy from Oz, back in my bed—murmuring over and over, "I count. No matter what I do or don't do, I count. I am important."

I got out of bed and, needless to say, was very distressed. I thought I was going to have cancer, because I didn't fully trust what had just happened.

Later that day, the man I was living with at the time, who knew nothing about what had transpired, suggested I listen to Dr. Gershon Lesser's radio show. I resisted, thinking I'd heard it all before, but he flipped it on anyway. What I heard changed me forever, as if I hadn't already been changed forever as it was!

Dr. Lesser said that millions of women die needlessly of breast cancer every year because they don't think they're important or valuable. Energy poured through my body as I sat there, stunned. I quickly flipped open Louise Hay's book *You Can Heal Your Life* and looked up breast cancer. It, too, alluded to low self-worth. Both of these were vehicles from Spirit to wake me up to what was going on in my body, and confirm what had happened on the inner planes.

One of the other things I needed to learn, I was told during that inner plane experience, was compassion. I guess there's nothing like a little cancer to open up the heart! "Is there another way for me to learn this?" I'd asked. "Yes," I was told. But they didn't tell me how, or at least I didn't remember what they'd said. So I had the opportunity to remain in a state of terror—which immediately summons compassion, as I've learned!

Shortly thereafter, I had another such experience. I was a little girl of five, and my father was standing beside me. I asked, "What kind of cancer do you want me to have, Daddy?" This sent me into panic as I sat there observing, because I realized I hadn't made up my mind yet. I also saw that at a very young age, I'd agreed to take on my father's illnesses—but that I was able to break those agreements, too. (Interestingly enough, my father did get cancer. I'm happy to say that we are both alive and well today.)

I desperately asked the beings who surrounded me, "What is this about? I need help. I don't want to die."

The answer quietly came back: "Compassion." Apparently I wasn't getting the message.

But how was I supposed to learn compassion? It's not like you can pick up a book and study it. I felt like I was being punished for something, but I wasn't sure what.

Mortal fear ran through me for the next few months—and in the process, believe me, I learned compassion. I didn't know I was learning it, but I found that the constant fear of my own death was making me look at others with new eyes.

But why were there so many people suffering on the planet, and so many of them from cancer? I had one more inner plane experience that somehow tied it all together. Here goes.

I'm walking through a beautiful landscape. Emerald green grass, soft as velvet, caresses my feet. Mountains in shades of purple, lilac blue, and violet tower majestically over me. I look around and realize that I'm in a cemetery. I come upon a tombstone carving of a tortured Jesus nailed to a cross. Blood streams down his legs and arms. His face is twisted in agony and ecstasy.

I drop to my knees and shriek at the top of my lungs, "No!" My voice echoes through the cemetery.

Then my aunt, who died of breast cancer, appears before me on a white horse—but they are both transparent. She offers me a vial to drink from. Instantly, I know she's giving me her recipe for life, except to me, it stinks of death.

I turn sharply away and say, "Get thee behind me, Satan!" The horse and my aunt instantly disappear.

Jesus comes down from the cross and stands before me, caressing my cheek. "It was all made up, Rachel. Be of good cheer. Go and tell the others."

And then he dissolves into a million tiny sparks of light.

The Joy of the Worlds

Deborah Chenault

Like a crocus pushing up through the last hard frost, March 1995 found me emerging from my own deep winter: a depression that had left me unsteadily poised on the brink of the abyss, ready to topple back in.

My mind spun with terms like seasonal affective disorder, existential depression, and dysthymia, all proposed as possible diagnoses of my condition. Prozac, Paxil, electroconvulsive therapy, and cognitive therapy were tossed about as possible treatments. I tried most of them, but nothing cured me. I improved slightly, combed my hair, and sometimes put on lipstick in crazy slashes of blood red, too dark for my blonde hair and fair skin. And I was no longer threatening to take my own life.

Still, nothing offered the answers I was seeking. Why are we here? What's the point of existence when life inevitably yields suffering? Why is the world growing colder, more violent? Is there a God? Why did He give us these physical bodies to lose ourselves in, to distract us, to hamper our divine spirit? It seemed an odd marriage, flesh and spirit. I longed to shed the one and ascend as the other, if there was a God and if He would have me.

"I think you have the classic artist's disease," my therapist said one day. "Virginia Woolf, Ernest Hemingway, William Styron. It got them all."

I nodded, but didn't care. "I need to feel the sun on my shoulders," I told him.

In the middle of that March, flu swept the university campus where I was running errands, photocopying articles, and performing general grunt work to support my writing habit. In my weakened psychological and physical condition, I succumbed to the virus. For a week my fever raged, eventually pushing to 103 for five consecutive days. Already worn and worried from battling that other sickness with me, my partner urged me to go to the hospital. I refused. To placate him, I drank the hot broth he offered and shoveled more aspirin into my mouth, telling him I felt better.

Secretly, I believed my prayers had been answered. There *was* a God who would have me, and He was surely letting me die in a way that would leave everyone blameless. In lucid dreams I could already feel my spirit leaving my body, paradoxically released from my physicality by the physical: a burning fever that allowed me to float freely over my sleeping self, slowly bidding farewell to the sad woman in the bed below.

On that fifth evening of fever, en route to the bathroom, I passed out. In the brief time between my collapse and the discovery of my limp, unconscious body by my partner, I found myself at the bottom of a high, sloping, softly curved mound. I knew I must climb the slope to reach the opening that I saw there at its apex . . . but then covered my mouth with my hand and looked down in embarrassed laughter.

The opening had the shape of a vagina—and I was hesitant, I said to no one in particular, to enter into another woman's womb. Some urge propelled me, though, and I took one step up to find myself suddenly in the opening of the womb. There was only enough room for me to stand in the fleshy doorway, which I could now see opened onto a new dimension.

Through there, somewhere worlds away, there was a warm light half hidden by a horizon. Was it sunrise or sunset? I could not tell. When I swung my arm and leg out from the portal where I stood, they lost all weight and mass, floating freely. Time fell away. I giggled as I watched points of light fly past me into the old world, their own laughter a high, musical vibration in my ear. I turned to look back. The warm light from worlds away fell on my shoulders, and I could feel its knowledge illuminating my body as I peered down into the world from which I had come.

There I saw things as they really were, in a new light. I saw worries and concerns of friends that had been hidden from me before; I saw the answers to their problems. If I could see their answers, then could I see my own? I turned back toward the new world, warmth washing over my face, to ask my questions. There was no need to formulate them, the answers simply came.

"There is evil in the world."

I wheeled back around to witness spots of darkness sprinkled like black pepper over the landscape. I saw them massed together, hovering just outside the portal through which they could not pass. I saw the points of light touching these spots, transforming them, changing their color to white.

"Your body is a lesson."

And I witnessed the pattern of my life's growth through the adversity of the flesh. I saw the forging of my strength and awareness.

One by one, the answers came.

In the days that followed, as I began to recover, I thought about the dream with wonder and delight. I believed I knew things that I had not known before, with absolute certainty. All the things I had asked for, I received. Then one morning in the shower, my skin peeled from my body in long, translucent layers—a result of the sustained fever, I supposed. This, too, I took as a blessing, a transformation, the symbolic answer to my desire to shed my physical self in order for my spirit to ascend.

In later weeks, I sought out my friends to tell them what I had seen, to offer solutions to the problems I had not known existed before. "How did you know that?" they asked, thinking their secrets had been carefully guarded. Hesitantly, a little embarrassed, I would recount the dream. "It wasn't a dream," some of them told me. "It was a vision."

I look back at that experience as the night the old me died, my baptism by fire. I've read enough about the subject and had enough therapy to know that the "experts" would say my high fever brought on my hallucinatory dream, that my subconscious was merely revealing to my conscious mind the subtleties it had filed away over the months and years. It was telling me things, they would say, that I already knew.

Perhaps. But this past autumn, the season that had always heralded my major depressive episodes, I waited to see if I was really better. I waited for the raven to perch on my head and fold her black wings over my eyes, bringing the inevitable darkness. But she did not come. Instead, I found myself working, writing again, laughing, living one day at a time in the light, squinting like a wrinkled, pink-skinned newborn with her eyes first open.

In the midst of my work, researching an essay, I stumbled upon a 1937 painting by Cecil Collins called "The Joy of the Worlds." It depicts a naked pilgrim in the portal of an amniotic womb, with a halo of light around his head. Beyond him, out among the worlds, white lights sail by. I remember gasping and shouting for my partner to come see, to come see what someone had seen before me.

Today, when I look at this painting, I can almost hear the high musical vibration of the lights, and feel again the weightlessness of my arms and legs. I wanted to write to

VISION 271

Cecil Collins, to ask him about the painting. To my disappoint, I discovered that he had passed on in 1989. But I talk
to him anyway, believing that on that other side, he can
hear me. Did you have my vision, Mr. Collins? Did you,
like so many of us, suffer from that nasty artist's disease?
And I laugh, because it doesn't matter that our lessons make
us suffer. The suffering is as transitory as our physicality.

I often step outside now, empowered with flowering
hope and knowledge, to witness the nearest phenomenon I
can find in this world to that wonderful illuminating
light—the sunrise. Or is it the sunset? The Alpha? Or the
Omega?

Christmas at the Oasis

Arielle Ford

I felt like I was heading for a total burnout. I was physically
and emotionally drained, and had suddenly realized that
I'd been going nonstop for about three years. If I didn't get
some deep rest soon, I thought, I'd be putting my health
at risk.

I decided to drive out to the desert to a little spa I'd
heard about for years. It was a small, quaint place known
for its healing waters.

I spent the first few days in silence, speaking only when
absolutely necessary. My days were spent soaking in the
hot mineral springs, receiving massages, eating nourishing
foods, reading a few spiritual books, and sleeping in my
little cabin.

Each day I would meditate in the early morning and late afternoon. On my final night, I decided to listen to a meditation tape in addition to my usual mantra meditation. Within seconds of closing my eyes, something very strange began to happen.

I saw a very large white rabbit sitting near my feet. As soon as I noticed him, he began to hop away through a very beautiful forest with tall, exotic trees. I began to follow, and he began to hop faster and faster. Soon I was running just to keep up with him, and before I knew it I was actually flying through the air. I followed the rabbit all the way to the edge of the forest, where he vanished—and I kept flying.

In front of me was a snow-covered mountain. There was a stream running down it, with a little wooden platform beside. I landed on the platform and found myself face to face with a monk wearing a deep burgundy robe.

He was a gentle, compassionate man. He thanked me for taking the time to visit him. I don't remember everything he said to me. After a while, he told me that it was time to continue on my journey.

Once again I found myself flying through the air, headed toward another mountain. It was green and tropical, with craggy peaks. I noticed a small golden temple next to a waterfall. I landed at the door of the temple and went in.

It was quite dark, but there was a skylight illuminating a giant orchid in the middle of the room. As I stood there trying to get my bearings, an older woman with very long gray hair emerged from the orchid and walked toward me. As I looked at her, I realized she was a much older me.

At that moment, a little girl emerged from behind her skirts: It was me as a three-year-old. She was wearing a black and white polka-dot party dress and pink Mary Jane shoes.

They both hugged me, thanked me for coming, and commended me for taking the time out of my busy schedule to rest and renew myself. Both of them seemed joyful and happy to see me, and I soaked up all the love that I felt from both of them.

The old woman then said it was time for me to go on. She showed me to a door in the back of the temple, and told me that when I was ready, I should open the door and step through it. It was quite dark. I closed my eyes, pulled open the door, and took a giant step forward. When my foot landed on solid ground, I opened my eyes.

It took me a minute to figure it out, but sure enough, I was standing inside the middle of a huge Christmas tree. All around me I could see twinkling lights, and Christmas ornaments I instantly remembered seeing on other people's trees as a child (we were Jewish, and never had a tree). And directly in front of me was Santa Claus, sitting in a big ornate chair.

He motioned for me to come and sit in his lap. I walked over, sat down, and put my arm around his neck. Looking at his face, I noticed his eyes and eyebrows, and realized that I was looking into my own eyes. Then he asked me what I wanted for Christmas, and I immediately began to recite a long list of things that I have always wanted.

"You shall have them all."

At that moment I noticed a large cross of white light coming down from the top of the tree. When the cross was hovering at shoulder height, I took my arm from behind Santa's and put it around the cross. The cross slowly lifted me up, up, up . . . through the top of the tree and out into the night sky.

Flying across the midnight sky, the cross turned into Jesus, and suddenly I was lying in Jesus's arms, being flown across the sky. I looked into his eyes and said, "It's true, you really do exist. You're real."

Jesus looked at me with an incredibly loving expression on his face, and simply smiled.

A moment later I found myself sitting in the chair in my cabin.

Medicine Woman

Carl Studna

Several years ago, my friend Andrea and I were in the midst of one of my favorite exercises. I call it "Soul Gazing": you simply look into each other's eyes without speaking for what seems like an eternity, observing whatever feelings, thoughts and pictures come up for you.

At one point while we were in this timeless zone, I had a strong memory of knowing Andrea in another lifetime. She was the revered Medicine Woman of our Native American tribe, and I was a shy and awkward young brave. She was formidable and all-powerful. I was in awe. I was scared of her.

Looking into Andrea's eyes grew more and more intense as the memories crystallized. I knew that she could see what I was seeing, and I began to feel frightened and very small.

It was time to end this exercise. In an instant we were back in my living room, safe in familiar territory.

I began to tell her what I'd seen. "Andrea, I was this young Indian brave and you were . . . the chief's wife."

Yes, I actually told her that she was the chief's wife, for in that moment I didn't want her to appear more powerful than me.

In response, she boldly looked me in the eyes and said, "No, I wasn't. I was the Medicine Woman!"

Initiation

Brent BecVar

During my late twenties, I returned to visit my family home after some far-flung travels in search of myself. I was able to rest there for a week or so, in the comfort of that most familiar environment.

Settling into my old bedroom that first evening, I recalled for a while, as I watched the fading sunlight move slowly across the walls, how many dreams had emerged in this safe enclosure when I was younger. Then I felt I wanted to close my eyes and begin to meditate, as was my custom around sunset.

As my body began to relax in the cooling darkness, I felt the deep fatigue and stress of so many miles, of so much searching, begin to fall away, seeping out of every pore. Diving deeper and deeper inside, I felt thoughts flickering briefly, now and again, as they rushed out and away. With each breath, restrictions, apprehensions, alarms, anxieties, heartaches and disappointments continued to melt and flow away in favor of that familiar peace, that silence where everything begins again.

Recalling this experience now, I don't remember exactly how what follows began, except that I was by that time deep in silent meditation. I only remember suddenly feeling as though I was moving through the air, accelerating quickly to great speed, flying headfirst with my arms at my sides.

My awareness was completely taken up by the sun before me, drawing me toward it, as though its desire and my own were one. There was no fear as I felt my whole being soaring at tremendous speed, over a great distance, straight toward the center of the sun. My heart and the heart of the sun were the same, as desire drew me into this blessing: the Solar Gateway.

I knew instinctively that this was a doorway of knowledge and purification. And as I burst through the sun, I felt worlds extending in every direction, beyond beyond—worlds I'd never known—and peace again gathered around me.

I found myself standing on the surface of a cool silver planet, empty and still as the surface of the moon. I felt that I was exactly where I should be, at precisely the right time.

Almost immediately, coming from a great distance at the farthest horizon, through the semidarkness, I felt rather than saw a solitary figure moving toward me. I was transfixed with anticipation, not knowing what manner of being this could be, not knowing what else to do, since there was nowhere else to go.

I strained to see, finally discerning the silhouetted shape of a human man coming closer, closer . . . but now seemingly with some trepidation, as though he too were trying to see who I was. As his face and eyes became visible in the soft twilight, I saw with surprise that it was another *me*—and I knew that he was having the same thoughts as I, at the same time, recognizing me as I was recognizing him!

In that moment of recognition I was overwhelmed with emotion. Compassion dawned, and our hearts melted, met, and were united. I knew I was complete. Love flowed through every part of me as I accepted myself as I was.

As my awareness came back to the room where I was sitting, I felt tears of joy streaming down my cheeks. And when I opened my eyes, I knew that something profound had happened to me, and that I would never be as I was before. I had changed—not into someone else, but into a clearer knowledge of myself.

It felt as though, at some preappointed time, the coding of my very DNA had allowed an awakening, like the chrysalis's transformation into the butterfly. I felt more a part of the human race than ever: Knowing myself as I had never known myself before, I knew compassion. And I saw that my life had prepared me for this event in unaccountable ways. I see now that every choice brings us closer to that next initiation, at a time no one can guess in advance.

Heart to Heart

Madelaine Roig

I was traveling through central California with a good friend, and we stopped for lunch at a favorite restaurant of mine in San Luis Obispo. Over our table was a painting of Jesus Christ smoking a cigarette, aptly entitled "Smokin' Jesus." Tickled by this deliciously blasphemous image, we had some good laughs, but soon thereafter found ourselves deep in a heart-to-heart about the significance of Jesus Christ in our lives.

I told my friend that I had no relationship with Christ because I'd been raised Jewish, and I asked him about his. His eyes got misty, and he smiled, saying, "It's one of the most beautiful things." I reflected for a moment, then said, "Well . . . I'd be open to having a relationship with Christ."

Our trip ended a couple of days later with tragic news. My cousin and her husband had been in a terrible car accident. My cousin, six months pregnant, was in critical condition. Her husband had been killed. I was grief-stricken, and my friend offered to stay the night with me, but I had to be alone. I went home, lit all the candles in my house, and began a prayer vigil for my cousin, her beloved late husband, and their unborn child. As I prayed, the faces of everyone I loved came before my eyes, and one by one I said prayers for every one of them, too. Then I went to bed, and soon to sleep.

The next thing I knew, Jesus was standing before me, radiant. So beautiful was his presence that it took my breath away. His eyes and hair were dark, not like the many pictures I'd seen of him with blue eyes and light brown hair.

Without hesitation I walked up to him and, one foot at a time, stepped onto his feet, the way children stand on adults' feet to dance with them. This put our hearts in exact alignment. I pressed my body against his, chest to chest, and I felt his heart open into mine.

I was instantly flooded with the most overwhelming love, which I can only describe as all-encompassing light and bliss. Through waves of ecstasy, I could feel Jesus's body in contact with mine, my arms wrapped around his shoulders.

I felt as if I had no will or strength of my own, yet I was holding onto him. All I knew was that this heart-opening, this merging, this loss of self, was more pleasurable than anything I had ever known.

Jesus then began to walk backward, and I, still on his feet, walked with him. But he was moving away from me, communicating with his eyes that it was time for him to go, to move on, to continue his work. I guess I should have been grateful that he'd stopped by to see me, but instead I began to panic. I felt my stomach clench and tears well up in my eyes. I tightened my grip and said, "Now that I have tasted of this love, you cannot leave me without it!"

Jesus continued to move away from me with a calm and reassuring expression on his face. I was not reassured. Like a child anticipating the agony of abandonment, I begged him not to go. Clutching at him, my tears turned to sobs, the sobs to wails. "Don't leave! Take me with you. Please don't go!" The unfathomable joy of only moments before had now become unspeakable anguish.

And then . . . all of a sudden, I was awake.

The first thing I was aware of was my breathing, and then my hands, which were folded over my heart. The anguish was gone. I felt at peace.

Then I felt the stirring. It was coming from beneath my hands. It was my heart, and it felt alive with an energy I had never known before, but have since grown accustomed to. I recognized this energy as love: compassionate, unconditional, unmistakable love! And it's with me every day now, not just when there is a miracle or a tragedy. It doesn't just appear when I am attached to someone, and it doesn't go away when I'm separated from those I love. It isn't something I have to earn.

So I haven't converted, and I don't read Scripture, but I know now that I was initiated into what is referred to as "Christ consciousness." After thirty-seven years on this planet, I can now honestly say, "Thank you, Jesus."

My cousin survived the accident and has recovered physically. Through time, and the love and support of family, friends, rabbi, and support groups, she is learning to live and love again. She buried her child with her beloved: Their infant daughter was placed on his chest, encircled in his arms—the two eternally heart to heart.

Nothing Matters

Neale Donald Walsch

I'd had words with my wife that night. Don't ask me what our tiff was about; I'm sure it was something silly, though, like whose turn it was to take out the garbage. It was always something silly when we had our disagreements.

I retired for the night early—and alone. My wife stayed in the family room, icily watching television. I hated this feeling of separation and disharmony, yet I felt powerless to stop creating the experiences in my life that produced it. My ulcer was bothering me again, so before turning in I marched to the bathroom for some medication. Passing the family room, I thought of apologizing to my wife, but something wouldn't let me give in. Instead, I began marshaling my arguments for the morning. I had already thought of a few things I could have said that night, but didn't . . .

Back in bed, I hit the pillow hard. Exhausted, frustrated, and more than a little upset that the evening had been lost to bickering and hassling, I cried out silently, "Why can't we just be happy?"

I tossed and turned for a bit, then, as suddenly as if someone had thrown a switch, I fell asleep. I remember a dim awareness, at the edge of wakefulness, that this would be the deepest sleep of my life.

It could have been many hours later, or just minutes, when I was abruptly awakened by an overwhelming sensation that I was falling off the bed . . . *upward*. That's the only way I can describe it.

My breath gone, my heart pounding, I opened my eyes—and all sense of panic melted. I don't know why. It just . . . went away, and I was filled with a certainty that everything was perfectly all right. I was perfectly at peace—even as I floated somewhere near the ceiling, *looking down at my body*.

There I was, on the bed, sleeping . . . but the part of me that I experience as "me" was not in that body. I was pure thought, pure consciousness. I was an awareness, not a physical being—and I instantly realized that this is what I have always been.

Looking down, I saw a lump of flesh that appeared very much like me, and yet, in a strange way, not like me at all. Rather like a corpse looks, but *doesn't* look, like the person it is supposed to be. I felt a great sadness as I contemplated my body, so limiting, so restricting, so unbelievably bound and heavy. I just couldn't imagine how anyone—least of all my very Self—could exist imprisoned in such an encasement. One thing I did know for sure: *No one was imprisoned there now!*

In the moment of that realization I was whisked out of the room with a noiseless *whoosh*—sucked backward right through the ceiling. I found myself racing at insane speed through a dark tunnel. Then, abruptly, I "popped" into a space of extraordinary wonder.

There were billions of tiny particles dancing before me, shining, shimmering, and pulsating with brilliant color. Some were blue, some red, some green . . . but not just ordinary blues, reds, and greens. These were the richest blues, the reddest reds, the deepest emerald greens, and my eyes filled with tears at the sight. I am, you see, color-blind.

Now I said my eyes filled with tears, but that was a *sensation*, not a reality. In reality I had no eyes, nor hands, nor feet, nor any body parts at all. I was only that part of me which exists behind my eyes. But it *felt* as though I had eyes. And when I "reached" for something, it *felt* as though I had hands. I know that, because I tried reaching for one of the shimmering particles. It was like reaching with invisible hands, like reaching out with your thoughts, if that makes any sense.

I wanted to touch, to hold these incredible shimmering particles of color. But I couldn't. Each time I tried to touch one, it moved away, tantalizingly out of reach. So I could only watch in awe as these countless particles of light danced and vibrated before me. It was then that I saw something I'd missed before. They were changing color and shape.

Each of these "particles" was connected with another, like pieces in a jigsaw puzzle. And now each was changing shape and size and color at will. As each one did so, the particles to which it was connected changed *their* shape and size and color as well, in a silent chorus of continuing accommodation. The whole of the action produced a breathtaking mosaic of pulsating, shimmering, changing colors and shapes, stretching as far as I could perceive in every direction.

I found myself literally in the midst of this. And somehow I knew then what I was seeing: It was life. The raw material of *life itself*. I was seeing All That Is, in its submolecular form. I was seeing pure energy. The Force of the Universe. The Source. The Power. The Cause and the Effect.

"How simple," I thought. "How incredibly, elegantly *simple*."

And now I wanted to get closer to it more than ever. I moved forward, but again it moved out of reach. I moved up and down, left and right, and with each move, it moved. I could not get any closer.

Then, in a flash, I understood why—and it seemed so obvious to me, I wondered why I hadn't figured it out sooner. I could not get any closer *to* it because I *was* it! As I moved, it moved. Of course: One can't get closer to one's nose by moving one's eyes!

I knew then that I was not looking at this mosaic, this pattern, from someplace outside of it, but from deep within it. I was It, and It was Me. I was looking at the rest of Me.

Just as this understanding dawned, my surroundings changed. It was as if something or someone *knew* that I had just reached comprehension, and so shifted the experience. At once, everything went dark. I felt I was in a vacuum, the only thing there. And then, in the very next instant, I felt . . . the only word that comes close is "embraced." I felt held, hugged, immersed in a feeling of total acceptance and total love.

First there was just this warmth; then it manifested as light. I seemed to be floating in a nowhere void, held in an egg-shaped cocoon of the softest, warmest light. The feelings of love and acceptance were overwhelming, and I bowed my "head" in reverence . . . and in shame. Again I experienced myself crying, this time not with joy, but sadness.

"I don't deserve this," I said with my thought. "No, not me. Not with all the black marks on my soul. This gift belongs to someone else. Someone far better, more perfect than I."

Then I heard a voice, the deepest, richest, softest voice I had ever heard. A voiceless voice I did not "hear" at all, but *experienced*. It said softly, ever so gently, with complete compassion and deepest understanding:

"You are my Beloved. And you are perfect, just as you are. In this moment and in this form, and in every moment and every form, I see only that which is good, that which is pure, that which is exquisite. You are my Beloved, and I know only love for you. I will never know anything else. I will never see you any other way. You are safe, now and always. Now . . . and always."

Once more I wept, this time with the relief of deep knowing. What was being said to me was true. I knew that. I knew it at the depth of my being, and my heart filled to overflowing.

Again the "scene" changed, and again in the same instant comprehension arrived. I was being given one more experience, one more awareness before I would have to go back to my body.

I found myself before a large book, the largest I had ever seen. Each page contained enough information to fill an encyclopedia. Each page was onionskin-paper thin, and the book had millions of them.

As I stood before the book, the Voiceless Voice spoke again. "Okay," it said. "All right. You've wanted to know, to really understand, for so long. Your search has been true. Your desire has been real and pure. So here. Here it is. Everything there is to know."

With that, the book opened and its pages flipped past with a gentle speed, as if blown by the breath of God itself. As each page passed, its contents were absorbed by me, totally, completely, instantaneously. It all happened in a nanosecond, and in this nanosecond I found the answers to every question I'd ever asked—and to questions I never knew existed.

When it was over, I said simply, "Of *course*." It was as if the obvious had finally become obvious to me.

Now my journey was complete, and as quickly as it had begun, it ended. I was back in my bedroom, back in my body. I felt incredibly heavy. It seemed impossible to move. I sensed my wife lying beside me. I could not guess how long she'd been there, or how long I'd been "away." It did not seem to matter.

I thought, *I'd better write this down. Wow, what an incredible dream!* I reached for paper and pencil on the nightstand beside me. Often I've awakened from a dream I knew I wanted to write down, but had never done so. This time I was not going to fail. It was important that this time I have a record of what went on, of what I had seen and learned. And I guess I wanted to prove . . . well, prove that I had "been there."

As I reached toward the night table a thought filled my head. It did not feel like "my" thought, but a thought coming from somewhere else.

"There is no need to do that. It would be as pointless as writing down two plus two equals four. The truth need not be proven nor disproven. It *is*. Simply know that you know it."

I found that my hand would not move, and I did not want it to move. I'd lost all need or desire to write down anything. I brought my arm back to the bed and allowed my head to sink into the pillow.

Then I heard the Voiceless Voice one last time. It said, simply, quietly, calmly:

"Nothing matters."

A great peace came over me. I let go not only of any anxiety I may have had to write anything down, but of all anxiety over anything. And I knew I need never have another argument with my wife, or with anyone, again. My time of arguing could be over. All I had to do was remember. In the moments when I could remember what I knew, there would be nothing to fight over, ever.

The next morning, and in the days and weeks that followed, I tried very hard to figure out what it all meant to me. Standing in the shower that following morning, I knew that something was different, but I couldn't figure out what. I felt (boy, I hate to use this word) transformed. I felt "at one" with the water—and strangely in love with it. I felt "at one," too, with the shower curtain to my left, the tiles to my right, the fixtures in front of me . . . everything.

As I stood there, I tried remembering my dream. Mostly I tried remembering what I had seen in that Book—and my mind was filled once more with the Voiceless Voice. It said, "You are not to remember."

Surprisingly, no sense of frustration followed that. I seemed to understand that if I were to retain all the wisdom and knowledge to which my mind had been exposed, I would be unable to handle it. My mind would "fry." The circuits would blow, or something. I just knew that, and accepted it.

But I also knew that anytime in my life I needed answers, I would get them. They had not been taken from me, but kept in "storage" for whenever I needed them. I knew, too, that I was not alone in this. I knew that *everyone* had access to this knowledge and this wisdom, and that when we needed answers, all we needed to do was ask.

Twelve years later I had occasion to test that theory. The result was an extraordinary series of dialogues with that same Voiceless Voice. I called these dialogues my own private conversations with God.

7

THE
OTHER
SIDE

Spiritual Courage

Joan Borysenko

The mystic poet William Blake said, "If the doors of perception were cleansed, man would see everything as it is, infinite." Psychological courage entails just such a cleansing of the doors of perception, allowing us to see things as they really are rather than through the distorted lens of the past. The more we are cleansed of expectations, the more we see what is and the more we can respond to it creatively.

In those moments when we are fully present to life—the moments of grace—we experience love, gratitude, awe, joy, security, and compassion. There is no fear. We know this when we are in the midst of a rapture, transported by the stark beauty of a mountain path or lost in the eyes of our beloved. We know this when we abandon our little selves and find our greater Selves in song or dance. We know this when an amazing serendipity delights us and we are reminded again that coincidence, as the old saying goes, is just God's way of remaining anonymous. Unfortunately, we tend to forget it the rest of the time. Spiritual courage grows through our willingness to keep on remembering, to keep on searching for the sacred behind all the seemingly mundane and even terrible facets of life.

Spiritual courage is more than faith that the universe is friendly and that, despite all earthly appearance to the contrary, we are ultimately safe. It is the *inner knowing* that this is so. That knowing is the composite of all our experiences, dreams, serendipities and practices of remembering—such as meditations and prayers as well as the "tingles of recognition" and "aha's" we feel when someone else's story awakens our remembering and becomes part of our soul-knowledge.

My own courage was given a considerable boost as a result of a remarkable series of events that surrounded the death of my mother in March 1988. Although her death from emphysema and congestive heart failure was slow and must surely have been quite uncomfortable as her heart and lungs failed and her body swelled like a water balloon, she rarely complained. Not a woman to show her emotions in life, she didn't reveal them at death's door either. In her final hours, Mom's manner of finishing old business was simple and direct. She turned her face up at me as we rode together in an elevator on the way back from one final test, saying, "I've made a lot of mistakes in my life. Will you forgive me, Joanie?"

I squeezed her hand and replied simply and in kind, "I forgive you, Mom. I've made a lot of mistakes, too. Will you forgive me?" She nodded, and we rode in silence to her room. My brother was there with his children. My husband and two sons were there. Other relatives, friends and the two loyal women who had cared for my mother during her long illness were there as well, all gathered to say their last good-byes.

The sun was setting already, casting long shadows on a cold Saint Patrick's Day evening that held the barest hint of the coming spring. The hospital windows overlooked the Boston skyline, and the lights of the city began to awaken in the violet twilight. It was the last time we would experience a sunset together. We held hands, she lying still and heavy on the white sheets, supported by pillows since she was too weak to keep herself from falling to the side. This formidable woman looked so vulnerable and yet so at peace.

"Mom," I began, looking into remarkably sweet and innocent eyes, eyes that used to sparkle with mischief and would often flash with anger. "Mom, I want to exchange gifts with you. I want to exchange a special quality, a soul quality that we admire in one another." I hesitated for a moment, wondering if this sensible, concrete woman would think I was crazy. She clearly did not. Moved by her vulnerability and by a feeling of mutual trust, I continued, "I have always admired your courage. I ask it as a gift from you."

She smiled at me and pressed my hand with her waning strength. "I give you courage," she said. "And I ask you for compassion."

There was so much love in that moment. She saw me as compassionate. (As I typed this last sentence, by the way, my unconscious reversed the letters in "saw." I typed "she was me as compassionate." That slip, perhaps, captures the essence of our bonding better than words do.) I felt seen, acknowledged, valued. I never thought of her as admiring compassion, nor did I expect she would have seen it in me since I had often been more angry than compassionate to her in the forty-three years of our relationship. Perhaps she was also surprised that I saw her as courageous, but I did. She personified that first kind of courage—indomitable will, the ability to keep on trucking no matter what.

Mom drifted in and out of consciousness for the rest of the evening. She sometimes spoke of seeing the Light, returning to consciousness fully in character, cracking a few last jokes before she slipped into a final morphine-assisted sleep. Our son Justin, my brother, Alan, and I stayed with her that long night as she labored to give birth to her soul. We sang to her, held her, prayed for her, sat with her and alternately roamed the hospital corridors.

At one point I sat meditating in her room and was suddenly overcome by a vivid vision that pulled me out of normal, waking consciousness into another realm. It was a luminous kind of experience during which every cell in my body felt wonderfully alive, and I knew that I was witnessing a deeper reality than is usually perceptible.

In the vision I was a pregnant mother, laboring to give birth to a baby. Remarkably, I was simultaneously the baby in the process of being born. Although the birth superficially involved pain and fear, it was deeply joyful, peaceful and transcendent. As the mother I felt the holiness of being a gateway into life. As the baby I was in wondrous awe of the bright, mysterious and awesome Light I saw at the end of the long, dark tunnel of birth. From the perspective of being both mother and child, I felt totally at one with my mother. Our life together—in all its joys, sorrows, angers and anguishes—made perfect sense. I was aware of her consciousness moving down the dark tunnel and leaving this world, already rejoicing in the splendor of her return to the Light. She had birthed me into this world, and I felt as though I had birthed her out of it.

I opened my eyes to a room that seemed to be suffused with the Light and alive with an indescribable, peaceful power. My twenty-year-old son, Justin, was also in the room. He turned to me and said in awed tones, "I feel like Grandma is holding open the door to eternity to give us a glimpse. Can you feel it?"

Although Mother's body continued to breathe for a few more hours until an oxygen tube was removed, it felt as if her soul had been born back to the Other Side in the silence of the night. The memory of our last exchange and of the extraordinary vision stayed with me, creating a new frame of reference through which our sometimes difficult relationship appeared whole and perfect. I no longer thought in terms of forgiveness—her forgiving me or me forgiving her. The deep acceptance and identification I felt with her during those last few hours left me with an expanded view of our life together. That fuller viewpoint, an expanded vision in which even pain and disappointment make perfect sense as part of the fabric of divine love, is really at the heart of spiritual courage. When I asked her for the gift of courage that night, I had no idea what a revelation would follow.

I dreamed of Mom several times in the weeks following her passing. Although they were varied—funny, mysterious, delightful, painful, symbolic and healing—each dream was like a jewel. In one of the dreams she reminded me that she was often a bitch and that I'd better not start idealizing her! In another dream, I collected her gift of courage, which allowed me to face both the pain of this life and of past lives. The experience of courage that was given to me in the dream imprinted a new story on my soul and sent me forth into waking life with a changed perspective.

In the dream I am in the mountains, passing through on my way to give a workshop. Noticing a hidden door in the side of the mountain, I enter a room full of people. I am told it is a cafe but soon discover that I am in a school for spies. Several old women are there. They tell me how the school has pushed them to their very limits of endurance—sometimes beyond their limits. These women glow with wisdom, confidence, strength, compassion and power. I feel a fierce willingness and desire to submit myself to the same tests they have endured. It dawns on me that I have just been accepted into a school for courage.

The time comes for the final exam. As the class passes through a room, I am drawn to a group of children playing. When I look up, I realize that the class has gone on without me. I have to find my way to the final test myself. I know only to look for a hole in the ground. Outside once again I come upon a hollow tree trunk. Inside looms a giant, dark, watery chasm. Surprising myself, I jump immediately inside, abandoning myself completely to the watery darkness. Unexpectedly I land on a raft and travel at breakneck speed through a dark underground tunnel of water. I feel complete confidence and know at some deep level that my relations to fear and to the unknown have changed. Emerging into a landscape of stunning brightness and beauty I awaken feeling joyful and very clear.

I recorded the dream in my journal and then got up to make coffee. There by the coffee pot was a round sticker, the kind that adheres when you peel the back off. It was, and is, about three inches in diameter, red with swirly white lettering that, at first glance, seems to spell "Coca-Cola." It doesn't. It actually spells "courage." The red badge of courage awaited me with the morning coffee. I asked my sons and husband where it had come from. No one knew. It is currently mounted in my office over my word processor. I can see it as I write. I often look at it or remember it in those moments when fear has narrowed my vision and I have lost a higher perspective.

Presence from Mom

Chérie Carter-Scott, Ph.D.

Nineteen-seventy was a difficult year. I was a freshman at the University of Denver. I had transferred as a junior, and now had to start over. I was living off campus without a car. I didn't fit in. I was afraid I had made a terrible mistake.

I let my parents know that I had mixed feelings about my situation. They said, "Come home!" This is what they always said when things seemed rocky. Then, to my great surprise, they announced that they were coming to Denver to see me. The shocking part was that my parents never went anywhere. They never visited any of their children, and rarely strayed far from their beloved home. The thought that they would leave New Jersey, get on a plane, and come to Denver, just to visit me, was almost overwhelming.

Only in hindsight did I realize how truly memorable the weekend was. We did tourist things: ate out, went sightseeing, and shared some special moments. I had never felt so close to both of my parents. I felt special, I felt important. I felt like I mattered to someone. All too quickly the weekend came to a close.

I never saw my mother alive again.

In March, she came down with some sort of extreme but nonspecific illness. She was hospitalized for tests and given some medication that brought on a negative reaction. By the time someone prescribed a third medication, she was in a coma. She stayed in that coma for over two months, and passed away on May 17. It all happened so quickly; she was only fifty-five years old.

I came home for the funeral, and felt strangely disconnected from the whole event. The total lack of explanation was appalling. My questions were dismissed. After a while I stopped asking what I perceived as "dumb" questions. We buried Mommy, I went back to college, and that was that.

Months passed. There was an emptiness, I felt alone, but this was all part of growing up.

In December of that same year, my sister Lynn, her husband Douglas, my fiancé Bill and I were home for the holidays. It was five days before Christmas. As we sat in our living room, we remarked that not a single piece of furniture had been moved since our mother's passing. Her portrait hung over the fireplace, and the straight-backed needlepoint chairs still flanked the oversized pocket doors. The coffered ceiling and bay windows gave a full panoramic view of the blue-gray Atlantic. My sister and I sat on the overstuffed couch, the boys in armchairs, and we reminisced about the past.

Suddenly all four of us looked at each other with immediate awareness. A presence had entered the room, and we all felt it simultaneously.

My sister looked at me and said, "It's Mommy!"

Without thinking, words came out of my mouth. "She wants us to know that she misses us. It's the first Christmas without all of us together. She says we shouldn't be afraid. She is happy just being with us. She will be with us just as she always has been at Christmas." I didn't know where the words were coming from. I wasn't thinking about what to say; they spoke themselves, without thought or effort.

My sister, brother-in-law and fiancé all looked at me with amazement. Then the presence moved through the living room and seated itself on the couch where Mommy always sat. Bill said, "She's sitting at your mother's place on the couch." A look of recognition passed between us, and silence filled the room.

After a few moments the words erupted from my mouth again. "She wants us all to know that she loves us very much. She can't imagine being anywhere else except with us at this time of year. She is happy we are home, with her, the way it always was."

There was a long pause. Everyone took a deep breath.

Douglas asked, "Why is she speaking through you?"

I didn't know what to say, so I guessed. "I think since I am the youngest, her baby, that she probably felt she could access me easier than Bobbi or Lynnie."

I didn't know how true those words were. For the next two weeks, Mommy was our constant companion. She was with us at dinner, she rode around in the car with us in the back seat, she sat with us when we played bridge. She only spoke through me, and only in response to questions in someone's mind. It was quite unsettling for me. I had never had an experience like this before. In fact, I wasn't sure that I really believed in an afterlife. I didn't know where I ended and she began.

After two weeks, there was an absence. We all felt the strange return to normalcy.

Her presence had been an overwhelming preoccupation for two weeks. Now her absence was mystifying. I found the courage to talk about this experience with my Aunt Mary and cousin Peter. It seems that Mommy made many appearances during this time. She sat in the back of my cousin's classroom while he was teaching class. She visited my Aunt Mary and my sister Bobbi. I guessed that she was bringing a closure to relationships that the coma had prevented.

Although the experience was unsettling, I was glad to have this closure with my mother. I could no longer dismiss thoughts of an afterlife. I knew with every fiber of myself that our spiritual essence is an unquestionable reality.

Joined Forever

Corinne Edwards

From the time I was a very little girl, I can remember closing my eyes and thinking there was someone inside me who was separate somehow. Not connected to my body. Someone who was there, who was me, but seemed totally distinct. Not dependent on my body. I wondered if anyone else thought things like that.

Then I went to school, and the nuns taught me the word "soul."

Aha! That must be it!

But it didn't quite fit. A soul seemed to be holy and floating around Heaven in a nebulous fashion. This person was me. Uniquely me.

I guess that was why it was easier to accept some of the unusual things that happened after my son Mark died. For a long time after his physical death, he didn't leave this plane of existence. That separate person, who was not his body, stayed around.

My son Mark was beautiful. Mark was a genius. He read *War and Peace* when he was in the fourth grade. But Mark was, became, a drug addict. A classic example of the culture in the 1960s and 1970s.

Mark is proof to me that we are not bodies. We are minds that temporarily inhabit a body. Minds that seem to be separate and yet also are connected to some Higher Power or Deity.

I want to tell you about some of the things that happened after he died.

It began with my feeling his presence with me. I could tell when he was in the room and when he left. Sometimes he would drive to work with me in my car. Sometimes not. I don't know how to explain this knowingness that he was there except through a sixth sense. It felt like the experience we have all had when we have been sitting quietly alone somewhere—and yet, although we didn't hear a sound, we were aware of someone coming into the room. We look up and there he is. That's the way it started.

I talked to a psychologist friend whose specialty is grief counseling. He explained that these feelings were part of the process of grieving, and not uncommon. That I was perfectly normal and that it would all pass in time. Not to worry.

But the events that followed were not explainable as grief. Mark was around.

A few months after Mark's death, my son Peter drove me to a large business meeting in the city. There were hundreds of people there, so the atmosphere was very animated. Part of the presentation was a video.

I was absorbed in this when I heard a kind of voice, though not an audible one. It was more like a flash of words in my brain.

It said, "Don't be upset. Listen! Don't be upset! He is not hurt!"

A few moments later, there was a tap on my shoulder. There was a phone call for me. It was Peter. He'd had an accident with the car and it had been towed. But he was not hurt.

Then the real messages started coming. They now did not come directly to me, but through a woman named Evelyn, who was the mother of an acquaintance of mine.

Evelyn was a sweet middle-aged Jewish woman with little formal education. She told me she had been able to communicate with the spirit world since she was a child. She always had playmates no one else could see. She always knew things that no one else seemed to know.

She told a story about the time she and her mother were in a candy store. Evelyn was about five at the time. She said to a child in the store, "Don't go outside. You will be killed by a truck!" The child ran outside and was killed instantly.

Her mother was very frightened. Other messages, other knowings, had preceded this dramatic event. Evelyn was taken to the rabbi, who told her not to tell these things anymore. For a long time, she didn't.

Evelyn is a gifted psychic. Although she was not well off financially, she did not charge for her services. She said it would be a misuse of her gift. She felt she would lose it if she asked for money. So I never paid her anything.

She told me that she never understood why she could communicate with the "other side," but she knew it was to help people. Sometimes she worked with the police, together with a few of her psychic friends, to locate missing children.

Evelyn had several children of her own in this dimension, and I don't know how many spirit children. She favored communication with young people who had gone over to the other side. I always got confused about which children were on which side. There were so many names.

She liked Mark. He was twenty-one when he died, which made him a natural addition to her family. I don't know who contacts whom in these cases, how they get together. I can't even believe these things happened. But they did.

The messages were meaningful. They were not, "I'm okay, Mom. Don't worry about me." They were specific.

I'll give you a couple of examples.

Evelyn had never been in my house. Our conversations were all on the telephone.

One day she called and told me that Mark was showing her a chest of drawers. It had three drawers. A small chest. She didn't know where the chest was in the house. There were drugs in that chest and I was to throw them out!

There was a chest like that in Peter's room. There were some drugs and drug paraphernalia in the middle drawer. Mark was watching out for his brother.

Another time, she called to tell me that Mark was showing her a long piece of paper. It was some kind of a form for school for another son, Paul. It looked to her like an application. She said to tell Paul he should not put my husband's income information on the form because he was his stepfather.

Paul was interested in a grant from the state of California. I am certain Evelyn did not know anything about grants.

I telephone Paul to tell him this information. But he had already mailed the application with my husband's income on it. When I reported this to Evelyn, she insisted the papers she saw were blank.

Two months later, Paul discovered that his application had been lost in the mail. They sent him a new set of forms. He filled them in as instructed. And he got the grant.

There were times when I decided this whole thing was crazy. These happenings were just coincidences. I decided to put it to a test. I would ask my own question.

I asked Evelyn to find out from Mark what his middle name was. He always liked his middle name and used it.

He answered in a way that would leave no doubt that these transmissions were real. He told Evelyn to tell me that his middle name was the maiden name of my mother.

I was stunned. How clever for him to answer that way! Mark's middle name was Stewart. It occurred to me when I asked that question that it was on his tombstone. Although Evelyn is not a devious person, and I don't think she knew where he was buried, that information was available. But there was absolutely no way she would know the history of the name. She knew no one in my immediate family. The rest of my relatives lived a thousand miles away!

There were many other not so dramatic messages. Like one where Mark told Evelyn he had been visiting in Greene

County. Mark's favorite aunt lived in upper New York State in that county.

These messages from Mark comforted all of us. It did not seem as though he was gone. I think when we hear of our oneness with God, we fear that we dissolve into an amorphous mass, no matter how joyful we hear it will be! Mark kept the same identity, the same personality, and the same interest in his family after his body was gone. Mark was still Mark.

We haven't heard from him for a long time. I have a feeling he is involved in some kind of continuing education on the other side. And Evelyn has gotten old. I saw her last year and she told me her work was done and she had to concentrate on her health now. But she has lots of guardian angels around in her children—all of them!

I believe these communications are not as rare as we may believe. I have been in groups where the subject has come up and several people sheepishly recount their experiences. They are afraid to tell them in normal conversations. They are sure that they will be judged as unstable or crazy.

My experience supports that we are eternal beings. We are minds who occupy bodies, just as I suspected as a little girl.

If my son lives in another dimension, none of us can die. We do not need more than one black sheep to prove that all sheep are not white. He cannot be the only one.

You may be wondering why you have not heard from a loved one who has died. I don't know. I have asked myself that question many times.

My dear friend Dee died a few years ago and I have not heard a thing from her. We were very close. And she was very bossy! It seems odd that she would not have something to say about some of my business dealings. She was my accountant and I know she would not approve of some of my decisions.

Maybe there are certain channels, like radio frequencies,

we have to tune into. Maybe we aren't on that frequency, or they are not. It is not that our loved ones don't care. Perhaps they can't get through—or it could be that it is not in our or their best interest to communicate.

I sometimes think that the reason we heard from Mark is that he died so suddenly and was very motivated to help his brothers, especially Peter, where drugs were concerned. Perhaps he felt responsible and didn't want him to make the same mistakes. And he did help.

These things happened years ago, but the telling of the story has flooded me with fresh sadness. With missing him as though he had just left.

But it has made it easier for me to understand that only minds can join—not bodies. I know that our minds are joined with his forever. And therefore, my mind is joined with yours, and yours is joined with mine.

Parting Gifts

Laura Goerlitz

In 1971 my father died suddenly from a heart attack, at the young age of forty-four. I was seventeen.

One morning a day or two later, my mother came into the front room where my grandparents, sister and I were gathered soon after waking up. Holding my dad's wallet, she sat down and said that he had come to her during the night. He had taken her to the dresser in their room and showed her his wallet, telling her there was some money in it that she hadn't found yet. When she woke up, she told us, she'd looked, but found no money.

I remembered hearing footsteps in the hallway throughout the night. Everyone else said they hadn't gone into the hallway, nor had they heard anything.

I was watching my mom rub her thumb back and forth over the picture on Dad's driver's license. Then she slipped her fingers under it and pulled out some money—folded up with a small handwritten note.

The note was a will she'd known nothing about, leaving everything to her in the event of his death.

On the night after Dad's funeral, Mom asked for some help returning the folding chairs we'd borrowed for the funeral reception from our neighbor two houses down. My grandmother and I volunteered.

I remember we were being very quiet as we walked over in the dark. It was late, and we didn't want to wake anyone.

Just as we got to the end of the house next to ours, we saw a brilliant glowing light rise from across the street by our church, a couple of houses down from where we were walking. It was the brightest light I had ever seen, and it was huge—about as wide as a house, and as long as two houses. It had a long oval shape that made no sound as it rose up and to the right, into the sky. As it crossed high above us it disappeared, leaving no trace.

It didn't look like anything I had ever seen before. It wasn't like those big spotlights they use at airports or store openings to attract attention. It had a beginning and an end to it. It didn't look like a meteor or falling star. It went up instead of down, almost in an arc across the sky. It didn't look like a vapor trail from a rocket or plane. Later that month, I even checked with the local observatory, and they had no record of unusual lights in the sky that night.

I was speechless. I knew it was Dad's spirit, showing us that he was still with us. It was the most wonderful experience I had ever had.

The three of us said nothing. We quietly left the chairs on our neighbors' porch and walked back home.

We didn't talk about what we'd seen until much later. When we did, we all agreed that we felt it was Dad's spirit.

Twenty years later, I was going through some difficult times and my faith in God was beginning to get shaky. One day I mentioned the experience with the light to a friend. At that moment, I realized that it hadn't just been Dad's way of showing us he lived on. By rising up from the church, it was his way of showing us that God was real.

A Butterfly's Goodbye

Dolores R. Hill

My sister Denise was nineteen when she died on May 21, 1991. She died at home in her bed from a heart attack. Denise didn't have a history of heart disease. It was very tragic and sad and totally unexpected.

When Denise died I lost my sister, my child, and my friend. She was everything to me, and I to her. You see, we lost our mom in 1980 to ovarian cancer. She was only forty-four when she died, leaving behind a large and grieving family: my dad and us six children. I was the oldest and the only one married at the time; Denise was nine years old, and my youngest brother, John, was only five. I sort of became their surrogate mother, even though I wasn't living at home. Denise and John came to rely on me for the parts of their lives that my mother would have been there for. So, with this in mind, you can see how much my family means to me. Especially Denise, my only sister, who was born when I was sixteen.

Because of the nature of Nisey's death, I felt out of sorts. I had a very strong feeling that she would come back to say goodbye. I wanted her to. Yet, being human, I also feared her coming. I begged Denise to come to me only if I was outside.

About a week after we buried Denise, I was working on a scrapbook of poems that she had written, memorabilia from high school, and other special things she had saved. I was writing a poem to her, to dedicate the scrapbook to her memory. It was, to say the least, a very emotional day for me.

I was still working on the book when my husband came home from work. He wanted to grill outside and went out to fire up the grill. When it was ready, he called to me to come out to help him. I was holding the platter of steak for him, and as he stabbed the meat with the fork, Tom happened to look into my eyes—and we heard "Lor."

I didn't say anything, because my husband just doesn't believe that these things happen. He placed the steak on the grill, then looked at me and said, "You heard it, too."

I nodded and said, "It was Denise."

"It sure was. It was her voice."

Nisey was one smart girl. She knew if she came to me when I was alone and I told my husband about her visit, he would scoff and say I was imagining things because I was upset. I was really happy that she came to say goodbye, and did it so that I would be believed.

A few days later, I was standing outside our front door when a strange feeling came over me. Turning around, I saw a duplicate of my sister's car in the street; same make and model, color and interior. I was a bit rattled, and in my mind I spoke to Nisey. I told her that I loved her and missed her and that I always would, but these "visits" were really shaking me up. I told her she could visit me one more time, and then she would have to leave me alone for a while.

On Denise's twentieth birthday, June 29, I went to visit her grave and give her some flowers. I cried a great deal that day. Later in the afternoon, I took my daughters over to my parents' home to go swimming. I was walking beside the pool, and out of nowhere this black and orange butterfly appeared. It flew around me a few times, and I stopped. The butterfly then landed on my left breast, above my heart. A feeling of peace overwhelmed me. I knew it was Nisey, saying a final goodbye and telling me that she was all right. What a wonderful gift she gave to me on her birthday.

I'm not the only person whom Denise returned to because she wanted to say goodbye.

One night soon after Denise died, she appeared before my sister-in-law, Sande. She and my brother Ed were asleep in their bedroom when she awoke, sat up in bed— and Nisey stood in the corner of the room. She was wearing a t-shirt and a pair of boxer shorts (her favorite summer attire); her hair was just the way she usually wore it, loose around her face. She was transparent, and Sande could see the wall behind where she stood. She didn't say a word, just stood there, and when Sande turned to wake my brother, she had gone.

Denise's boyfriend was working at his job in a warehouse when she came to him. Jeff worked alone on the night shift; there wasn't anyone else in the building except the man in the office. Jeff told me he was walking down one of the aisles when he heard Denise say his name. Nothing more, just his name.

One evening after work, my brother Michael was at the cemetery. He was sitting in his truck in front of the headstone, just thinking about Mom and Denise. Out of nowhere, a black and orange butterfly flew into his truck and settled on the dashboard. He told me he knew it had to be Nisey.

The day after Denise's birthday, Tom and I and our daughters Stacy and Vicky went to the cemetery, to be sure the flowers we'd placed on Denise's grave still had water. My dad pulled up right in front of us; my youngest brother, John, was with him. It was extremely hot that day, and we weren't going to be long at the cemetery, so we decided to leave the car running with the air conditioner on, so it wouldn't get too hot inside. We got out of the car and shut the doors right away, and went over to greet my Dad and John.

I told John about what had happened with the butterfly the day before. John said that he hoped she wouldn't come to him, because he was too scared. You see, John was the one who'd found Denise when he returned home from school. I told him that she would never frighten him, that she just wanted to have a chance to say goodbye.

With that, John turned toward the car and said, "I'm hot. I'm gonna get some cool air."

When he opened the car door, a black and orange butterfly flew out.

Since then, to my knowledge, Denise hasn't returned to anyone. I hope one day she will return to me, but I know she's at peace—and she did, in her way, say goodbye to everyone.

Not an End, but a Beginning

JulieAnna

There have been many times when I have questioned why certain events in my life were taking place, only to have it become perfectly clear to me in six months or a year, sometimes even five years later. All except for this one time.

I had always marveled at the type of relationship my grandmother and my mother had. It never made much sense to me at all. They had completely different ways of seeing the world, and were very often at odds with one another. There were many times when they actually lived together: during World War II, when most of the men were away, and again at various times and for various reasons over the decades. They seemed to need to be close to each other, and yet the undercurrent of discord was always present.

I had lived away from our hometown most of my life when, through a set of what I thought were mere circumstances, I relocated back there, and ended up living very close to them. They were living together again. Granny was getting up in years, about ninety, and was not, shall we say, steady on her feet. She was still very bright, watching game shows on TV and answering most of the questions before the contestants did.

I began to see that even though they usually seemed to be at odds about something or other, they depended upon one another a great deal, emotionally.

Mom suddenly became ill with cancer again, and I felt it necessary to shield Granny from what we all knew was going to be a rough year. Granny went to live with her other daughter, many hundreds of miles away. Even though she loved both daughters equally, she became quietly frantic at being unable to be at Mom's side to help. I could hear it in her voice when I called her.

There came a time when I moved in with Mom, and we began the journey toward that door we call death. I had come to believe that death is not an end, but a beginning. It was probably a good thing that I did believe so strongly in a loving God, and in the fact that our souls do continue. I also believe that sometimes our spirit gets tired, and we want to go home and rest for a time, to try again later.

As the time drew near, my aunt came to town to say her goodbyes, leaving Granny home with a nurse. One morning shortly afterward, I spoke with Granny on the phone. She knew that it would be a hard trip for her to make, but she wanted to be with Mom. Even though we'd tried to tell her Mom was doing fine, she knew in her heart that she wasn't.

At the end of the conversation, Granny told me that she was tired and very "blue" that day, and was going to take a nap; she would call again later. She went to her room and fell asleep, and never woke up.

My granny was a great light in my life. Coming in the midst of my caring for Mom, her death was quite a blow.

We decided not to tell Mom, as she was so weak. Soon after that day, Mom lapsed into a coma.

Meanwhile, my aunt had made all the arrangements to have Granny buried next to her husband in our hometown. Granny's coffin arrived just minutes before Mom passed away.

In my heart I know she came to get Mom, probably a few days before. She was always the brave one. She, too, believed in a loving God, and in all that is good—and she knew Mom would be frightened. I felt as though Granny's coffin arriving just at that time was to let me know that all was well, and that she would take over from there.

Soon after all of this, I met a seer of sorts who asked me it I had lost anyone to death in the past few months.

Before I could answer, she said, "Two . . . there are two. They are together, and are very happy, and are not arguing." She paused. "Does that make sense to you?"

I answered, "It sure does."

Grandpa Charlie

James David Seddon

I never really got to know my Grandpa Charlie. Cancer took his voice when I was eight; a couple of years later old age robbed him of his mind, and he died before I turned twelve. My memories of him are foggy fragments of the times we shared, but those were enough to create a bond that took years for me to discover and understand.

My grandparents lived in a big white house on a little hill, across the street from my parents in a small town called Cincinnati, Iowa. Charlie Harrison had come to Cincinnati as a young man. He met, fell in love with, and married the beautiful Chloie Beer. They bought and moved into the white house on the hill and spent the rest of their lives there. Five children were born in that house, and three children died in that house. My mother and her older sister were the two that survived.

Nothing of importance ever changed in my grandparents' house. The white iron bed was always in the south upstairs bedroom. The piano was always on the east wall of the parlor. The same pans were in the pantry, and the Shirley Temple cup was always in the kitchen cupboard.

The center of the house was a large dining room. In the southwest corner of that room was my grandpa's desk, a huge dark oak rolltop that was off limits to all grandchildren. That desk was a monument to my grandpa's life. Its cubbyholes and drawers were full of ledgers and postcards, maps and odd sheets of paper, and "Elbert Hubbard's Scrap Books." There were pictures and pins, pens and pencils from all over the country. It was my grandpa's corner of the world.

It was a great honor to be invited into that world. Every once in a while I would stand at Grandpa's elbow, and he would reveal some of the secrets of his desk. Secrets that were memories, of coal mines that he had dug, trips he had taken, and people he had known. Somehow it all added up to bits of wisdom he liked to share. I always felt a little bigger, a little more grown up, after spending those times with Grandpa.

In the center of the dining room was a round oak table, large enough to seat a dozen people. Most of the time, it was my aunt and uncle, my parents, my cousins, brothers and sisters, and Grandma and Grandpa. There was something infinite about the circle of people around that table.

After Grandpa died, the circle was changed, yet still complete. It took me forty years to discover why Grandpa always smiled at that table.

When I was twenty-two, like many young men of my time, I went to Vietnam. I could not have gotten further away from Cincinnati, Iowa. The peace that was southern Iowa became the terror of war in southern Vietnam.

I spent a year in Southeast Asia. I saw humanity defiled. I saw friends die, and I killed other people's friends. And, like a good many other young men, when my time was up I silenced the screams, stored the terror in the back of my mind, and came home. I came home thinking that once again I would find the peace of southern Iowa. But the demons of war do not die as easily as young men do. They are a secretive, insidious bunch who invade the dark recesses of the mind and hide there for years. They disguise themselves as smells and sights and sounds. They invade the night, steal the peace from sleep and replace it with the terrible memories of war. Once they have conquered the night, they invade the days, and turn life into one long nightmare.

Like many young men of my time, I became a victim of the demons of war. And like many young men, I decided the only way to conquer the demons was to destroy myself. But the soldier in me did not have the courage to kill again. I had to find another way to destroy the demons. That is when I found the power of words. By writing my story of war, I exorcised the demons—but the exorcism came with a terrible price. I had to relive every memory. I had to relive the pain one more time, and sometimes I had to face pain I had repressed for twenty years.

One evening, when my mind no longer wanted to recall the pain and my hands refused to write the words, I went outside and stood in the dark at the edge of the woods. It was fall, and a gentle rain was falling. I lit a cigarette, and as I blew out the match, my eyes adjusting to the darkness, I saw an old man standing at the edge of the woods. His white hair was being tossed by a breeze that was not blowing, and although it was raining, I could see that his white shirt was not wet. He looked at me, yet beyond me, and spoke in a voice that I knew, but could not remember. There wasn't a sound, but I understood what he said.

"You know what you have to do."

And with the same silent voice I responded, "I know, Grandpa."

Grandpa had been dead for over twenty years, and I realized that what had happened defied reality, but it didn't matter. For the first time in a long time, I felt that there was a purpose in living. There was a peace in the pain I felt about the war—a paradox that I didn't need to explore. I wrote my book, told my story, and put my trust in Grandpa.

Grandpa and I have had several visits over the past ten years. I have learned a lot from him, but last winter I think Grandpa left. I think I'm finally on my own.

On a Sunday afternoon last February, I went to visit my parents. As I opened the back door and walked into the kitchen, I could tell no one was at home. I was about to leave when I noticed one of Grandpa's "Elbert Hubbard's Scrap Books" on the stove on the back porch.

I opened the book to a page where Grandpa had written in the margin, "Some men draw circles to keep people out, other men draw circles to keep people in." I smiled, closed the book and left.

The next day was a cold Monday morning, and I was short of breath and dizzy. I found out ten years ago, after my first heart attack, that I have coronary artery disease. I had a second heart attack last November. Now it was just four months later, and I was having that familiar dreaded feeling again.

I remember going in the house and sitting down in my recliner; I remember my wife coming home; I remember asking her to call 911; and I remember being loaded into an ambulance. But somewhere between 911 and the ambulance, I died. I don't remember my wife screaming my name, I don't remember her pulling me onto the floor. I don't remember the paramedic zapping me with his paddles.

I remember thinking to myself in the back of the ambulance, on the way to the emergency room, *You just died. It was easy.*

I arrested two more times during the next two days. Each time the magic paddles brought me back. It was during those first days that I began to see the circle, the circle around my bed. There was my wife and my daughter, my parents, sisters and brothers, aunts and uncles, cousins and friends—and Grandpa.

I began to remember the dining room in my grand-parents' house, the round oak table, and the circle of family that used to gather there. I came to realize that the circle can never be broken, it can never be destroyed. It can only be forgotten.

"I know what I have to do, Grandpa."

Grandpa smiled.

A Ghost Story

Rick Wright

This was many years ago. I'm now a psychotherapist and hands-on healer, but at this time I was working for a tele-marketing firm and concentrating on my own personal spiritual investigation.

Through my work, I met a very interesting woman. She talked about the afterlife and reincarnation, spirit, souls. . . . One time she was talking about "lost souls" and told me a little about how to release ghosts—spirits—from homes and other places.

She talked a lot about intuition, too, and I began to practice following my own. One day when I was in my car, I very suddenly had a strong feeling that I should drive out to see some friends, an old friend and his wife, who lived in the country. It wasn't that I suddenly wanted to see them, but an urgent thought that something was wrong.

I arrived forty-five minutes later. My friend's wife answered the door, in tears.

She had just been in the master bedroom of the house,

she told me, trying to pray. My friend was at work. I could see how truly shaken she was as she told me what had been happening, and what I'd just stumbled into.

They'd never felt right in the room, she said. Lately, she'd been following a path of prayer and meditation—and whenever she tried to pray there, she felt a terrible presence, sometimes weaker, sometimes stronger. Just now, she'd been praying for a long while and had been very upset to feel the presence grow *very* strong. She'd come downstairs, and I was there at the door.

I told her about my feeling an hour earlier that something was wrong. I said I would go investigate, while she stayed downstairs in the kitchen.

There were butterflies in my stomach as I started up the stairs. As I went up, the air seemed to get stuffier, thicker. By the time I reached the room, the light was dimmer, and I was already wondering what I'd gotten myself into. I opened the door.

I couldn't believe my eyes. The room was filled with spirits.

I'd never seen spirits before, but I knew what I was looking at. I was instantly much more afraid. They actually looked like gremlins, ugly gremlins . . . luminous, but with a dark shading around the eyes and mouth. There was a four-poster bed there, and one of them was perched on a bedpost, leering at me. There was another I could see clearly in a corner of the ceiling, and more of them seemed to be moving around the room, although it was all a blur. When I heard something scrabbling around what looked to be a small bathroom, I started thinking I'd gone nuts.

I wanted to run, but I held myself there. Gradually, where before I'd just seen shadows, I started to see shapes. It was chaotic, disorienting, but I saw them.

It looked as though they were tossing things around the room. Etheric things, not the furniture and books I could *see* there. It was like madness. The spirits were spitting something like saliva, or actually more like goo.

They were ecstatic. I could tell that they were still enjoying having scared my friend.

I literally blinked my eyes. But they were still there.

Then I remembered my other friend saying, "There are no 'bad' spirits. Some are just lost." They'd only become caught, she said, in their transition in death, and attached to a place that seemed familiar or at least safe to them.

I felt a little bit calmer, and I tried to make myself as calm as I could. I knew that these souls or "ghosts" could sense fear, and I saw they enjoyed it. They were still running around like Casper's mean brothers, kicking up their heels over scaring my friend. I struggled to recall what my friend from work had said to do.

"You are no longer among the living," I told them. "You aren't here with us. You are dead. You are spirit."

I kept on like that, and felt them eventually quiet down. It seemed like it had registered, like they were listening.

I felt a great compassion for all of them, and wondered what had come over me. I asked for help—from anyone, anything—to guide them to their proper place. And then I knew I had to perform a ritual there, in the room.

I went downstairs to find a box of table salt. I told my friend what I'd seen, that she wasn't crazy. I told her what I was doing. Then I called my office. Luckily, the friend who'd been instructing me was there that day.

When I got off the phone, I didn't know if I was inspired or crazy, but I went back upstairs. They were still there.

I salted the room, all the way around the baseboards, reciting the prayer I'd just been given. I salted the loft someone had built in there, and salted the door.

Glad to close the door behind me, I went downstairs.

I said that they should leave the salt there for twenty-four hours, then vacuum it up and dispose of it somewhere where nobody lived. Even a Dumpster would do. I sat there, collecting myself, as my friend told me she'd been praying fervently the whole time I was upstairs.

Two days later, she called me. She'd done as I said, and the room felt calmer. She'd slept there, and woke to sunshine filling the room, and she'd just prayed there for the first time. The presence was gone, the room warm and bright.

"It's full of love!" she said.

Transitioning: Mystery of Spirit

Mary Amrita Weed

Mother had only a day or so to live. Our family could feel it.

We were all there: my two brothers, their wives, their sons, my daughters. We took turns reading to Mother from the Bible. Could she hear us? We weren't sure, but we felt it was easing her transition out of her cancer-ridden body. We were invoking Christ consciousness, and surely that was tremendously powerful in and of itself.

We were so deeply bonded with her. She was beloved by so many—for her generous spirit, her storytelling, her wisdom and compassion, her courage. What could we do to keep her alive? We wanted her with us—for all time. And yet we knew we needed to let go.

As we finished dinner, the sun was just setting on the bay in this beautiful Jersey Shore town. We felt drawn to go back to the room we'd fixed for her off the kitchen.

How did we know the time was coming near? We must have heard her labored breathing. Breathing—it gives us so many messages. Inspire comes from *spiritus*: the breath of life. After my father died four months before, Mother had talked of the death rattle she heard in his throat. We all heard it in hers now, and shuddered.

And then it happened. Her breathing stopped.

And I was amazed and awestruck by what I experienced next. I felt my father's presence, directly above her bed, and the whole room was flooded in the sweetest, softest blue light. I was flooded with ecstasy. The bliss I felt was wondrous and delicately deep.

When had I experienced something like this? In giving birth to my daughters!

Transitioning from spirit to matter (the birth of my daughters) and transitioning from matter to spirit (the death of my mother): Each generated the deep joy that holds tears, and the open heart that holds bliss.

I stayed in her room for the next hour—still, prayerful, and pondering on the mystery. Then my brothers wrapped her in a sheet, and she was put in the mortuary car.

I walked on the beach and looked up at the heavens. Lo and behold, the clouds were in the shape of an enormous angel! "You need never fear death" is the message I heard. Even in her death, Mother was still giving to me.

I honor the mystery of transitioning. There is blessing and grace always.

He Watches over Me

Marilyn Camacho

"His eye is on the sparrow," says the hymn. And through His wondrous nature, the sparrow's eyes were on me.

I had not intended to go to St. Augustine, but while having coffee on the Saturday morning of Labor Day weekend,

I had this feeling I should go there and visit my husband's grave.

Camacho had been the love of my life. I met him when I was forty-six and followed him into a new life, even though it meant abandoning my financial security. I'd never regretted my decision. Whatever material comforts I'd left behind, he and I rebuilt together. Every moment of my eighteen years with him, I knew I was loved. But now he'd been dead four and a half years.

Something told me to go to St. Augustine, even though my car was in such bad shape that my son was horrified when I told him I was going. Over his protests, I took off the next morning.

I hadn't been at the cemetery very long when, to my surprise, one of Camacho's ex-employees drove up.

"Jose, what are you doing here?" I asked.

"I come here every so often to check the grave and pay my respects."

As we sat on a bench by the grave and reminisced about our beloved Camacho, I noticed a sparrow wandering around at our feet. I thought it might be wounded, because even when we shifted our legs it didn't fly away. Shortly the sparrow started pecking at my little toe. "Goodness, what're you doing?" I cried.

The sparrow jumped on my foot and started pulling on my gold ankle bracelet, which had once been Camacho's. Then he flew up to my arm and pulled on my wrist bracelet. A gift from Camacho, it spelled out my name in diamonds. The sparrow pulled on it and pulled on it, then jumped on my knee. After he'd sat there for a while he flew up to my head, then down to the back of my neck, where he gave me a couple of pecks. Camacho had loved to lift my hair and kiss me there. The sparrow then perched on my shoulder for a few moments before proceeding to walk down my whole body.

After that, he flew briefly to Jose, and from him to a tree. As I stared at that little sparrow, I was overcome by a certainty that he had to be Camacho . . . but I wasn't sure how

I felt about what was happening. I was more in a state of shock than anything else.

The sparrow flew back from the tree to the bench. We sat together for another half hour.

The next morning I went back to the cemetery. This time I was ready for the sparrow, but he wasn't there. But that didn't mean he wasn't still looking out for me.

As I was leaving, my car suddenly overheated just outside the cemetery. I pulled into a gas station only to discover that they couldn't fix it: it was Labor Day. I was forced to stay overnight.

The next day, Tuesday, the mechanic made a temporary repair because he didn't have the right size hose. He urged me to have the right one put in as soon as I got home, and although I was short of money, I followed his advice. *That* repair cost me $220.

That very same Tuesday, I received a check in the mail for $240: A piece of furniture I'd left on consignment had just been sold. I couldn't understand it. Before I'd left that Sunday, I'd called the shop, and they told me it hadn't been sold yet.

I knew it had to be the sparrow. I knew it was Camacho, watching over me.

Try to Remember

Jenna L. Adamo

It was almost the middle of August 1994 and my grand-mother, whom we called by her first name, Lily, was dying of cancer. I had last seen her in July when I had gone with my mother, brother, and son to visit her at her home in Arizona.

During that visit she often took three-hour naps in the afternoon. This was unlike Lily, who was always the kind of person you had to practically tie down just to make her sit and eat dinner. In fact, when I was little I would tie her apron strings to her chair at dinner. Each time she'd pretend she hadn't known, then laugh and say, "I'm going to get you, you little minx." But on that last visit there wasn't much left of the playful woman with the sparkling blue eyes and strawberry-blonde hair.

Despite the changes in her behavior, it didn't occur to me that the cancer that had been removed a little over a year before had returned. I wanted to believe my Lily would live forever. By the end of my visit, though, I did wonder when I kissed her goodbye if it would be for the last time. It wasn't until my mother returned home to get more clothes that I learned the cancer had returned, and was in an advanced state.

The weekend before her death, my father decided that he should go visit Lily, his mother-in-law. We knew now that she was slipping away. I was given the option of going with my dad, but there were a lot of things to consider. My two-year-old son, Joey, wouldn't be able to stay at my grandmother's home. Everyone was too immersed in grief to take the stress of having a toddler bouncing all over the house. I could leave Joey at my aunt's house, an hour's drive from my grandmother's, or I could let him stay overnight with our neighbor. But I was apprehensive about either option, since my son had never been cared for by anyone other than my mother, my father, and myself.

I finally decided to stay home with Joey, because I felt that was what Lily would want me to do. She always put children first.

The night before my dad left I wrote Lily a letter, thanking her for her unconditional love and for always believing in me. I asked that my mom read it to her. Still, I was uncertain that I had made the right decision. I wished I could have a sign that I was doing the right thing, though I never thought I'd actually get one.

It was Sunday. My dad was on his way home from my grandmother's, while Mom stayed behind. Only Joey and I were in the house. It was a warm, windless, eighty-five-degree day in San Diego, one that seemed unusually quiet and peaceful. I was getting ready to put Joey down for his nap when I heard the tinkling of music coming from my parents' room.

I cautiously went in. There on my mother's dresser was the music box that my uncle had given to my mother. When I was two or three years old my grandmother had given it to me to play with, and I had broken the head off the figurine. Now it was spinning slowly on its crooked axis. I sat down on my parent's bed, stunned, as the music played. The song was "Try to Remember."

After putting Joey to bed, I anxiously phoned Mom to tell her what had happened. I explained to her that there hadn't been any wind, and nobody had been in the room.

She told me that the music box hadn't worked in over ten years.

Lily died two hours after I received my sign. But I know that her spirit is still with us, as it was with me that day.

When All Else Fails

Chérie Carter-Scott, Ph.D.

Everything seemed to be going wrong. We found out that we had rats in the attic. Then there was an infestation of mealworms throughout the dried foods in our pantry. Then the toilets started backing up, the washing machine erupted, and finally an opossum died under the house and gave off the most awful stench.

We called the plumber, who couldn't find a source for any of the problems. We called the fumigator and the exterminator—and soon after they'd finished, it started again.

With incident coming after incident, we started to scratch our heads and wonder what was going on. After weeks of anxiety, we started to look at alternative causes.

In a conversation with my sister, I said, "This reminds me of the movie *Poltergeist*. It seems like there is no rational explanation." She told her friend Anne, who immediately exclaimed, "Cortland, he's the person you should call! He takes care of situations like this." My sister got his phone number, called him, and scheduled a house call.

When Cortland arrived, we were obviously uncomfortable. Not knowing how to behave, we acted a bit like self-conscious schoolchildren. I explained the situation to him.

Then he walked from room to room, saying in each one, "This room is clean." After he had covered the entire first floor, we went upstairs. Again, from room to room he continued to say, "This room is clean."

Finally we entered the master bedroom, and Cortland blurted out, "This is the room!" He looked around. "Twenty years ago, someone died here. He is trapped in this reality. He is not angry . . . he's trying to get your attention so that he can transition. He is just doing everything he can to be noticed, without scaring you to death."

I asked what he could do to help this person. He said that he would say the words to usher the entity to the next world, and that we had to "sage the house." We walked from room to room with a burning twist of sage, cleansing the entire house. When we were done, Cortland gave us some more sage and told us to do it again in three days. Our problems would now stop.

We offered him money, but he refused. He said that this was a service he offered, and he wasn't supposed to take money for it.

As if a switch had been turned off, the incidents stopped. The odor disappeared, the plumbing worked, and the mealworms were gone for good.

Not long after, I ran into the woman who had sold us the house. I asked her if she knew of anyone ever dying there.

"Yes," she replied. "Twenty years ago, the sheriff died in his sleep in the master bedroom."

Someone on the Other Side

Micki East

My dad was dying.

I could not accept it. The doctors had to be wrong.

Yet here he was, dying.

"No heroics," he'd said to the doctor. "Just let me go in peace."

I was in turmoil. Dad, how can you say that? You can't die!

But I looked down at this man who was once so tall, so handsome, so healthy. What right did I have to ask him to continue living?

I took his hand. "I love you, Dad," I choked out through stifled tears.

With what little strength he had he squeezed my hand and whispered something.

"What, Dad?" I bent close.

"Please let me go."

"What?"

" . . . "

"Do I need to let go for you to die, Dad?"

"Yes."

"Do we all need to let go?"

A second, barely audible "Yes."

"Even Mom?"

His eyes took on an anguished look. "Please," he gasped, "don't force her. Let her do it on her own."

Oh God, I prayed, *please give us the strength to do what is right.* Dad closed his eyes, I squeezed his hand. He tried to squeeze back but didn't have the strength. I bent down and kissed him on the forehead. He did not respond.

My family came back from dinner. While our mother went in to see Dad, I shared his request with my brother and sisters. Kathleen told us he'd asked the same of her. We all agreed that for his sake we needed to let go—but what about Mom? With unwavering faith, she continued to believe he would get well. How could we help her see that his love for her was so strong, he couldn't leave without her blessing?

That evening, the words clumsily tumbled out. Mom's face clouded in disbelief.

"How can you give up on him? How can you ask me to let go? I need him," she pleaded. "How can you be so cruel!"

I tried to hug her, but she wouldn't let any of us near. Everyone's eyes were brimming with tears we couldn't release. We left the hospital in stony silence.

The next day, as Dad drifted in and out of coma, each of us said our goodbyes. All except Mom.

As evening fell, she asked to be left alone with him. I kissed Dad goodbye. My sisters and I went home; Mark stayed at the hospital.

Alone together in his room, Mom took Dad in her arms. And, with all her incredible love for him, she let him go.

My mother and brother had just arrived home when I felt my father's presence in the house. The phone rang, and the hospital told us he was gone.

I closed my eyes only in pain at first, then in growing curiosity. I could still feel Dad there.

I didn't say anything to anyone, but went into another room. Sitting down, I began to meditate. I promptly got an image of his face. He looked healthy again.

"Are you happy, Dad?" I asked, and his beaming smile told me he was.

"I love you, Dad. I'm glad for your sake that you're out

of pain ... but I am really going to miss you!" I began to sob. Then a troubling thought occurred to me.

"Dad, are you really here, or am I just making this up so I can feel better about losing you?" He assured me that he was there, but I still thought I must be suffering from an overactive imagination.

"Okay, but ... do me a favor, will you?" I bargained. "When it's Mom's turn ... will you come and tell me ten days before, so I can prepare the family, and myself?"

Nodding affirmatively, my father's image faded.

Nineteen years later, I woke one night with a jolt. Standing next to my bed, bathed in blue light, were my father and my maternal grandparents.

I closed and opened my eyes several times, and each time they were still there. Finally I stammered out something, and my father spoke.

"You need to tell your mother that it is okay to let go."

"Is she holding on for us kids, Dad?"

"Yes. Tell her it is okay to let go."

And then they were gone.

I began to cry. Mom was seventy-nine and had Parkinson's disease. It had wasted her body to the point where death was something she seemed to welcome. But was she really just holding on for the four of us?

In denial, I went shopping the next day for her Christmas present. When I returned from the store I called my brother to tell him what I had purchased, and he suggested I return it. "The nursing home doctor called today," he said quietly. "It won't be long now."

I thought of my visitors the night before. I told my brother about them, and we agreed it was time to tell Mom she could let go.

I said goodbye to Mom on Christmas Day. I told her that each of her daughters wanted her to know that we loved her, but that it was okay for her to leave us now. I promised that Mark would visit later in the week.

The evening Mark said his goodbye, she passed on. It

was exactly ten days after my father and grandparents' nocturnal visit. I have no doubt they were with her as she crossed over.

Our loved ones are always with us in spirit, and when our time comes we do not die alone. There is someone waiting on the other side.

Perfume in Heaven

Frank A. Alamia

My niece, Melissa Ann, passed to the other side on June 11, 1995, at the tender age of twelve. For over five years she had fought a valiant battle against a childhood cancer called rhabdomyosarcoma. Melissa was, in a word, a saint during her short stay on this earth, and we dearly loved her and her valiant spirit. Needless to say, her death devastated my family. The pain her parents and little brother went through was unspeakable. We couldn't imagine why someone so young and wonderful had to undergo such a difficult illness. We prayed constantly for her and supplicated daily to God to give us a sign that she was at last at peace and happy.

Now, it was my regular practice to pray for all those friends and relatives that have passed on over the years. On this particular night I lit a candle by my bedside, and asked these dear ones to come to me and give me a sign that Melissa was with them and happy.

I retired for the night, and the following dream came to me.

* * *

Melissa stood before me. Somehow I knew, as you do when you experience a true vision, that this really was Melissa. Standing with her was my twin brother, who had passed on in 1989.

I was overcome with joy and I hugged Melissa, shouting, "It's her, it's Melissa! Do you see her? It's really her!" My brother forgotten, I held Melissa, and a warm and pleasing sensation shot through my body, like nothing I have ever experienced before or since. I can never accurately describe what it was like, but a surge of love, warmth, and happiness filled me.

"Melissa," I almost shouted, "do you know how much everyone misses you? Do you know how much your dad and mom miss you? Do you know how much your brother misses you?"

Melissa looked at me in the same knowing way she always did when someone stated the obvious to her, thinking she was just a child and couldn't understand the ways of the world. "I know," she said. "But there just isn't enough time to visit everyone who is calling to me. Everyone keeps calling me! And besides, I am with them every night."

"Are you all right?" I asked. "Are you happy?"

Her angelic face kind of squinched up, and she said, "Oh, yes. Except I can't get the perfume I like!"

"Perfume?" I remember thinking that this didn't make sense: this was heaven, you ought to be able to get any perfume you like. But all I said was, "Well, what kind of perfume do you want?"

Without a moment's hesitation she said, "Cody, Ex—." I couldn't seem to understand the rest of the word. It sounded like "extravaganza" or something like that, but it made no sense to me.

At that moment, another little girl appeared. She seemed younger, and the two of them appeared to be close playmates. They began walking away, and I followed.

They went up to a house that I had never seen before, climbed the stairs to the front door, and went in. I waited on the sidewalk in front of the house, not knowing what to do or say, hoping to see Melissa again. Shortly the two came out of the house and down the stairs, and started walking away down the sidewalk.

I called out, "Wait, Melissa, wait!" But they vanished, leaving two small pools of silver where they had stood. Just as quickly, the pools of silver disappeared as well.

I awoke, at first feeling confused and sad. *What a strange dream*, I thought.

Then it hit me, powerfully, from my soul. That was no dream! That really happened. I just knew, with a sureness that cannot be expressed, that it was a visitation, not a dream. I really had spoken with Melissa.

I began to sob uncontrollably. This was too much for me. Her words made me tremble: "There just isn't enough time!"

It was one in the morning, but I called her parents anyway. They didn't answer, but through hysterical tears I told the story to the answering machine.

At seven in the morning the phone rang. It was Melissa's mother. I recounted it all again and asked her, "Did Melissa like perfume? Did she have a favorite?"

"Yes, she did," her mother told me, but she couldn't remember the name. She told me that Melissa had received a stuffed toy Scottie dog with a bottle of perfume tied around its neck. She would go through Melissa's room and find it, and call me back. She then told me that another child in the neighborhood, younger than Melissa, named Chelsea, had passed on. She thought that the other little girl in the dream might have been her.

The description of the steps leading to the house they'd entered piqued Melissa's father's interest. For some reason, this was the part of the dream that rang true for him, making him believe that it was no mere dream. I told him that the steps had confused me, because I knew of no house in their neighborhood that had such steps leading to the front door. He didn't elaborate, and we rang off with a promise from them that they would call back when they found the perfume.

A few hours later they called back, tears evident in their strained voices. They had found the perfume hidden away in Melissa's makeup and jewelry box. It was a bottle of Cody "ex' cla ma' tion" that had been tied around the stuffed dog's neck.

There was no way that I could have known about that dog or that bottle of perfume, and it convinced me that Melissa had actually spoken to me the night before. I surmised that Melissa knew I would have no knowledge of that perfume (indeed, I had never even heard of "ex' cla ma' tion"), and she was giving me a sign so that her parents and little brother would know it was truly her, and that she was okay and doing well.

A few months later, I was visiting Melissa's parents. I was about to head home when my brother said, "I want to take you to Chelsea's house to see if you recognize it."

Off we went. I followed in my car, as I planned to leave after visiting the house and then the cemetery where Melissa's body had been laid to rest. I was confused, as her parents drove out of their neighborhood to a house some two miles away. As we turned into a street I had never been on before, I saw the house I had seen the two children enter in my dream.

They didn't stop in front of that house, but in front of the house next door. I got out of my car and approached theirs, and tentatively pointed to the house they had stopped in front of. "Is that Chelsea's house?"

"No," they said, and pointed to the house that I had recognized immediately. I knew then that Melissa had truly been with me and had delivered her message to her family, and I began to cry uncontrollably once again. I knew that she was fine and happy and that she had joined her young friend in heaven. A peace came over me, and I marveled at the gift I had received.

Night Shift

Allan Thomas

I was with my friend Sandy when the radio began playing "The Night Shift," a tribute by the Commodores to some well-known deceased singers. We both commented on how beautiful and sad it sounded.

Three days later, my mother called me in the morning to tell me that my sister Judi had died in her sleep during the night. An hour later, Sandy called from work and asked right away, "What's wrong?" Still weeping, I told her about Judi and that I would be going home to Virginia for her funeral. I was about to hang up when I realized there was no reason for Sandy to have known something had happened. I asked what made her call. She said she had just heard "The Night Shift" on the radio, and knew "something was wrong with Allan."

Growing up as Army brats who got relocated every three years, my sister had been my best friend while we were kids. We grew apart in later years, especially after her drinking got so bad that it was difficult to be around her. Because her husband had died while he was in the Army, she was entitled to a military funeral at Arlington National Cemetery. During the service, I read a poem she had written about herself in junior high school. I hoped it would help explain her short, painful life, as it described someone who even then was already yearning for the peace of Heaven.

After the honor guard had fired its volleys and the ceremony was over, she was laid to rest with her husband. I waited until everyone had left, and then said out loud, "Judi, if there's any way you can let me know that you're all right, please do it." As I looked down at the flowers over her grave, I saw a red rose standing out alone—and decided I would have to settle for that as a communication, while wishing there could have been something more certain. I needed to know that my little sister had finally gotten her peace.

I walked back to the parking lot and got into my car—it was the only one left—and just sat there for a while. Finally, I started it up and turned on the radio for distraction. It was silent. I reached to fiddle with the knobs, but before I could touch them, "The Night Shift" began to play.

The Song in David's Court

Maryann Candito Wilkin

David was a very special friend who passed away from AIDS at the age of twenty-six. He was a remarkably positive individual despite all the prejudice, discrimination, and hatred he faced. He was also the most kind, compassionate man I'd ever known. When I found out he'd tested positive for HIV when he was only twenty years old, I was devastated.

But David just went on with his life, working, going to college, striving for his degree. When it was discovered he was HIV-positive, he lost his job and his health insurance. Because of the high cost of treatment, David was afraid his parents would be left penniless, so he reached tirelessly for work where he'd be assured of medical coverage—even if it meant not reaching his goal of getting a degree. Finally, though, he found a job at the university that would provide coverage and still allow him to pursue his studies.

Eventually he became too ill either to work or finish school. He moved back to his parents' home in a little town in the Florida panhandle.

After being feared by the medical professionals at his hospital, and treated without an ounce of compassion by certain members of the clergy, he decided to start up OASIS: Okaloosa AIDS Support and Information Services. David's dream became a reality, and it is still providing love and support to those who need it today.

I can hardly express how much joy and laughter this young man brought into the lives of everyone he met. He was (is) a beautiful soul.

When he passed away, I flew to his services.

He'd said he wanted everyone in festive colors. No one was to wear black! And he didn't want any organ music at his viewing, that was just too gloomy. Instead, he wanted a tape of all his favorite songs playing. That was David.

Whenever I remember his service, the only song I recall—imprinted in my mind so vividly, as though it was the only one being played—was Louis Armstrong's "What a Wonderful World."

After I went back home, I was extremely depressed for quite some time. Four weeks went by, and I still couldn't face life. Then, one evening, all of that changed.

I was sound asleep in my bed when all of a sudden I heard my name being called. I wasn't dreaming, although my physical body was not awake. What kind of strange and wondrous state of consciousness had I entered?

I couldn't believe what I saw. It was him, it was David, and oh, how beautiful he looked! His eyes shone like stars in a clear summer sky, and his smile penetrated through to my soul in a totally natural connection. He looked radiant, kneeling there beside my bed. He was completely transparent, and the room glowed from his presence, in a warm and loving embrace of energy.

David put his hand out toward mine, and waited patiently for me to place my hand in his. It was a struggle for me to break through the boundaries of my physical body. Finally it happened, and I was able to break free of my shell. As my hand joined his, it was the most exhilarating experience I had ever known. It felt like a merging of vibrant, loving energies. The rest of my soul followed as I stared at David and literally felt his smile filling me with warmth, unconditional love, and the comfort of knowing he was still with us, and very happy.

Before I knew it, David and I were off on a magnificent journey, flying at incredible speed. A kaleidoscope of colors surrounded me, sparkling dust reflecting the brilliance of the lights in all the spectacular colors of the rainbow. Oh, what a wonderful world!

Throughout our journey I still saw David's smile, for it was as bright as any star around. When we communicated, it was through our souls rather than with words.

We entered a long dark tunnel. At the end of the tunnel was a bright light. I stopped, slightly frightened. David "told" me to come with him.

I believe now that he simply wanted to show me more. Out of fear, I didn't go. I let go of his hand, and he continued to smile radiantly at me as I was pulled back with a tremendous force unlike anything I've ever felt. Suddenly I was back in my body, awake and full of wonder.

After this, it was as though a great weight was lifted from me. My life went back to normal—as normal as it could be after that—and I went on, my depression gone, knowing there's more out there than we could possibly fathom.

A couple of months passed, and I was in New Orleans with my fiancé, sister and brother-in-law. We were eating at the Court of the Two Sisters, which was David's and my favorite restaurant. We used to go there when David made the trip from Tallahassee to New Orleans for his experimental AIDS treatment.

As Greg, JoAnn, Chuck and I were eating, a familiar song came over the sound system. It was Louis Armstrong singing "What a Wonderful World"—and in that moment, I knew we were not alone.

I felt that same presence penetrating deep into my being, filling the room with light and love. David was with us, celebrating life.

In the years since, there have been other times when I've felt his presence, and I welcome the love and guidance he sends me. Although I miss him very much, I have set him free: free to learn what he needs to learn in his world, as I am learning what I need to in mine. But when I least expect it, he continues to remind me . . . what a wonderful world.

Esther's Song

Kim Weiss

We were warned: Regular study of Kabbalah—the ancient mysticism of Judaism—could and would lead to miracles. As a student at the local Kabbalah Learning Center, it was no different for me. One particular Friday night, my miracle happened.

I must tell you first that although I was born a Jew, my relationship with my own religion lagged far behind my dalliances with the mysticism of foreign cultures. My orientation to Judaism amounted to two years of yawning at

Sunday school, the annual sips of wine at Passover dinner, and the proverbial hunt for cash known as "Hanukkah gelt" each winter.

The company at these occasions almost always included my maternal grandparents, who identified themselves as Jews first, Europeans second. Weekly visits from Grandma Esther and Grandpa Benny created a sort of backdrop of Jewishness, replete with warmth and comfort, Yiddish soundtrack intact. For their amusement, I contributed a few piano numbers from *Fiddler on the Roof*. On the sofa, a winsome Grandma Esther swayed and hummed along in her high, sweet voice.

When I was old enough to start thinking for myself, in adolescence, I reached out to Eastern traditions: the writings of Krishnamurti, Kundalini Yoga, macrobiotics—you name it, if it came from anywhere outside the Western world and seemed exotic, I was interested. Praying at a synagogue was not part of the counterculture program. It would be years before I would discover what was hiding in my backyard.

But this path of spiritual studies finally did lead me to the Kabbalah Learning Center. The first crumbs along the trail were from a book recommended by my sister called *The Jew in the Lotus*. This true story of a number of rabbis in dialogue with the Dalai Lama piqued my curiosity about Jewish spirituality. I enrolled in a basic Kabbalah class, and was immediately smitten.

It seemed that Kabbalah carried a formula for living that made perfect sense. What Kabbalah offered was the "why" behind what we call religion, and an ancient yet practical style of spirituality that proposed real mastery over our lives. Kabbalah even claimed to unlock true secrets of immortality. By decoding the mystical powers of the Torah (the Jewish Old Testament), Kabbalah held all the information one would ever need to understand the past, present and future. The basic tenets seemed rather simple: love thy neighbor; stop being reactive (learn restriction); everything is energy, so all we really want is energy.

My favorite part occurred during the first class when Shaul, my teacher, opened class with the statement, "Don't believe anything I tell you." Coupled with the more subtle physical and metaphysical feelings I experienced in my own energy and body, this seemed to fit. It felt like home.

At the time of my "mystical experience" I had been attending classes for about three months. Still a novice in the lessons of Kabbalah, I attended my second Shabbat (Sabbath) service at the Kabbalah Center. Unlike the services of my childhood at a Conservative synagogue, these services were lively, spirited, almost evangelical—a sort of Southern Baptist version of Judaism. These services in the Orthodox tradition were perhaps the most exotic spiritual expression I'd ever witnessed.

During the services, as an obvious beginner and not literate in Hebrew, I was "tutored" by some of the seasoned students. They would guide me through the prayer books, tell me when to lean, when to bow, look up, look down—and, most important, when to scan phrases of Hebrew letters, considered to have a deep, almost holy effect on the consciousness of the reader. Interspersed with spoken prayers were some lovely songs with phonetic pronunciations included in our books. I followed along as best I could.

I am somewhat musical, so during the singing I found it fairly natural to gravitate to the melody of the prayers. I began singing simple "la, la, la's" along with the Hebrew. In a higher register than is usual for me, I began to get comfortable with the music.

Almost instantly, I heard a startling yet familiar sound coming from my throat. It was clearly not my own voice.

Each time I opened my mouth with another "la, la, la," I heard the voice of my grandmother. Not an imitation of my grandmother, but *my grandmother*.

I would begin a phrase, hear Grandma Esther, and become too choked up to go on. Again I would start with a "la," and the lump of emotion would grip my throat. Another "la, la, la," and I was near tears—over and over, until

I feared I would lose control and begin to wail uncontrollably in the temple.

I was filled with something not quite sadness, not quite fear, something that touched me so very deeply I could not give it a name. It was as if I had just had a direct experience of immortality. Grandma Esther was alive and well and celebrating her love of her Jewish faith through me.

What followed next was the perfect ending to my second Shabbat at the center. We moved from the praying area to a large rambling table where Shabbat dinner would be served. I had a few moments to compose myself, and a tiny window to doubt what had really happened to me. Maybe I was imagining things, making too much of something small.

More prayers were said, songs were sung, and bread was broken. Warmed by the rich tradition of Sabbath services, we celebrated the night with laughter and conversation. Lost in the festivities, I glanced across the table at a small, shining-eyed elderly woman who sat smiling at me.

Speaking with an indistinguishable accent, she immediately engaged me in loving dialogue about her many grandchildren. I introduced myself and asked her name. She drew closer to me and said, "My name is Esther."

Fancy Nightmares

Beth Witrogen McLeod

Tenderly but reluctantly, my father delivered the news: It wasn't arthritis that had been crippling my mother's hands, but Lou Gehrig's Disease. Now it was also creating an Alzheimer's-like dementia.

I'd never considered that my mother could waste into nothingness, so robust and energetic had she always been in her sixty-nine years. At sixty-eight, my father had been the one battling dragons for twenty-five years, always beating the odds, Mom at his side. My parents had never allowed the unthinkable to pass into our consciousness, so it was easy to believe that they would never really leave my sister and me.

Now, in a breath, that security was destroyed. As I sat at my workplace, grasping onto my father's strength, I felt my life force drain away. I was desperate to hold onto a past and a future that no longer existed. Suddenly both my parents were dying at the same time, two thousand miles away, and I hadn't a clue how to handle it. My only hope was that love somehow would carry us through.

I come from a family of dreamers. My father's mother held great store in dreams; we often talked about them. So it was no surprise that two weeks after she died, Grandma appeared in a dream and said, smiling, that she wasn't worried about me, I'd muck on through somehow. That faith in my mucking has sustained me in the worst of times since.

My father's sister also had a dream shortly after mother died, ten years ago. Grandma was radiant, standing in a hallway in a flowing white gossamer gown with a long train, at the end of which perched a beautiful red cardinal. Sam knew then that her mother was all right, and the cardinal became a symbol of deep spiritual significance for her.

And oh, how often my mother and I talked of our dreams, remembering them in great detail. She always said, "Our love will never end." As she grew more ill—her body becoming warped and bent, her speech slurred, her hands paralyzed—she repeated it to me every night when I tucked her in. "Come to me in dreams, Mommy," I said. And I could only hope she would find me somehow.

But my own dreams became tortured. Sometimes I watched waves break onto shore, freezing in midcrest to form shapes like the carved women perched on the bows of ancient wooden ships. I stared at the frozen figures as they glared back at me, cold as ice and filled with a mocking hopelessness. And I awoke screaming, exhausted, claustrophobic.

My sister and I were raised in an Orthodox Jewish tradition; neither of us held to it, yet we were both influenced by it. As a child I found security in the old synagogue, the rituals and songs giving me peace. There was no foundation in my life for such beliefs now—yet my certainty that there is deep meaning in losing parents this way, that there is more to this experience than meets the senses, could not be shaken. I watched my mother lose her mind, her body—everything but her faith. Worse, I watched my father lose both his body and his spirit. He couldn't make sense of a God who would cause the love of his life to be stricken so harshly; he could no longer put stock in either faith or reason.

For me, faith was all I had left.

I dream that I am floating into a huge synagogue with many rooms. I walk into a classroom and my mother is there, whole and healthy and beaming at me mischievously through those long-forgotten rhinestone-covered eyeglasses from the 1960s. No words are spoken, but she wants me to know that she will be okay, that she already is all right. Then we are driving along a highway deep in the Plains. As I watch fields of tall grass swaying in the breeze, a tornado funnel begins to form. I tell her to pull over, but she can't follow directions. Finally we crawl into a ditch, but as we start to lie down, the wind whips up and she runs like a crazy person into the open—and I can't save her. I cannot save my mother.

After my fourth trip home in seven months, my father had a reaction to an accidental overdose of morphine and a bad combination of drugs. He wasn't expected to make it another twenty-four hours. I had only just gotten back to California, in a state of complete exhaustion and despair, and decided to wait it out at home with my husband. I went to bed still searching for equanimity. All the tools learned in twenty years of seeking had lost their magic.

That night, I am with my father in the hospital. I notice he's reading *Hamlet*. I ask him if there's any significance to that, and he replies, "Victory digs deep."
"You've certainly dug a lot," I say. "Now it's my turn."
"You look like a little girl, standing there waving goodbye."
"I am."
Deeper into the night, all night, in fact, I am with him. Now he is lying naked on a slab-like surface in a sterile white room, telling me he has to go, alone. I know that, and thank him for my life. He tells me that everything that has happened is perfect, that all of life is perfect, and not to worry.
Then he just ceases to be, and I am captured in his explosion of light. I disappear, too, but am conscious as I rocket backwards at warp speed through a light brighter than

anything imaginable. A thought occurs: "But what about Mom?" And suddenly my father and I are back.

The next morning, Sunday, the phone rang. It was Dad. "Did you see Calvin and Hobbes today?" My husband and I looked at each other in disbelief: We were talking about the Sunday funnies! Dad was okay, although he allowed he was a mess. "I almost got there," he said, with a morphine-induced slowness so antithetical to his crisp mind. "These are some fancy nightmares!"

And so it went, down and down. That August we moved Mom and Dad into a nursing home, the only way to beat the $15,000-a-month bills for two-person, twenty-four-hour-a-day home care.

One night, I dream they are sitting on the deck outside their condo. It's twilight, and the air is limpid and comforting. Dad is smoking his trademark cigar, smiling at me, the wisps of aromatic smoke wafting slowly into the trees. As he flicks ash to the ground, staring at me with a mischievous but intense smile, he says decisively, "We've had wonderful times."

The next day, Thanksgiving, my father passed away, in agonizing pain.

On New Year's Eve, I dream that people are pouring into the funeral home. Someone is giving a eulogy, but I can't hear it because some guests are chatting loudly. When I go over to ask them to be quiet, I see my father sitting on top of Mom's coffin, youthful and vibrant, throwing his head back and laughing with delight.

The next morning, Mom died peacefully in her sleep, weighing fifty pounds and totally paralyzed. We all knew they would go close together.

The following June, I held the ceremony to unveil the headstone. On a whim, I returned one last time to my parents' condo, site of many wonderful summer vacations with my husband. I heard an unfamiliar sound out on the deck. When I went to look, I was greeted by two cardinals, male and female, chirping insistently at me. These had been my parents' favorite birds when I was growing up, but never in the fifteen years they lived in that condominium had I seen one.

Yet there they were, as if to tell me I was not alone. I went outside and the female flew off. But the red male stayed in the branches above for three hours, as I sat on the bench where my father smoked his cigars and watched the leaves, the golden Kansas light filtering through them in a soft prairie breeze.

A month later, I had this dream:

I am sitting at a table with my parents, and my father keeps repeating a phrase. Finally it registers: "The red cardinal only comes out in the winter." I jump up, exclaiming, "So it *was* you at the condo!"

And as they rock back in their chairs, laughing, "Yes, yes," and holding out their arms, I run to them and we hug until I wake up.

A New Way to Say Goodbye

Kristina Paradis

It was one year ago today, as I write this, that I got the call.

I had received the same type of call several times before. First it was when they discovered my mother had breast cancer. Later, when she had heart surgery; then intestinal surgery. Then when her lungs collapsed. For nearly twenty years the calls had come. Each time I would get in the car or on a plane and off I'd go.

For some reason, I was never afraid. I would hold a vigil at the hospital. At night I would return to my parents' house to fix dinner for my father and keep him company—then back to the hospital the next day, just to sit, and read, and be there.

Mom and I would talk, sometimes even laugh. Like the time the nurse wouldn't bring the bedpan. I struggled to lift all five-nine of her off the gurney, but neither of us was strong enough to make it all the way to the bathroom. Mom just had an accident right in the middle of the hall. Such a difficult thing to endure for such a dignified person—and my mother was the essence of dignity. It was unbearable to see her embarrassed by something that wasn't her fault. That's when I had the idea: We would just move the gurney a few feet down the hall. When the nurse came and saw the mess, we just pretended we didn't know a thing. The spin that threw the nurse into was worth a million dollars, and we laughed about it for the next hour.

It wasn't easy to laugh in a hospital, but if you looked around, you could see a lot of pretty good jokes. Sick jokes, but then we both liked sick humor.

When the phone rang this time, my father's voice nearly broke my heart.

"Come to Kentucky. I need you."

I wandered through my house with the portable phone as Dad described the events of the last few weeks. Suffering from intense stomach pain and no sleep, Mom was exhausted. He didn't know what to do.

I hung up and stared before me at the bookshelves in the living room. They were loaded with family portraits; my gaze fell on the large black-and-white portrait of my mother in her wedding gown. She was twenty-three. Wavy light-brown hair framed her face and cascaded past her shoulders in the style of the mid-forties. She was a real beauty. So young, and yet so regal in her carriage. Perhaps it was something that came from being constantly admired.

How must it have felt to have been that lovely? Then to have doctors cut pieces out of you, have the years wear you down, until you were just one more old lady, frail and sick? My mother had lived through seven childbirths and four major surgeries. She had so many scars that she called herself "Frankenstein." She once told me, "You'll have to run me down with a bus if you ever want to get rid of me."

The sky was gray and it was raining lightly as I landed that evening. I stopped at the hospital just to tell my mother I was there and wish her good night. Mom was conscious when I entered the room, but not terribly responsive.

"Hey, Mom," I said, giving her a light kiss on the cheek. "How are you feeling?"

"Let's make a rule. You don't ask that question, and I won't answer it. Okay?"

"Okay."

I sat by my mother's bed and just held her hand for a while. We didn't talk. I knew she was in a lot of pain. An expression of something resembling concentration held her face almost immobile.

Finally Mom said, "Go on now and be with your father. I need some rest." I left.

In the days that followed, friends found out Mom was in the hospital and the casseroles and flowers began. There were no answers to their questions. No one really knew what was wrong—at least, if the doctors knew, they weren't saying.

After a week, Mom announced she wanted to go home. "I am dying, and I want to die at home."

I rode home with her in the ambulance. We had her in bed at five o'clock that evening. As the six o'clock bells rang from the church next door, my mother sighed her last sigh and was still.

She was seventy-two, but she looked ninety. So small and gray. I kissed her forehead and stroked the side of her head. Her hair still smelled the way it had when I was a child.

Three weeks later, I met my mother in a dream.

At first the dream was soft and unclear, but it felt somehow familiar. As I wandered, I suddenly saw my mother before me. A graceful being of celestial lightness, she appeared as she did at twenty-three, with long, silken waves of hair and serene sapphire eyes. I looked at this angel and was at once certain that it was my mother.

In the presence of this lovely creature, I felt a calm that was unlike anything I had known before, a sense of release that seemed infinite. It was joy. In that joy was a complete absence of pain, fear, or worry. I felt that I could swim in this lightness forever.

As I relaxed into this way of being, I could see my mother hovering around me. She was more lovely than the photograph. She was exquisite in her perfection, complete in her peace.

My mother did not speak. She just showed herself to me.

As I floated halfway between waking and dreaming, tears filled my eyes and fell to the pillow. I was overwhelmed by the joy of seeing my mother this way. I was overwhelmed with the joy of knowing I would be that way, too, someday.

Contributors

Dr. Michael Ackerman is in private practice in La Jolla, California, where he specializes in removing the emotional and psychological roots of disease, in addition to holistic chiropractic care. Contact him at (619) 692-7247.

Jenna L. Adamo is a single parent and struggling writer who resides in Virginia Beach, Virginia. She hopes to give her son the same unconditional love she received from her grandmother. She can be contacted at (757) 431-1400 or paged at (757) 670-4472.

Frank A. Alamia is a health care executive and registered nurse currently working for the Navy Surgeon General at the Bureau of Medicine and Surgery in Washington, D.C., as director of the Navy's Health Care Risk Management Program. He resides with his two children, Dan and Anisa, in Washington, D.C. E-mail Frank at Benfrankly@aol.com.

Linda C. Anderson is a spiritual adventurer and ordained Eckankar clergywoman. An international speaker, author, and winner of national awards for playwriting, she writes and talks about the extraordinary spiritual experiences of ordinary people. Her book, *35 Golden Keys to Who You Are & Why You're Here*, brings spirituality alive for today's truth seekers. Find out more about her book by contacting Eckankar, P.O. Box 27300, Minneapolis, MN 55427; calling (800) 568-3463; or visiting Eckankar's Web site at http://www.eckankar.org.

Carol Willette Bachofner is an award-winning poet living in California. She teachers poetry workshops, and her poetry is widely anthologized. Carol is married to Bill and is the mother of six and grandmother to five grandsons. She may be reached at 7781 SVL Box, Victorville, CA 92392.

Karena Delite Bailey is a video producer and healer, creating media to remind us that we are each and every one a miracle. She believes that even at its darkest moments, life is a continuous stream of miraculous events. Write to her at P.O. Box 19545, Plantation, FL 33318.

Heide Banks is an author and expert on the healing power of interpersonal relationships and quantum living. Her work has been featured on *Oprah!*, *Entertainment Tonight*, and ABC and NBC News. Based in Santa Monica, California, Heide also maintains a private counseling/consulting practice for businesses and individuals.

Brent BecVar, M.S., has worked as a psychotherapist, health care administrator, and university administrator and holds a Master's Degree in Educational Psychology. Mr. BecVar has worked for Dr. Deepak Chopra since 1991 in both Massachusetts and California as an administrator and educator. He has also been a certified Yoga instructor since 1970, and was trained by Dr. Chopra as a teacher of Primordial Sound Meditation and Principles and Techniques of Ayurvedic Healing. He currently resides in Los Angeles, California.

Rama Berch, listed in *Who's Who* for 1997, is the creator and supervisor of the yoga program at Deepak Chopra's Center for Well Being, as well as the founder and director of Master Yoga Academy in La Jolla. Teaching since 1976, she has an exceptional understanding of how the body and mind work, and how they work together. Rama travels extensively throughout the U.S. and Canada, conducting advanced courses for yoga teachers and yoga seminars for the general public. Svaroopa Yoga™ is the name of her healing approach to yoga.

Marc Boney is a teacher and practitioner of Jyotish, the astrology of ancient India. He resides in Southern California, and can be contacted at (619) 944-7323.

Victoria Bullis has been doing psychic readings and holding seminars on self-improvement for over fifteen years. She produces audiotapes for meditations and has been a regularly featured guest on hundreds of radio shows throughout the country. She also appears frequently on TV. Victoria is currently completing her first book. To schedule a phone session please call (415) 978-8447 or toll free at (888) 686-2200.

Nick Bunick, a prominent Pacific Northwest businessman, learned from nine different sources over a period of twenty years that two thousand years ago, he lived as the Apostle Paul. He was reluctant to share this information, concerned about public ridicule and the effect it would have on his business and private life. Beginning on January 14, 1995, Nick had the first of many angelic experiences, which compelled him to come forth with the extraordinary story in his bestselling book, *The Messengers*.

Chaz Burton, after many years working in the field of business, recently became a middle school teacher. He is working to create an Earth-centered, transformative program for adolescents. Contact him with your ideas and for information at 22 Senisa Way, Irvine, CA 92715.

Andrea Cagan has done editing and collaborated with such talents as Diana Ross, Marianne Williamson, Lynda Obst, Grace Slick, and many others. She currently lives with her husband, Greville, in Los Angeles, where she is working on her first novel. She can be contacted at (213) 654-3877.

Dennis Calhoun lives in Tulsa, Oklahoma, with his wife, two cats, and two Irish wolfhounds. He works as a safety engineer, and is a member of the Eckankar clergy.

Chérie Carter-Scott, Ph.D., is an international speaker, author, consultant, trainer, and teacher. Her books include *Negaholics: How to Overcome Negativity and Turn Your Life Around; The Corporate Negaholic: How to Deal Successfully with Negative Colleagues, Managers and Corporations; The New Species;* and *The Inner View: A Woman's Daily Journal.* She is also a co-author with Jack Hanfield and Mark Victor Hansen of *Chicken Soup for the Global Soul.* She has worked since 1974 with individuals and organizations worldwide and can be contacted at 145 Canon Drive, Santa Barbara, CA 93105; (800) 321-NEGA or (805) 563-0789, ext. 27; Cherie@the_mms.com; or at www.the_mms.com.

Lisa Chan and her screenwriter/producer husband, Edward Kovach, reside in L.A., where she teaches and practices reflexology, spiritual art, and energetic healing. She also makes videos about alternative healing and has just completed a novel entitled *The Healing Channel.* She can be contacted at 745 E. Valley Blvd., #823, San Gabriel, CA 91776, or at (213) 891-3980.

Deborah Chenault is a fiction and freelance writer whose work has appeared in various literary journals, newspapers, and magazines. She is currently at work on a collection of essays about the mythology and lore of the garden. She can be reached at 219 N. Walnut Street, Cynthiana, KY 41031, or faxed at (502) 868-5100.

David G. Cooper has been living and traveling extensively throughout Southeast Asia, Australia, and Brazil as a spiritual explorer since 1991. His heart-centered true life adventures have been shared through his stories, photos, television appearances, workshops, and public appearances. In addition, David conducts spiritual tours to sacred places in

Bali and Southeast Asia. He can be contacted at P.O. Box 1632, Naples, FL 33939.

Verlaine Crawford, author of *Ending the Battle Within,* is an international speaker and conducts workshops in the U.S., Europe, and Asia. She has pursued spiritual growth for over twenty-five years. She lives on a lovely mountain estate in Southern California and can be reached at P.O. Box 3038, Idyllwild, CA 92549 or (909) 659-3594.

Jyoti Dar is the granddaughter of Mme. Vijaya Laxshmi Pandit, the first woman president of the United Nations and sister of Indian Prime Minister Jawaharlal Nehru. Dar has lived in many parts of the world and is fluent in English, French, Swedish, and Hindi. She has written for travel and food publications, and is currently working on a novel dealing with East–West issues.

Nancy Cooke de Herrera is the author of *Beyond Gurus.* As a Beverly Hills mother of four, she would have seemed an unlikely sponsor of Transcendental Meditation, which spread spiritually from the East to the West during the 1960s. However, a personal tragedy started her quest for knowledge in India. Captivated by its people and spiritual heritage, she returns there yearly. She can be reached by fax at (310) 274-7463.

Dr. John F. Demartini is the creator of the Concourse of Wisdom School of Philosophy and author of *Count Your Blessings,* which carries his compelling message that gratitude and love can heal. He travels extensively to teach his Breakthrough Seminars to Fortune 500 companies and to private citizens searching for personal fulfillment. He can be reached at (713) 850-1234.

Kathi Diamant is a freelance writer, actress, and Emmy Award–winning television talk show host and producer. She lives in San Diego, California, with her husband, Byron LaDue, their dog, Jett, and two budgies, Kim and Nan. She is hard at work on the third draft of her book about Franz Kafka and Dora Diamant. E-mail to scribe@connectnet. com.

Marcelene Dyer is a mother of seven and the wife of Dr. Wayne Dyer, with whom she co-authored *A Promise is a Promise*. Her book on a spiritual approach to pregnancy, birth, and infancy care will be published in 1998.

Micki East, M.A., is a counselor, writer, teacher, and professional speaker. Her joy in life comes from serving as an advocate for children and helping them discover and share the innate gifts they each bring to this world. She is the site coordinator for mental health services in a school-based program for emotionally disturbed children.

Corinne Edwards is the host of the popular *Corinne Edwards Interviews* TV series. She is the author of *Love Waits on Welcome . . . and other miracles*, *Low Pain Threshold*, and *A Woman Without a Man*. She can be reached at Corinne Edwards Interviews, 1 East Delaware Place, Suite 24B, Chicago, IL 60611; at (312) 642-7453 or (312) 642-7493; or at miraclecor@aol.com.

Deborah Ford is an author, coach, consultant, teacher, and integral faculty member of the Chopra Center for Well Being in La Jolla, California. Her book *The Dark Side of the Light Chasers* will be published in May 1998. She is a graduate of JFK University with a degree in psychology and emphasis in consciousness studies. You can fax her at (619) 454-3319.

Robert Gass, creator of the *Opening the Heart* workshops, is a frequent speaker and teacher at conferences, growth centers, and universities. Robert works at the most senior levels in major corporations, government, nonprofits, and activist groups. A musical recording artist, he has released twenty albums with his well-known group, On Wings of Song. He is currently coaching leaders who want to integrate their spiritual life and work in the world.

Frances Heussenstamm, Ph.D., is an artist, writer, clinical psychologist and consultant, and former professor of art and education at Columbia and California State University (Los Angeles). Her *Blame It on Freud: A Guide to the Language* *of Psychology* was published in 1993. Her paintings of "the territory behind her eyes" are in collections in Australia and the U.S. Now semiretired, she convenes a monthly women's group, sees a few clients, and paints. She can be reached at 219 Broadway, Suite 136, Laguna Beach, CA 92651.

Dolores R. Hill resides in Berlin, New Jersey, with her husband and two daughters. She has run an in-home day care center for the last twelve years, is very active in volunteer church activities, and enjoys singing and all types of crafts. You may contact her by writing to 49 Dunham Loop, Berlin, NJ 08009.

Bruce Stephen Holms is an author, film composer, radio and television host/producer, and songwriter with over 1,000 songs to his credit. Since 1989, *Timeless Voyager Radio* has been broadcast to over 50 countries and more than 150 cities in the U.S. He can be reached at TVR, P.O. Box 6678, Santa Barbara, CA 93160, or at bsh@west.net.

Dina Tevas Ingram is an Emmy-winning writer-producer and author of *Answered Prayers,* a collection of inspirational true life stories of celebrated personalities and ordinary people whose lives have been touched by the miraculous healing power of prayer. Ingram also writes a regular column about extraordinary experiences with prayer and interviews celebrities for *Body Mind Spirit* magazine.

JulieAnna is the author of *A Practical Way to Find Peace.* Through her writings and on a one-to-one basis, she has become a quiet advocate for a peaceful, loving, sharing world. She enjoys presenting modern ideas of old wisdoms to people who want to make a difference. She can be contacted at Julieanna Productions, 7007 Mission Gorge Road, Suite 200, San Diego, CA 92120.

Patrice Karst is the author of *God Made Easy*, which is also an audio book read by Ellen Burstyn. She lives near the ocean with her son , Elijah, where she writes, speaks, and continues striving to get closer to God. You can write to her at P.O. Box 103, Pacific Palisades, CA 90272.

Ara Ketenjian, a man with multiple professions including author, physician, scientist, singer, and lecturer, pursues his life's passion—personal enlightenment—through the understanding of the workings of the mind. He loves to share his experiences and knowledge to facilitate spiritual enlightenment in others. He can be reached for lectures and seminars at 2349 Rue Adriane, La Jolla, CA 92037.

Dharma Singh Khalsa, M.D., and **Kirti Kaur Khalsa** live in Tucson, Arizona. They have been American Sikhs for over ten years. Dr. Khalsa's first book, *Brain Longevity,* was released by Warner Books in May 1997, and his second book, *Feeling Great/The Pain is Gone,* will be published in 1998.

Sri Harold Klemp is the spiritual leader of Eckankar, Religion of the Light and Sound of God. As an inner and outer spiritual master, he teaches students of Eckankar through dreams, spiritual guidance, writings, and talks. A pioneer of today's focus on "everyday spirituality," his mission is to help people find their way back to God in this life. He is an international lecturer and author of over thirty books. You can find out more by contacting Eckankar, P.O. Box 27300, Minneapolis, MN 55427; calling (800) 568-3463; or visiting Eckankar's Web site at http://www.eckankar.org.

Michael Peter Langevin is the co-founder, co-publisher, and co-editor of *Magical Blend Magazine.* He has contributed chapters to *A Magical Universe: The Best of Magical Blend* and *Solstice Shift: Magical Blend's Synergistic Guide to the Coming Age.* He lives with his wife and two children on a farm in Chico, California. He can be contacted at P.O. Box 600, Chico, CA 95927; via e-mail at magicalblend.com; or through the Web site, http://www.magicalblend.com.

Alexandra Light and **S. A. Forest** are personal metaphysical teachers, authors, and stress management consultants based in Seattle.

Becki Linderman is the author of the book *Complicated Child? Simple Options*. In it she shares the journey she has traveled with a child who had severe emotional problems, while other families also share their children's successes. She can be reached at P.O. Box 835, Darby, MT 59829.

Diana Loomans is an international speaker, spokeswoman, journalist, and best-selling author of eight books including *Full Esteem Ahead, The Lovables in the Kingdom of Self-Esteem*, and *The Laughing Classroom*. She has delivered over 1,200 programs for corporations and universities and is a frequent guest on national television and radio. Her stories & poetry have been featured in numerous publications and several of the best-selling *Chicken Soup for the Soul* series. She can be contacted through: Global Learning, P.O. Box 1203, Solana Beach, CA 92075. To order her books, call (800) 833-9327.

Julia Loomans is a college student, writer, actress, and co-author of the best-selling books, *Full Esteem Ahead: 100 Ways to Teach Values and Build Self-Esteem in All Ages*, and *Positively Mother Goose*. She has been a frequent guest on national television and radio, and her short stories and poetry appear in numerous books and publications. She can be reached through: Global Learning, P.O. Box 1203, Solana Beach, CA 92075. To order her books, call (800) 833-9327.

Judy Martin is an Emmy Award–winning television reporter who, through Judy Martin & Associates, has combined her love for and knowledge of books, the media, and people into a diverse career promoting and representing authors who are dedicated to a healing purpose. She has authored numerous articles on spirituality and work ethics and is currently finishing *In Search of the Father*, the book from which her story came. She can be reached at (561) 845-8441 at the Palm Beach Center for Living in North

Palm Beach, California, where she volunteers as Public Relations Director.

Beth Witrogen McLeod is the award-winning author of the Pulitzer Prize–nominated series "The Caregivers" (*San Francisco Examiner,* April 1995). She leads a weekly chat on AOL, consults on caregiving and aging, and is currently at work on a book. She can be reached at 4418 Deermeadow Way, Antioch, CA 94509, or at bethcare@aol.com.

Rachel Naples is the author of the upcoming novel *Flying Lessons,* an upbeat female journey of self-discovery, and the screenplay and book *The Door,* a magical journey through time. Rachel attributes the many mystical experiences she's had to the opening of her creative channels through her work as an actress, massage and energetic therapist, and now as a writer. She resides with her husband, Scott de-Moulin, in Los Angeles. They have one child, Taz, a beautiful white angelic being with four legs.

Judith Orloff, M.D., is a psychiatrist and psychic, and author of *Second Sight.* She is an assistant clinical professor of Psychiatry at UCLA and has a private psychiatric practice in Los Angeles. She's been featured in *Elle, McCall's, New Woman,* the *New York Post* and *L.A. Times,* and has appeared on CNN. She lectures nationally on the integration of spirituality and psychic abilities with traditional medicine. Dr. Orloff can be reached at 2080 Century Park East, Suite 1811, Los Angeles, CA 90067.

Kristina Paradis is a freelance writer/editor who lives and works in Naples, Florida. She has written and edited for regional publications and contributed to a book on the area. She recently completed her first screenplay and is working on a science fiction novel. Kristina holds a master's degree in creative writing from the University of Louisville.

Eric Scott Pearl, a Los Angeles chiropractor, discovered in August 1993 that he was blessed with an unusual gift. After twelve years practicing traditional chiropractic, he suddenly became a healer of a different kind. An international healer, author, and lecturer, Dr. Pearl is a frequent guest on radio and TV talk shows, including NBC's *The Other Side*. His patients' healings are documented in three books to date. He can be reached at 8615 Santa Monica Blvd., West Hollywood, CA 90069, or at (213) 658-8400.

Thomas Pecora is an Intuitive Astrologer living in Chicago. He also hosts his own radio program that can be heard in Chicago and over the Internet. To listen to the program or to contact him, please visit his website at http://www.thomaspecora.com.

Freddie Ravel, keyboardist and multi-platinum composer, has collaborated with the greats of the spiritual and musical world, including Deepak Chopra, Tony Bennett, Quincy Jones, Sergio Mendes, Earth, Wind & Fire, and Madonna. His most recent album, *Sol to Soul*, has reached the top of the charts nationwide, embraced by college radio, top Latin stations, and the "Smooth" Jazz format. He can be reached at (818) 386-5866 or through his Web site, http://www. ravelation.com.

Charles Lewis Richards, Ph.D., is a psychologist specializing in non-hypnotic past life therapy. He resides in Del Mar, CA, and can be reached by calling (619) 755-5185.

Madelaine Roig, M.A., M.F.C.C., is an artist, writer, teacher, and psychotherapist in Los Angeles. She teaches creative arts as an expression of the Divine, and consults with individuals, groups, and corporations on living a mystical life in the material world. She can be reached at 650 Haverford Ave., Pacific Palisades, CA 90272, or at (310) 288-6401.

Harry W. Schwartz is the host of public television's celebrity cooking show, *Chef Harry & Friends*, and is a regular guest on NBC's *Today Show*, Lifetime's *Our Home*, and the Home Shopping Network. He is a feature writer for several publications, author of three cookbooks, and is about to launch a line of food and cooking products. He can be reached at 23852 Pacific Coast Highway, Suite 917, Malibu, CA 90265.

Stephan A. Schwartz is the author of two books, *The Alexandria Project* and *The Secret Vaults of Time*, as well as chapters in other books, technical papers, and television documentaries. For more than twenty years he has been actively involved in the academic community studying extraordinary human functioning and consciousness. He is currently doing research for a new book, *Mysterious America*.

James Seddon, a poet and author of *Morning Glories Among the Peas*, lives with his wife in southern Iowa. He can be reached at 708 W. Washington St., Centerville, IA 52544.

Les Sinclair is a former TV producer, vice-president of BrainTainment Resources, a cognitive diagnostic company, yogi, and certified teacher in "The New Warrior Network." His personal mission statement is: "To create a safe and compassionate world by healing myself and others." He can be reached via e-mail at les@brain.com.

Linda Tisch Sivertsen is an author and celebrity biographer, currently living high in the mountains of the Southwest with her husband, Mark, and their six year-old son. Luke, the cat portrayed in her story, loved his new forest home. He recently passed away at the age of nine. When his family was told his story would be printed, they cried tears of joy that his little life would continue to touch others.

Jerry Snider is co-editor of *Magical Blend Magazine*. His writing has appeared in numerous books and publications, both nationally and internationally.

Carl Studna's photography of the music industry's legends is known worldwide, gracing the covers of CDs and magazines alike. Currently Carl is working on several photographic/ text books with the primary emphasis on revealing the sacredness of life's journey. For inquiries and appointments, call (310) 475-6175.

Daniel Tardent is an Australian currently living in California, where he works as a marketing manager in the Silicon Valley telecommunications industry. For the past twelve years he has been a member of Eckankar, Religion of the Light and Sound of God, and his study of the ECK teachings has brought him more love, wisdom, and spiritual freedom than he has ever known before. He lives with his wife, Josse, and can be e-mailed at taffy.c@ worldnet.att.net.

Allan Thomas resides in Santa Monica, California, where he practices massage therapy, dances, sings, writes prose and poetry, and channels Sacred Geometry into human movement. Allan is dedicated to raising his spine to the divine by following his own kundalini path. E-mail to handyman@wla.com.

Carol Tisch grew up in the San Francisco Bay area and holds a degree from University of California, Berkeley in Social Welfare. She is a professional Vedic Astrologer and Reiki practitioner, and is working on her first novel. She can be reached at 1276 S. Cloverdale Ave., Los Angeles, CA 90019; (213) 896-8111.

Doreen Virtue is a fourth-generation metaphysical healer who holds a Ph.D. in counseling psychology. For information on her books, *The Lightworker's Way: Awakening Your Spiritual Power to Know and Heal* and *Angel Therapy: Healing Messages for Every Area of Your Life,* and her audiotape, *Chakra Balancing: A Morning and Evening Meditation to Awaken Your Spiritual Power,* or to receive Dr. Virtue's workshop schedule, contact Hay House at (800) 654-5126 or visit their Web site, http://www.hayhouse.com.

Mary Amrita Weed, M.P.H., is a health educator dedicated to facilitating people to live life in full self-expression through integrating mind, body, and spirit. She teaches the

Hoffman Quadrinity Process in San Anselmo, California, is an associate with Mannatech, Inc., and does personal coaching. She can be reached in Palo Alto, California, at (415) 858-2602.

Ellen Lieberman Weil is an internationally known psychic and psychotherapist with twenty years of experience in combining practical problem-solving and emotional healing with psychic/intuitive wisdom. Her telephone and in-person consultations address personal, business, and relationship problems, as well as spiritual/metaphysical questions. She can be reached at Aspen Consulting Associates, 4337 County Road #113, Carbondale, CO 81623; at (970) 945-3078 (phone) or (970) 928-8185 (fax); or at gunther@rof.net.

Kim Weiss divides her time between music, yoga, her work in the communications field, and her study of Kabbalah. She has represented many books devoted to personal growth and spirituality, and has worked with Jack Canfield, Mark Victor Hansen, Thomas Moore, John Bradshaw, Stuart Wilde, and many others. She is currently working on a project with Rabbi Berg of the Kabbalah Learning Center. She resides in South Florida and works for the progressive publisher Health Communications, Inc.

Marcia Wieder lectures worldwide on dream fulfillment, DreamTeams, and visionary planning. She is the author of *Making Your Dreams Come True, Life Is but a Dream*, and *Doing Less and Having More*. She has been featured on *Oprah!* and *Today*. Contact her at (800) 869-9881.

Rick Wright, M.S.W., is a highly respected teacher, healer, and consultant to individuals and organizations. Trained in both Eastern and Western modes of healing and personal transformation, he has a successful international healing practice based in Los Angeles, California. (800) 311-5246.

Maryann Candito Wilkin is the manager of the Chopra Center for Well Being in La Mesa, California. Since her "contact" with David, she has dedicated her life to helping others find their path. She can be reached at the Chopra Center for Well Being, 8270 La Mesa Blvd., La Mesa, CA 91941; (619) 667-9355.

Tom Youngholm is author of the visionary fiction *The Celestial Bar: A Spiritual Journey* and its sequel, *In the Shadow of the Sphere* (working title). He is an international speaker and presents workshops on the need for balance of P.E.I.S.: physical, emotional, intellectual, spiritual. Contact him at Creative Information Concepts, P.O. Box 1504, Lemon Grove, CA 91946; (619) 698-9462; CreativeIC@aol.com; or http://www.celestialbar.com.

Have You Had a Mystical Experience?

If you have had a personal mystical experience you'd like to share for a future volume of *Hot Chocolate for the Mystical Soul*, please send it to:

Arielle Ford
P.O. Box 8064
La Jolla, CA 92038

or fax it to: (619) 454-3319

Please make sure to include your name, address, and phone number!